c2

THE ITALIAN SUMMER

Golf, Food, and Family at Lake Como

R O L A N D   M E R U L L O

A TOUCHSTONE BOOK
PUBLISHED BY SIMON & SCHUSTER
NEW YORK   LONDON   TORONTO   SYDNEY

Touchstone
A Division of Simon & Schuster, Inc.
1230 Avenue of the Americas
New York, NY 10020

First Touchstone hardcover edition April 2009

TOUCHSTONE and colophon are registered trademarks
of Simon & Schuster, Inc.

For information about special discounts for bulk purchases, please contact Simon & Schuster Special Sales at 1-800-456-6798 or business@simonandschuster.com

Designed by Jamie Kerner

Manufactured in the United States of America

10   9   8   7   6   5   4   3   2   1

Library of Congress Cataloging-in-Publication Data
Merullo, Roland.
   The Italian summer : golf, food, and family at Lake Como / Roland Merullo.
      p. cm.
"A Touchstone Book."
   1. Como, Lake, Region (Italy)—Description and travel. 2. Golf—Italy—Como, Lake Region. 3. Como, Lake, Region (Italy)—Social life and customs. 4. Cookery, Italian. I. Title.
DG975.C7215M47 2009
914.5'2310493—dc22   2008026229

ISBN-13: 978-1-4165-6353-2
ISBN-10:   1-4165-6353-9

For Amanda, Alexandra, and Juliana
and for Craig Nova

ACKNOWLEDGMENTS

MY THANKS TO MY great traveling companions, Amanda, Alexandra, and Juliana; to Jeffrey Forhan for reading an early version of the manuscript and offering suggestions; to everyone at Touchstone Books, especially Zach Schisgal, my fine editor, and Shawna Lietzke and Jessica Chin; to my wonderful agents, Marly Rusoff and Michael Radulescu, and everyone at Marly Rusoff and Associates.

Special thanks to Judy Veale for a wealth of advice about living at the lake.

CONTENTS

If a man insisted always on being serious, and never allowed himself a bit of fun and relaxation, he would go mad or become unstable without knowing it.
—HERODOTUS, *HISTORIES*, BOOK II

Tell me what you eat and I shall tell you what you are.
—ANTHELME BRILLAT-SAVARIN, *THE PHYSIOLOGY OF TASTE*

I simply wanted to do nothing. . . . My nothing meant simply to play golf. . . . This may seem incredible to those who have never fallen hopelessly in love with the game; but I can see the charm and temptation even now, for golf or any other pastime can be much more than a mere hitting of the ball; it can be, however a poor one, a life to be lived.
—BERNARD DARWIN

INTRODUCTION

A SUMMER IN ITALY

I went to Italy to learn to relax. A type-A personality who plays golf too fast and eats too fast and writes three books at a time, I was hoping the Mediterranean air would shift me down into a slower gear, not just for the summer we spent in Italy, but permanently. The plan was to enjoy the food and wine and golf courses, to have the kind of uninterrupted family time that is almost impossible to get at home, with the girls' school schedules, and the ordinary domestic and work responsibilities of the middle-class American life. Amanda and I chose Lake Como because it was said to be one of the most beautiful places in the world, because it was a part of Italy we hadn't yet seen, and because a warmer place—Tuscany, Sicily, Sardinia—would have been difficult for our older daughter, who has cystic fibrosis. And we chose Italy in the first place because, whatever their weak points might be, the Italians like children, are usually kind to visitors, and seem to have made a five-thousand-year study of the art of enjoying life. We had been there seven previous times, winter and summer, north and south, alone and with our young daughters. We spoke a fair amount of the language, we were used to the wild rules of the road. In short, we knew enough about Italy to know that it is a place you should go if you feel your life has fallen under the harsh modern dictatorship of work and worry. It seemed to me that a summer of golfing and eating there would serve as a lesson in a slower, richer way of living, and that I could carry that lesson back across the Atlantic.

We left home the day after the girls finished school for the year, and we spent most of their summer vacation in a rented house near the western shore of Lake Como, not far from the border with Switzerland. It was a simple house, stucco and tile, with three bedrooms, a shared swimming pool out back, and a unique assortment of neighbors. But if you opened the tall glass doors of the living room and stepped onto the patio where we ate our meals, you could look out and down at one of the most spectacular landscapes on earth—a branch of the blue lake, with tile-roofed houses clumped and scattered along the base of forest-covered mountains on the opposite shore. Rising behind that first range of mountains, farther east, were taller peaks—eight thousand feet, some of them—that caught the bottoms of cumulus clouds as they drifted past and turned from smoke gray to pink in the late northern dusk.

It was wonderful to lift the brass clasp on the shutters in our bedroom, swing them open, and start the day with that view. And it wasn't so bad either to lie on a chaise lounge in the warm, dark air when the girls were asleep and study the stars and planets, and the lights of the towns across the way—Lezzeno, Bellagio, Varenna. Once a week in fair rotation one of the towns would put on a fireworks display. Late one Saturday night we heard wedding music from a boat decorated with Chinese lanterns and drifting around not far from shore. A dog barking at phantoms, two young neighbor boys resisting bed, the faint drone of a motorcycle on the lakeside road—these things would momentarily break the quiet of the Italian night the way speedboats and ferries ruffled the lake's surface during the day. But then the silence would swallow them up again, and a particular kind of peace would descend over the sloping front yard and over me.

Even enveloped by that peace, I remembered, of course, that life has its harsher side. I have written about war, addiction, illness, failure, and experienced some of those things. But I decided, this time, to write a happy book, a book that might serve in some small way to counterbalance the constant bad news we live with. Not an exhaustive analysis of Italian culture; not an instruction manual on playing golf better; not even a gourmet's guide to food and wine. Just the story of a slice of time in a beautiful place, where I had a lesson in living more slowly.

I

LA BAITA

From several different sources we had heard about a restaurant called La Baita, and one night in July, when we'd been at the lake for a while, we decided to have dinner there. La Baita was difficult to get to, our sources said, reachable only by a road that was not for the timid, tucked into a high valley above the Menaggio and Cadenabbia Golf Club—my home course during that summer—with a view of a piece of Lake Como and of the alpine landscape near the lake's northern end.

We were advised to make reservations and to arrive hungry. We had also been advised to hire a taxi driver to take us to La Baita because we'd heard—and would later learn firsthand—that there were roads climbing into those hills that connected to other roads, that turned into dirt tracks with steep drop-offs, no lights, and no guardrails, and wandered so far into the high valleys, so deep into the rugged landscape between Italy and Switzerland, that the idea of heading out in the evening, without a taxi driver leading the way, or an Italian friend familiar with the terrain, with two young children in the car, without provisions, weapons, first-aid kit, or at least a few days' supply of fresh water . . .

I'm exaggerating, of course. And yet it was true that an American acquaintance who'd lived on the lake for twenty-five years, and knew we'd have a rental car, had given us the names of several restaurants back in the hills and suggested we let a cabdriver take us to them. Later in the summer, we would discover how easy it was to get lost up there, and how treacherous the roads could be. As we came to know the high country behind our house, we found it surprising that there were any roads up there at all, given the steepness of the grade; and next to unbelievable that people had decided to make their homes in such places and start restaurants in those remote hills and hollows, when there was plenty of perfectly good and much flatter land just a few miles north along the lake.

Still, we wanted to try La Baita and we decided it was worth the risk. On that warm July evening, Amanda and the girls put on nice dresses. I changed from sneakers to shoes, T-shirt into short-sleeve dress shirt. With an old emergency kit and a bottle of water but no weapons or provisions or guide, we headed out, in our rented Renault, in search of dinner.

From our house on the slanted western shore of the lake, we started out north along a side road called Via Pola. This unlined street, with weedy fields and orchards and a few houses to either side, brought us past the spot, marked by a simple black cross, where Benito Mussolini had been killed in 1945, then dropped us down to the *statale*, the lakeside road. We turned north on the *statale*, with the lake to our right, and to our left a brief parade of old stone buildings standing shoulder to shoulder. There were shops and small eateries on the street floor of these buildings—

including a place called Bar Roma, where I liked to go for cappuccino before an early-morning round of golf—shuttered windows and doors above. On the small balconies there you might see a man in a white T-shirt that looked as though it had been carefully washed and ironed, and he would be watering the tomatoes in his flower boxes. Or you might see an elderly woman wearing a flower-print dress, leaning her fleshy arms on the railing and staring down and across the road at men fishing from the promenade with long poles, a few small boats at anchor, then the expanse of blue water, the green hills and gray cliffs beyond.

It was just after seven p.m. Though it would still be several hours before darkness settled around the lake, the sun had already fallen behind the hills on the western shore, our shore, and huge, looping shadows were reaching across toward the famous resort town of Bellagio on the other side. As always, Bellagio sparkled in the last sunlight, as if it were proud of itself, set apart there on the triangular spit of land that separated Como's two spindly legs. And as always the more plebeian *statale* was lively with evening traffic: blue German tour buses with pale-complected retirees gazing out the windows at the chaotic Italian roadway. *Driving like that, how can they survive long enough to raise a family?* you imagined the Germans and Swiss and Dutch visitors asking themselves, because, like so many Italian roads, the *statale* was a crazy Roller Derby of motorcycles cutting from lane to lane with the drivers leaning hard into the curves and the passengers holding on tight; BMWs, Porsches, Fiats, and Peugeots zipping along so fast you would have thought the ancient road were lined, or wide, or straight; cyclists in professional-looking shirts and shorts pumping the pedals in a bright yellow or blue line with a foot or so to spare between their knees and the buses' big wheels. *How do they do it? Why do they do it?* We'd asked ourselves the same thing so many times and come up with a dozen answers: for fun, to show off, to test the machines they drove, to test their own nerve, because they did everything else in such a relaxed fashion. After a while, we stopped asking and started having some fun ourselves.

Past the row of tourist hotels we went, past an elegant villa set back behind a grand lawn of palms and flower gardens, past another sprinkling of restaurants, a ferry dock, a favorite swimming spot, then into the shadows and through a short tunnel that spilled us out on the edges of the town of Menaggio. At the Bank of San Paolo, where the road split, we took the left fork, away from downtown, away from the lake, made the hairpin turn in front of Pizzeria Lugano, then started to climb the switchback road that led, if you followed it farther than we would on that night, across the border and into Switzerland.

This was a true mountain road, a test of nerves, skill, and patience. On the first mile alone, there were eight hairpin turns. Between those turns lay straight stretches where the Italians liked to pass with great stylishness and daring. Once we had successfully navigated this first winding uphill stretch, we reached the village of Croce, near the Caffè Peace. There a sign on the wall said simply GOLF, and we cut across the highway, carefully, choosing our moment, and zigged and zagged up a much narrower road—Level II of the La Baita driving test—in first gear mostly, sounding the horn three times as we neared each corner and watching for whatever might be coming the other way. Bicycles, Audi Quattros, cement mixers. Seven more harrowing turns and we arrived at the edge of the golf course property, which called to me, as always. But on that evening, instead of passing through the tall wrought-iron gates and up toward the clubhouse restaurant, we veered left, onto a road wide enough for a single car—Level III. This road soon turned to rutted dirt and offered, every fifty yards or so, like a series of apologies, small cutouts where you could pull over and let another vehicle squeeze past.

Up and up we went, dust powdering the roadside leaves behind us. And then, at the crest of a hill, the climb abruptly ended and we turned sharply right, and down, following two dirt tracks that snaked through the trees. No cutouts here, no guardrails, no streetlamps, no signs. In another minute this road cast us forward into a gravel parking lot next to a two-and-a-half-story, white stucco and gray stone house that seemed to have been set there, on its small promontory, by helicopter. There was nothing to indicate we had arrived at a restaurant. No sign. Apparently no entrance door. I brought the Renault to a stop, turned off the engine, and looked across the seat at Amanda. "The food must be spectacular here," I said in a hopeful way, "or else who would ever come?"

It took us a minute to figure out how to gain entrance to La Baita—up a set of stone steps at the side of the house, then onto a covered porch that looked out over treetops to a fresh view of the folding mountains and a small piece of the lake. A fluttering of *buona seras* filled the air around us, as if, in crossing the threshold that separated the stone landing from the wooden porch, we had startled a small covey of happy birds and they were brushing our ears with their soft, warm wings. This feathery greeting came from the owner of the place, a sturdy, middle-aged woman named Marissa, who had reddish blond hair and a smile like sunlight.

A warm welcome is the first step in eating well away from home. The Italians understand this principle of the culinary science in the same way they seem instinctively to understand everything else that has to do with food: growing it, preparing it, serving it, accompanying it with the proper wine, eating and digesting it, and talking about it: You can't expect to fully enjoy a meal, they seem to say, if your first moments in a dining establishment consist of a welcome that is short on eye contact and long on surliness. In the chain restaurants back home (Italy has yet to be overrun by them) this essential first step has not been forgotten, but it has mutated into a standardized greeting: *Good evening and welcome to Mickleford's. Hi, I'm Brent and I'll be your server tonight. Can I start you folks off with something to drink?* As sincere as some of these pleasant offerings might be, you still have the feeling they've been written up by a management consultant somewhere in Orlando or San Jose, and that they're delivered under I-might-lose-my-job duress.

Marissa had no management consultants and was in no danger of being fired. She seemed genuinely happy to see us, and, a minute later, to welcome our friends Andrus and Elsa. She had started La Baita twenty-one years earlier after the sudden death of her husband, turning the family home into a restaurant as a means of making a living. Now she kept it open six days a week, year-round, serving mainly tourists and vacation-home owners in the warmer months, and mainly locals in winter, when the cool rains came, the tops of the surrounding mountains were clothed in white, and the menu tilted in the direction of heavy stews, polenta, and the richer red wines.

She motioned us toward a rustic table set for six, with that wonderful view over the treetops—Lake Como held in a basin by steep mountains to either side. There were four other tables on the porch. Near the back wall sat a man with tattooed biceps that were wrapped around a squirmy, pretty, year-old daughter dressed in pink. And beside us sat a party of eight. For most of the evening, one of the members of that party fixed her eyes on our younger daughter, Juliana. I could not tell if it was desperate longing for a child (something I'd seen more than once in Italian women, living, as they did, in a country that was known for its familial affections and yet had one of the lowest birthrates in Europe) or if her persistent visual attention was a kind of reprimand, a signal that she expected our ebullient six-year-old to sit perfectly still with a napkin on her lap, her eyes forward, her attention given completely to the task of eating. Had the woman asked, we could have told her that we sometimes cherished the same hope, that we were often advising Juliana as to the joys of stillness, encouraging her to eat sitting down rather than standing up, suggesting she move slowly and deliberately instead of scooting, racing, zooming, and banging into things. Had the woman asked, we could have told her that certain personal characteristics cannot easily be changed by the admonitions of parents, or the stern looks of strangers.

Marissa moved among us in a deliberate fashion, with an understated graciousness that came, I suppose, from so many years of encouraging guests to feel at home. She made sure Alexandra and Juliana were comfortably seated—at least for a few seconds; she complimented them on their dresses, asked their names, smiled and noted that they were Italian names, *i nomi italiani;* in short, she gave them the required amount of attention, making them feel as if they were full souls, not merely miniature accompaniments to the paying guests. That having been done, our hostess asked how many of us would be interested in the antipasto, and if—you are their parents, you would know best—the girls might be happier with a simple *penne al pomodoro.* She inquired about our preference for wine. And then, as if it were a two-woman act they had practiced many times, she stepped aside and let Nadya, our waitress, take over.

There was no menu at La Baita. Or, more accurately, there was an unwritten nightly menu of ten small courses from antipasto to dessert. We could, Nadya told us, choose as many or as few of these courses as we liked. I noticed that the tattooed father and his little child had come only for drinks and something sweet. They disappeared shortly after we'd begun. At the opposite end of the spectrum, I had skipped lunch in anticipation of La Baita, had enjoyed an active day of golf and swimming, and was prepared to do battle with the forces of dietary caution.

Nadya, I suspected, had been witness to many world-class eaters in her career; after her first few inquiries, she seemed to understand that my answer would always be the same: Yes, I would like some of that. Yes to that, also. Yes, again. *Sì, sì, sì certo.* She ducked into the kitchen for a few minutes, then reappeared carrying a wooden platter on which glistening pieces of salami and strips of thin-sliced prosciutto had been arranged in circular patterns. With her other hand she set down a bowl of roasted onions. While we were admiring them, she brought a mélange of vegetables—roasted red peppers, olives, pickles—accompanied by a crusty peasant bread. Because Amanda suffers from an unfortunate allergic reaction to red wine, Marissa had recommended a pinot grigio, and once that was opened and poured, we started in on the food in earnest. A piece of prosciutto, a whole onion, sweet as honey, a forkful of the vegetables, a bite of bread (with the rich, cold butter we always have to ask for in Italy because it is assumed you take your bread with olive oil), a sip of wine, some talk, an olive, a soft, succulent pepper, more wine.

Andrus and Elsa, our dinner companions on that evening, were retirees who had been born and raised and still lived in the Netherlands, but owned a vacation home on another hillside not far from where we sat. They made several long visits to Lake Como every year, driving nine hours across Europe with golf clubs in the trunk of their Mercedes. He was tall and trim, with bright blue eyes that beamed out of a florid, northern-European complexion, and she was brown-haired and classically pretty, with a direct gaze and a manner that was at once dignified and blunt. We had met them watching golf in the clubhouse at Menaggio and Cadenabbia and had become friends playing golf there, and had decided to try La Baita for the first time together as a way of deepening our acquaintance. They were accompanied by Max, their long-in-the-tooth, long-haired dachshund, who found a comfortable place on top of one of Andrus's shined loafers and didn't let out so much as a squeak of complaint when the girls ducked under the table and fondled him half to death.

When the papery slices of meat and the bread and onions and pickles and olives and peppers had been eaten up, slowly, and with the greatest of appreciation, and when most of the pinot grigio had been consumed, Nadya arrived with a freshly made carrot-and-celery coleslaw, dressed in oil, then a plate of grilled eggplant and zucchini, sun-dried tomatoes, artichoke hearts, and a light pastry that bore a close resemblance to spanakopita. The girls' pasta arrived in huge platters. Amanda and I exchanged a glance that said something like *Good thing we skipped lunch.*

As the meal moved slowly along and the last hours of daylight thinned, as the adults were served the next course—two pastas, *arrabbiata* and *boscaiola* ("Yes, I'll have both," I told Nadya, *Sì, sì, tutti e due*)—the conversation turned, naturally enough, to golf. You come to know people quickly if you drink with them or go through something difficult with them, and, as every golfer knows, at least as well and quickly if you play golf with them. Andrus played to an 11, with a smooth swing that accelerated smartly just as the clubhead reached the ball. Elsa, having played since she was a young girl, carried a handicap of 6 and had one of the sweetest, most perfectly rhythmical swings I'd ever seen. ("She often beats me, you know," Andrus said, after I watched Elsa hit her first tee shot.) They played a precise style of golf, and they played at a smart pace, like people who were expert at the complicated dance of the game: how to have your club chosen when it's your turn to hit; when to help a playing partner search for an errant tee shot and when to go find your own ball first, in the rough on the opposite side; how long you can reasonably (and legally) look for a ball; how to mark your ball on the green and let the other person putt undistracted; how to say "I'll wait" if you are waiting, or "I'll finish" if you aren't; all the unwritten rules that made the game move along at a brisk but comfortable tempo.

They were gracious, too, in the small touches that had nothing to do with speed: bringing an extra bottle of water in case I forgot that there is rarely drinking water on Italian courses; fixing someone else's ball mark without being asked and without making a fuss of it; retrieving a divot; lifting a wedge off the green and handing it to another player after he'd finished putting out; tending the flag, standing still on the tee box, raking a bunker.

And they were gracious with each other, too, a spousal courtesy you don't always see on the course. Once, after we'd made the long downhill walk from the eighth green to the ninth tee at Menaggio and Cadenabbia, Andrus realized he'd left a headcover back on the eighth, and Elsa hustled up and over the hill and brought it back to him without having been asked. They were complimentary without being saccharine, not afraid to tell each other when one had hit a poor shot, not timid about sharing swing advice. Far from being tour-level players, they were nevertheless world-class companions on the course, and they enjoyed good food as much as we did.

Arrabbiarsi means "to lose one's temper" (something I did not see Andrus or Elsa do, even when their games faltered), so *pasta arrabbiata* is "angry pasta," I suppose, though "hot," with its dual associations of anger and spiciness, might serve as a better English translation. It's one of my favorite dishes, the small prickle of pepper working nicely against the solid ordinariness of the pasta itself. On that night at La Baita, it was paired with *pasta boscaiola,* which is likely linked to the word *bosco,* or "woods," because the creamy sauce is rich with porcini mushrooms. Set together on the same dish, they made a perfect pair, something like a fiery Italian-American husband and his calm WASP wife, for example, or like the mix of emotional elements you need to play golf well: hot enough to care, to try; smooth and creamy and cool enough to stay calm amid the quick explosions of success and failure the game throws at you.

As always, Amanda stopped drinking after the first glass, but once the pinot grigio was finished, Andrus, Elsa, and I moved on with enthusiasm to a bottle Marissa suggested, a weighty Veneto merlot that went well with the *arrabbiata*. The girls moved on from sitting at the table and eating, to scrambling around somewhere under the table and tickling Max's ears. They were already inquiring about dessert options, which would have been perfectly reasonable at any other meal. "It looks like we still have a ways to go before dessert," I told them, and they said, "Really, Dad?" as if I were making a joke.

Clearing away the empty pasta dishes, Nadya asked about the meat course, and I said yes to all of it, yes to the pork, and yes to the beef, and even yes to the veal, which I don't normally eat at home. In his working days, Andrus had been an executive with a large food wholesaler in Holland, and he told us about a European Union law that controlled the treatment of veal calves and let them run free. So I said yes to the veal and pork and beef in a light wine sauce, and yes to the garnish of carrots and greens, and yes and yes and yes to anything and everything that came out of the kitchen on that summer night.

The girls had given up on eating by that point and were lavishing all their affection on Max the long-haired dachshund . . . whether he liked it or not. At the far end of the table, Amanda and Elsa had fallen into an animated conversation and were nibbling away at the slices of meat, cutting off pieces of the nicely browned potatoes that had been served with it, and sampling the vinegar peppers. We were doing a decent job on the Veneto merlot, too, and with his typical enthusiasm for things Italian (and perhaps for things in general) Andrus was telling me about some local friends of theirs he wanted us to meet. "Fine, fine people," he said. "He's a world-class painter, she's a writer. I know you'd like them," and giving me his impressions of other golf courses nearby—Monticello, Lanzo, Villa d'Este.

When the larger plates had been cleaned, Marissa swung by with a selection of cheeses—a Parmesan, a Tarleggio, and a cheese they made there, at La Baita, which she claimed did not have a name. "It's just our cheese," she said. In taste it fell somewhere between blue and Brie, a dry, crumbly cheese you wanted to let melt on the tongue. Dusk was settling over the hills. The tempo of the meal had changed the way the tempo of a day changes, from the busyness of the working hours to the contemplative mood of evening. After the cheese and another glass of wine, I did not think I could put any more food or drink into my body. But then Nadya brought chocolate mousse and a *torta di frutta di bosco* that I'd had my eye on since we walked in, and drawn by those sugary delights, the girls returned to their places as if the magnets that had once held them there had been turned back on, and I found myself with room for a few forkfuls of sugared pastry and various berries. Cream, butter, flour, chocolate—how could something with these ingredients be in any way detrimental to one's health?

Darkness had not yet fallen over the view from the porch, so when we were finished eating, at last, really finished this time, we sat back, ran our hands across our midsections, sighed, looked at the pattern of crumbs and the last drops of wine, and then Andrus suggested we pose for a family picture. We assembled ourselves at the porch railing, and the photo sits in our home now. You can see that all of us were well fed, but my face in particular bears an expression almost of shock. Pleasant shock. But shock all the same. Could I have eaten that much, really?

We walked out through the kitchen for some reason—to meet the chef, to pay homage to the pots and pans, I don't remember—kissed Marissa good-bye there, went through a different door and down a different set of stone steps, then shook hands in the parking lot and wished each other a solemn good luck on the dark ride home. "We'll see you tomorrow at the course," Andrus said.

"Either that or come looking for us up here in these hills."

But once we had navigated the dirt track that led from La Baita down toward the gates of Menaggio and Cadenabbia, the rest of the winding ride into town and then back along the lake felt like child's play. It was late, the girls were tired. The first discomfort of overeating had passed. We got them home and into bed, then I took one of the chaise lounges out into the front yard, lay there and looked at the stars, and occupied myself with the art of digestion.

2

FAHNTAHSTIC, FAHNTAHSTIC

I cannot go any further into the story of that summer without introducing our friend and real estate agent, Harold Lubberdink, who probably deserves an entire book to himself. In fact, I sometimes think that, in years to come, when we look back at our time at the lake, the spectacular view will be the first thing we remember, and Harold Lubberdink the second.

Because we were determined to avoid a repetition of a previous family vacation in Italy, which had been an unmitigated disaster—wrong house, wrong time of year, bad directions, two trips to hospital emergency rooms in two different cities, an infected eye, a badly bumped head, a virus, an infection, a substantial financial penalty for flying back early, and so on—we had spent many late-night hours at home, making Internet searches of places we might rent. We began this search well in advance, in late October, and for a long while we were thinking of Tuscany or Umbria, until we realized how hot it would be in those places in July and August, and how unpleasant that would be for Alexandra. Friends who were even more experienced Italian travelers told us that Perugia and Venice would also be hot, the latter overcrowded and overpriced in the height of the tourist season. So we widened the search: Rome, Orvieto, Aosta, the Dolomites, Lake Garda, Lake Maggiore, Lake Orta, the stretch of coastline north of the Cinque Terra. We had visions of a pool, a comfortable house, interesting scenery. I wanted good golf nearby. Amanda wanted to be within walking distance of a town, not isolated far up in some hilltop village where, however quaint and fascinating the life might be, you'd still have to get into the car every time you wanted a box of pasta or a quart of milk.

During one of these late-night searches—it was the middle of March by this point—we came upon a page of rentals connected with a company that seemed to have British roots and an Italian office. Happy Holiday Homes, it was called, and the listing agent was the memorably named Harold Lubberdink. By then we had more or less narrowed the search down to the lakes district, preferably the middle part of the western side of Lake Como. Harold, it turned out, had an office right there. We sent him an e-mail. He replied. We went back and forth about the type of property we wanted, and soon he was filling the wires between us with photos of a house in Musso, close to the northern end of the lake. Perfect for us, he thought. Pool, views, parking.

We didn't like it.

He tried some other apartments and houses, and we didn't like those either, not because we are that picky, but because, bruised and scarred from the previous vacation, haunted by it, we wanted to be as attentive to what the Internet photos did not show as to what they did. We'd once rented a capacious apartment in Lucca that was directly above a nightclub: Would the condo in downtown

Menaggio be so noisy the girls would never get to sleep before midnight? Planning a vacation in southern France, we'd come across an advertisement for a chalet with an ocean view and rented it—and found, upon arrival, that the "chalet" was in a trailer park with a scum-covered swimming pool, a broken tennis-court net, and a system for heating hot water that required an engineering degree to understand. The ocean—visible, as promised—was thirty miles away. During our Italian search, we'd seen elegant villas right beside a busy road, and wonderful old stone houses high up in the hills, where you'd have to keep your car parked half a mile away.

So we were careful, probably even to the point of testing Harold's deep reservoir of patience.

At last, a few weeks into our correspondence he sent us a note with this opening line:

"We found it!!"

Which was typical Harold.

What he had found turned out to be the Mezzegra house, and once we let him know we were serious about renting it, Harold, working with his wife, Sara, turned out to be a sort of dream agent, sending not just three or four photos showing the property from its best angles, but pages of pictures: bedrooms, kitchen, pool, patio, and the lake. During the months between those early exchanges and our arrival, he made contacts at the golf course for me, recommended restaurants, excursions, activities for the children. He offered his own work space if we needed to check or send e-mails, agreed to carry on our correspondence entirely in Italian so I could get my language skills up to speed.

Our plans, complicated as always, called for us to fly into Paris, rent a car there, and make the drive east across France (Harold outlined the best route), then southeast through Switzerland. The route would have us leaving the highway at Lugano and crossing the final mountain range on a much smaller road that led directly into Menaggio, where HHH had their offices. With the exception of Virgin Atlantic Airlines' forgetting to put my golf clubs on the plane (they compensated for this trauma by delivering them, unharmed, to Harold's office an hour before my first tee time), everything went perfectly well until we reached Lugano, Switzerland, and could not find the road that led across the mountains into Italy. We stopped and asked a bus driver, whose confident directions sent us circling down and around and back to the bus stop again. We asked a friendly young Swiss woman in a gas station, who absolutely knew the way: up through a place called Paradiso. Go to Paradiso and you'll see the sign for the state (*cantonale*) road. But, with two tired children in the Renault, and nine hours of highway travel behind us on that day, the trip to Paradiso more closely resembled the trip to Hades. Once again, after a short nightmare of making turns and looking for signs, of stifling the occasional front-seat curse and quelling the periodic backseat rebellions, we were surprised to find ourselves passing the same service station where, twenty minutes earlier, we'd asked the friendly woman for help.

It was ten p.m. by then, too late to disturb a rental agent under ordinary circumstances. But when we'd spoken earlier that day from a phone booth in central Switzerland, Sara had insisted we call from Lugano no matter what the hour if we had any trouble finding the road. Fortunately, our cell phones still had service there, so, parked by the busy lakeshore, close to the edge of our patience, we dialed. Harold answered. He spoke and did business in English, Dutch, German, French, Spanish, and Italian and had the unfortunate habit of speaking tremendously fast in all of them. It was as if he believed himself to be forever on a phone whose battery was going to expire any second. This habit did not soften even when you were speaking to him face-to-face. To complicate matters, he spoke a brand of British English ("Everything is chockablock there at night, you know") with a medium-size Dutch accent, and this, over the phone, late at night, was a challenge.

Adding to the challenge was the girls' perfectly justified impatience—expressed in the language of childhood, which consists of an unself-conscious whining, screaming, and weeping—and another of Harold's habits, one he must have picked up during his years in Italy, of imagining that the road map of the earth is etched into the crust in straight lines. We have driven thousands of miles in Italy, asked directions hundreds of times, and almost without exception the Italians have been more than happy to oblige, whether, like the Swiss woman in Lugano, they actually knew the correct way to go or not. In just about every instance, at the end of their well-meaning recitations, these kind direction-givers have used the phrase *sempre diritto*—"always straight." This habit can be traced back to Columbus's first voyage, the psychological strains of which must have imprinted themselves on the Italian gene pool. After pushing off from Genoa with his small, brave fleet, and losing sight of the European mainland, Cristoforo must have consoled himself on the vast Atlantic with that mantra, *sempre diritto, sempre diritto.* While his actual route ended up being a sort of horizontal question mark down along the West African coast and then across the sea to Santo Domingo, still, there were long straight stretches where all he and his men could see was the fierce gray ocean, and all he and his captains could hear were the ringing doubts of those left safely behind on land. *Always straight, always straight,* they must have said to each other on those storm-tossed nights. And perhaps, returning home in exhausted triumph, they passed the words on to their descendants, who, while they surely know the world is not flat, don't always seem to appreciate that its roads can be crooked.

In any case, the Italians have a different concept of the road map than I do. This is further complicated by the fact that road signs in Italy never show the direction. You don't see A7 AUTO-STRADA EST or OVEST; you see A7 AUTOSTRADA—GENOA, AOSTA, and it is up to you to know where you are, at present, on the compass, in relation to those places. When it comes to verbal directions, in almost every case, Italians make the route seem much simpler than it actually is: just go along here, take your first left, then *sempre diritto,* and you really can't miss it, they will say.

But, of course, you can.

Dutch born and bred, Harold nevertheless seemed to have been infected by this happy overconfidence during his years in the *bel paese.* "Just follow the lake in the direction of Gandria, you can't miss it," he said, as we idled by the shores of Lake Lugano in a stew of frustration and exhaustion. "You'll get here to Menaggio in no time." Though, at his record-breaking speed of speech it sounded like "JusfollothlakeGandriacan'tmissit." He also had the amusing habit of beginning and ending every phone call with the phrase "Fahntahstic, fahntahstic."

So our actual conversation went like this: "Hi, Harold, it's Roland. Sorry to call so late."

"Where are you?"

"Lake Lugano, we're really—"

"Fahntahstic, fahntahstic. You're so close."

"Well, we're really lost. We can't seem to find the road to Menaggio. We've been going around in—"

"JusfollothlakeGandriacan'tmissit."

"Well, someone told us to go via Paradiso—"

"Paradiso? No, no. JusfollothlakeGandriacan'tmissit. Okay? We'll be here, no matter how late. It won't take you long now."

"Okay, we hope to see you soon. If it gets to be too late, we'll just find a hotel—"

"What! No, no, no hotel! We're waiting for you. Jusfollothlake Gandriacan'tmissit."

"Okay. Thanks."

"Fahntahstic, fahntahstic. Excellent, excellent."

But, somehow, following the lake via Gandria wasn't as easy as Harold made it sound, what with the dead ends, the roads that funneled us into parking garages, the forks that might have led toward the Italian border or might not have had we pursued them another twenty minutes, the demonstrations of pain and dissatisfaction from the backseat, the friendly Swiss policeman who pointed us past a construction detour with a few sentences of guidance and got us lost yet again on a hillside of neat, square homes and carefully groomed yards.

At last—it was almost inevitable—we found the right road and began our ascent, zigging and zagging in a kind of practice run for the real mountain roads we'd encounter once we arrived at Lake Como. If we ever did. We found Gandria and climbed toward the border. There, Amanda exerted herself unnecessarily digging out the passports from beneath piles of snacks and maps and guidebooks, because the Swiss guards waved us through their customs checkpoint with barely a glance, and a few yards down the road the singing, humming, foot-tapping Italian guard made some kind of a movement with his chin that could have been interpreted as shorthand for "Passports? What are you talking about, passports? It's late. You're driving a Renault. French license plates. Kids in the car. Go through, go through!" (Here, I have to confess a special affection for Italian border guards; it seems that every time I cross into or out of Italy, one of them is singing.)

Safely through customs, marveling at the way the roads narrowed and the stone walls beside them pinched at the fenders the minute we were on Italian soil, we descended another switchback road, angling back and forth like skiers on a black-diamond slope, past the turn that led to the golf course, past the hospital, past Pizzeria Lugano and the Banco San Paolo, and, at last, into the town of Menaggio itself.

When we'd asked Harold where his office was, he said, "Right here in the center of Menaggio, you can't miss it." But it turned out that we could. The address was Number 4 Via Fourth of November, so we stopped amid the bustling nightlife and sidewalk cafés and asked a partygoer. He said there was no street by that name in Menaggio. To further complicate the situation, it turned out that our phones no longer worked. The girls had come to the sensible conclusion that there was no such place as Mezzegra and our rented house, or, if there was such a house in such a place, it was hundreds of miles away.

Midnight by then, we stopped at the Caffè Centrale for change and called Harold's cell phone from a phone booth on the nearby piazza. Before I could walk back across the piazza from phone booth to car, Harold was there in his Audi convertible (parked illegally behind our illegally parked Renault), hugging Amanda and the girls, speaking his rapid-fire English, mixing in some Italian to give me practice, pointing out that one of the towns across the lake was having a fireworks display, "in honor of your arrival from America." Tired to the point of stupefaction, we watched the splashes of light and color for a moment, then Harold was zooming away, south along the *statale*, sweeping around the corners and racing through the straight stretches, putting half and then three-quarters of his car into the opposite lane, talking on the phone, waving at friends, strangers, and potential clients, marveling at the nighttime view. And then making a sharp right and leading us up the hill to our new home. Which was, as he had promised, perfect for us.

WE SLEPT LATE THE NEXT MORNING and awoke to the sounds of birdcalls, church bells, and someone laughing in the front yard, and the unforgettable view from our bedroom window. A note and two cell phones had been left on the outdoor table. These were Harold's own phones, and he was going to let us use them for the summer and had even filled them up with paid-for minutes.

He and Sara had stocked the refrigerator with milk and coffee and left a bottle of champagne and a bottle of Chianti on the counter. Weeks later, when the washing machine went cranky, Harold had someone there to fix it within twenty-four hours. When I bumped into him in the bank across from his office (where he told us we could always park, even though the signs indicated something quite different), he made off-color jokes with the teller and signed for my exchange so I wouldn't be charged the commission. He took us to a restaurant he liked up on the hill near the golf course and paid for our lunch; he introduced us to another eating place along the shore in Cadenabbia and took out his wallet again. A windsurfer and judo champion, he liked to pick up our girls by their wrists and spin his body around like a hammer thrower so they had a sort of amusement ride every time they saw him. And he could swim two laps of the big pool in our backyard without taking a breath.

Bald and brash, pushing forty, continuously on the cell phone in this or that language, Harold seemed to us to be running for mayor of the Tremezzino—the middle section of the western shore of the lake. One time when I played golf with him at Menaggio and Cadenabbia, he arrived late, talking on the phone, brimming with apologies, then answered sixteen calls in the first nine holes as he batted his scuffed-up Pinnacle this way and that through the trees. You'd see him in front of his office hugging the cleaning lady, or teasing Dalila, his young Italian assistant with the movie-star looks; you'd see him crossing the road with his golden retriever, Suli, on a leash, her two front feet held up off the ground; you'd find him in the bank making jokes with the teller, in the restaurant next door smoking a cigar, or walking up the lawn in front of the house in Mezzegra just as darkness fell, his nine-year-old son, Kevin, two steps behind. They'd been passing by and thought they'd stop in and see how everything was going. A drink? Of course, why not? Golf tomorrow? Yes, absolutely. Dinner afterward at the Lido di

Lenno? He'd make the call. A carrot cake with cream-cheese frosting for Juliana's birthday? Sara would take care of it.

Once, when I had the car for an early-morning round at the golf club, and Amanda and the girls wanted to head into Menaggio to see about some photos Amanda had left there to be developed, they decided to make a low-key adventure out of it and take the bus. They were waiting at the stop in Mezzegra when who should drive by? Harold, escorting a Danish couple interested in buying a three-million-dollar villa. It was the Danish couple's car, and they did not know my wife and children from the president of France, but Harold made them stop and squeezed everyone in. Forget the bus. Why would you take a bus?

The phone would ring at ten a.m. or three p.m. or after dinner, and it would be Harold, asking how everything was going. Were the kids happy? Had we seen anything interesting? Had any good meals? Fahntahstic, fahntahstic. Excellent, excellent.

It took us about a week to understand that Harold said yes to everything, sometimes agreeing to two or three events scheduled for the same time. An hour before we were supposed to meet for lunch, the phone would ring and it would be Harold. "How are you? . . . Fahntahstic, fahntahstic. Listen, we aren't going to be able to get over to Alberto's for pizza after all." Or "We can't make it tonight." Or "Sorry we couldn't be there yesterday. Everything went crazy here." Or he'd show up twenty or thirty or forty minutes late.

But in some way we never completely understood, our contentment was a personal matter to the mayor of the Tremezzino. After we'd been at the lake for only a short while, he and Sara concluded that, since we all liked to swim so much and loved the ocean, it was necessary for us to make a side trip to the Ligurian coast. They had an apartment there, right in the middle of the ancient town of Dolceacqua. Why didn't we just stay in that apartment for a week, no charge?

"All right, we'll go down there for a night," I finally agreed, after they had mentioned it several times.

And Harold said, "A night? All that way for a night? You have to stay three nights, minimum. Wait till you see Dolceacqua. It's fahntahstic, fahntahstic, I tell you. It's excellent. It's perfect for you."

"All right," I repeated. "But we're going to pay you for it."

"Nothing. Just pay the cleaning person, that's all. Nothing for us. It's our gift to you. Just go. Enjoy yourself. You'll love it there." Justgoenjoyyerselfloveitthere.

"All right, but we'd like to stay here for a while longer before we make any trips. I want to play some golf, check out some of the other courses nearby."

"Fahntahstic, fahntahstic. I'll go with you. We'll play together."

"I insist on paying you rent for the Dolceacqua apartment, though."

"Fine. Pay me twenty million euro. Will you forget about the payment and just go?"

As we were driving away from their office, Amanda said, "Doesn't seem like they'll accept any money."

"We'll get him a gift certificate for a couple of golf lessons at the club," I told her. "God knows he could use them."

3

TOURNAMENT GOLF

Not counting one rushed, solitary round I played on a humid afternoon between rain showers, the first time I played at Menaggio and Cadenabbia Golf Club was in a tournament called the Coppa di Consiglio, which, loosely translated, means the Advice Cup. This had originally been scheduled for the day after we arrived in Italy—in fact, I had arranged our arrival so I would be able to play in it—but, for unspecified reasons it had been postponed. Doris—the *segretaria,* a position that does not really exist at American clubs and that involves the making and canceling of tee times and the soothing of club members' bruised egos, but does not include giving golf lessons—had been kind enough to notify me of this cancellation, via e-mail, and to assure me that I would automatically have my tee time switched to the new date. However, when I called the day before the Coppa di Consiglio to double-check, Francisco, the other *segretario,* told me that he could not find my name on the list of tournament tee times. I was not signed up. He'd fix it, he promised.

Kind and reliable as Francisco would turn out to be, I did not know him at the time and did not really know Doris, so, with Amanda and the girls along as pretournament supporters, I drove from Mezzegra up the lake to Menaggio in a cloud of uncertainty. Uncertainty is not the most desirable quality for a golfer in a tournament or a driver on Italy's mountain roads, but I made the climb from Menaggio to Croce mostly without incident (one or two Mediterranean madmen roaring past on the short stretches, that's all; a deliveryman who kept tooting the horn; a bus driver and motorcyclist stopped at one corner, blocking traffic, arguing about who should back away first and let the other pass, since the bus driver had cut the corner, making his awkward turn, and the motorcyclist hadn't waited).

A strange sight greeted us at the start of club property; I had not paid much attention to it on my first visit. Just past the tall, black wrought-iron gates stood a modern sculpture that consisted of two pieces. The first of these was a five-foot-tall stainless-steel disk, probably a foot thick, standing on its edge. A round hole had been cut in the center of the disk, so that, for a second or so as you drove onto the property, you could see, through this hole, the second piece of sculpture, which was a shiny, stainless-steel, realistically dimpled golf ball, three feet in diameter, perched on a metal tee about ten yards behind the disk. Interpreting this modern art installation graciously, I might say that it had been made in the tradition of the old sundials one sees in courtyards and on the sides of buildings everywhere in Italy: a certain alignment of the sun with the protruding metal piece and the thrown shadow had a certain meaning. One o'clock, for instance. Just as, from a certain position on the entrance road, you could see the ball perfectly outlined in the "hole" in the disk, an optical hole-in-one. It is possible that the sculpture had been commissioned to mark the celebration, that summer, of the club's hundred-year anniversary, but the ultramodern work of art and the staid, old golf course went together about as well as peanut butter and osso buco. I will say nothing more about it, wishing only that I could insert here a photograph of the expression on the face of my friend Andrus, a somber Dutchman and frequent player at M&C, when I asked his opinion of the sculpture on the day before we had dinner with him and Elsa at La Baita.

But now we were past the gates and on a gravel drive, curling to the right and uphill, with the pumpkin-colored stucco wall of the elegant clubhouse coming into view. There was an overflow parking lot down a bit to the right. Up the hill straight ahead was the main parking area, suitable for twelve cars. By the time we arrived for my 10:50 tee time, those spaces were filled, so Amanda dropped me and my bag near the clubhouse steps and went, with the girls, to park in the lower lot so they could be witness to the grand moment of my Lake Como competitive-golf debut. I climbed the steps that led between the practice green and the corner of the clubhouse, then went across a stone patio that bordered the eighteenth hole, and toward the *segretaria*'s office, into which three people could squeeze at one time.

Doris was standing behind the counter there. She was a beautiful black-haired woman, somewhere in her late twenties or early thirties, with a slight build, a wonderful, if rarely seen, smile, and some kind of shadow across her. Over the course of our acquaintance, which lasted most of the summer, I would never get even the smallest hint as to the origin of that shadow, but I would notice it without fail every time I encountered her. It was as if some immense weight were leaning against her from the back, and she had to push against it with all her strength to keep from being crushed. Once or twice during the summer I would be in the small office, second or third in line, and Doris would be speaking to one of M&C's 345 members, and the member would be dressed with a certain casual elegance and would be perfectly handsome, or stunningly beautiful, and would have gotten out of his Maserati or her Porsche in the parking lot, and would be upset about this or that slight, and would seem to be changing the chemical makeup of the small room by the merest flicker of a facial muscle. Anyone who has ever played golf at an exclusive American club will recognize this person—privileged, demanding, probably better with investment portfolios than long irons to elevated greens. Doris would be listening attentively, but her smile would temporarily have disappeared. Her fingers would nervously be working the sheet on which tee times were made. After a few minutes, the dispute, or slight, would be smoothed over with promises or apologies, the man or woman would stride out onto the patio and toward the clubhouse restaurant (which offered, from its handful of beautifully set tables, a magnificent view of the mountains to the north), the line would move up, and Doris's smile would reappear, but slowly, the way a blade of grass, crushed for a moment by a passing boot, will eventually regain its posture and sheen.

In any case, as Francisco had promised, all was more or less in order on that day: my name was there next to the 10:50 slot, or so Doris assured me. A bit later, when I was handed my scorecard at the first tee, I would see that my name had been written down as Jack Merullo. Even allowing for pronunciation problems on my end of the phone line, I could not see how Orlando, as my father had been named, and as I called myself in Italy, could be heard as Jack. But I decided to let it go. In the extremely unlikely event that I won the Coppa di Consiglio, I would ask them to engrave the cup's silver surface with my correct name. Otherwise, I would let it go.

Doris finished checking me in and asked me for 80 euros, roughly 112 dollars at the current exchange rate. I had 30 in my pocket. I took out a credit card and handed it over. She fingered it dubiously for a moment, then said that, *in generale,* the club accepted *la carta di credito,* but that the machine was temporarily broken.

"I don't have the cash," I told her.

And she said, "That is not a problem. I am sure you will pay. You can pay later. The next time."

Which is not something you typically encounter at American golf clubs, no matter what kinds of cars are in the lot.

I thanked her and asked about the possibility of renting a riding cart. I knew from the previous day's round that the course was hilly. The day was hot and atypically humid, and thinking about the tournament as I'd been trying to get to sleep the night before, I'd had visions of losing my first drive in M&C's heavy rough and having to hike back up to the tee to hit my next shot, with sweat dripping down my shirt and foursomes backing up behind me like cars in Mezzegra's center as you tried to find a safe opening on the *statale.*

"I'm sorry," Doris said in her capable English. "But the carts are just for seniors only."

"At what age is someone considered a senior?"

"How old are you?"

I told her and felt vaguely flattered to have missed the age by two years. Let the seniors have their rides, I thought. Young, fit players like Jack Merullo will walk. I asked for a pull cart, or *carrello.*

"You have to ask at the caddy master's. You pay him there." She paused, glanced down at my shoes. "It is only a little money."

Just behind the clubhouse, a few yards below and to the right of the eighteenth green, the caddy master's quarters were housed in a musty, tile-roofed shed crammed tight with members' bags, small piles of lost hats and headcovers, tools, hoses, *elettrici,* and *carrelli.* All this was presided over by a young man I would come to think of as The Smiling Matteo. Twenty-five or twenty-eight, with brown curly hair and a high forehead, The Smiling Matteo spoke a slurred, rapid-fire Italian and went about his duties capably and efficiently, but with as much enthusiasm as an alpine Ivan Denisovich, counting off the days. He took one of the pull carts out of the shadows of his domain, wheeled it into the light, and thanked me for the one-euro tip on top of the three-euro fee. I asked about the location of the driving range. "Just down this path," he said, gesturing. I loaded my bag onto the *carrello*, accepted an embrace from Juliana and Alexandra, wishes for a good round from my wife, and headed down the path.

At Menaggio and Cadenabbia's driving range on that day there were the customary mats to hit from, and the familiar empty plastic buckets lying around, but no balls. I tried asking one of the boys who was milling about, but he responded with a puzzled, perhaps even a suspicious, look. How do you get balls? What do you mean, how do you get balls? I examined the shed behind the mats, the stacked plastic buckets there, just like home except that there was the word *gettone* on a sign beside the metal dispenser. I knew this word from other golfing trips in Italy.

"Where do you buy the tokens?" I asked an older boy.

"At the caddy master's."

There were only twelve minutes or so until I teed off, not enough time to walk up the hill to The Smiling Matteo's place, ask him why he hadn't said anything about tokens, buy one, come back to the range, and warm up my swinging muscles. But, by some familial magic, Juliana, Alexandra, and Amanda came walking down the path at that moment, at least as excited about the tournament as I was, anxious to see their father or husband in all his golf glory.

While I refined my chipping technique, Amanda hurried back to the caddy master and purchased a *gettone*. I hit half a dozen balls, kissed the girls, then headed over to the first tee.

A small-built young man named Antonio and middle-aged man called Francisco, my playing partners for the day, were waiting there. I could see from their posture and their greetings that they felt the same way I did about the tournament. To begin with, it was small change (*denaro spicciolo,* as the Italians would say), and we knew it: Menaggio and Cadenabbia's Coppa di Consiglio was not exactly the kind of event that has its results posted on the ticker tape at the bottom of ESPN's *SportsCenter* screen. Second, we understood that we had little or no chance of winning. Middle handicappers (Antonio played to a 12, Francisco was a 15; I carried a 10.2 at the time) don't win tournaments like this. Really good players—the 2s and 4s and 6s win the gross competition; and the really bad players—the 30s and 40s—have a good day, shoot 126, and take home the net prize. But a tournament is a tournament, an opportunity—in certain lives a rare opportunity—to test yourself under pressure. Succeed or fail, triumph or falter, I enjoy the challenge, and judging from the excitement on the faces of my playing partners, they enjoyed it as well.

We made our introductions, exchanged scorecards, and waited for a slow foursome in front of us to clear the fairway.

The first hole at M&C, like many of those that follow, is a beautifully laid-out piece of golf landscape, a long, tricky 432-yard par four. The fairway drops off sharply from the elevated tee box, slanting to the right as it curls and flattens. At about the 130-yard mark, it drops again toward a two-level green, invisible from the tee box, that is guarded by bunkers right and left. Only two shots can work from the back tees: a long driver with a fade on it, or a fairway wood or long iron hit in a high draw over the treetops. Neither is a particularly comforting way to start a tournament. Mistakes on this first hole were costly because of the thick woods to the right side, where the ground beneath the trees sloped off steeply, and the grass was six inches deep and speckled with pinecones and fallen branches. To the left a service road ran on top of a sort of levee, and beyond the levee was another hillside covered in trees and brush.

It was decided that, as the only foreigner in the group, I should hit first. With the girls and Amanda watching from the edge of the parking lot, behind the tee, I addressed the ball. Cleared the mind, made the regular three waggles—and then, just as I was about to start the backswing, Francisco, who had been standing behind me, said something in Italian that I did not understand. Actually, I understood one word, *molesto*, "bother." After a second of getting over my surprise, and after watching Francisco cross to the other side of the tee, where I could see him, I understood that he was worried that he'd bother me if he stood behind me. I have a good friend who would be bothered, but I am not. My friend doesn't like anyone to stand behind him when he swings because he is afraid he will accidentally hit them, and he is such a tenderhearted fellow that the thought of accidentally hurting someone—even an inattentive someone—on the golf course is more than he can bear. But I prefer to trust my playing partners to protect themselves, and I don't mind at all if they stand where I can't see them. It was useless to say that to Francisco, however, who had already moved, and it was unpleasant at that particular moment to hear a word such as *molesto*, even though I knew the Italian meaning differed in certain ways from the English cognate.

I stood up to the ball again, settled my feet, made my waggles, and tried the high draw. I got the first part right. The ball flew high enough to go over the trees, but there was no draw. After a few seconds, we heard the disconcerting sound of a golf ball working its way through foliage. I looked back at my threesome of supporters, forced a smile, shrugged. Not good.

Francisco, up next, hit a nice enough short drive down into the middle of the fairway. Antonio, who probably had the best swing of all of us, pushed a tee shot long and not quite as badly right as my own.

"I'll hit a provisional," I announced, though I used the word *provvisione*, which probably means something like "food supplies."

Francisco was kind enough to make me aware of my mistake. "*Provvisorio,* you mean," he said. I hit a *provvisorio,* safely left, waved to the girls and Amanda, and my fellow competitors and I started off down the slope.

I found the first ball—thanks to a lucky bounce off the trees it was in deep rough but playable—but, instead of punching out safely into the fairway and playing for bogey, I tried a tricky cut with a four iron and hit an eighty-yard grounder to the equivalent of second base. Second base was located under an apple tree. I managed to chop the ball out of the deep grass there and into the front bunker. Splashed it out. Two putts. Double bogey. Antonio made par. Francisco a five.

The second and third holes were both par threes that came back along the right-hand side of the first. One of these par threes was steeply uphill, and the other steeply back down. On two, I hit a six iron into the front left bunker and made bogey. On three, it was a seven iron just right of the putting surface, a weak chip, and a three-putt for another double.

It was not a promising way to begin the Coppa di Consiglio, and if I could have offered myself any advice at that moment it would have been to try to relax. I had not played in any tournaments that summer, and the air of competition seemed to have worked its way into my tendons and ligaments, winding them one notch tighter than usual. My full swings, chips, and putts were all tentative, and tentative doesn't work in golf any more than it works in heart surgery. I knew this, but I wasn't able to pass the information from brain to body.

Compounding the situation was the fact that, as the only outsider, the American, the American golf writer, I felt some kind of strange pressure. As if Antonio and Francisco would be judging the standards of American golf by my performance on that day. I imagined them thinking, He says he's a 10. Let's see what an American 10 plays like.

And so, of course, I played like an American 20.

On the elevated fourth tee, as we were waiting, again, for the group in front of us, I decided that a bit of conversation might loosen me up, so I asked Francisco if he could bring me up to speed on the Italian golf vocabulary. I had played in Italy before that trip, but it had been several years, and the words had slipped into the recesses of memory, and they weren't the kind of words you could dependably find in your average English/Italian dictionary. "Remind me how you say *fairway, rough, green, driver,* would you?" I asked.

He grinned and said, *"Ferrway, ruff, grin, driver."* Rolling the Italian *r*'s.

"All right. Got it."

"A hook is a *gancio,* though."

"All right. We'll try to avoid the *gancio*'s."

The fourth was a short hole, easy to like. Played from the elevated tee, it ran straight for most of its 329 yards, with a large fairway bunker crossing the landing area. At the 260 mark, a stand of trees pinched the short grass from the right side, and the hole angled slightly right from there to a green with a steep drop behind it and bunkers in front.

I managed a par and felt my game coming back, the muscles loosening, the fog of nervousness beginning to evaporate. Jack Merullo was making a charge from the bottom of the first division.

And then on the reachable par-five fifth, I made eight.

Seven over par after four.

Francisco was not faring much better and seemed, if anything, even more nervous than I was. He had an abrupt swing (*movimento* is the word in Italian, and it sounds better than it looked in Francisco's case), an almost violent stroke in which he reared back and then whipped his club through the downswing. As is true with most awkward swings, sometimes this worked and sometimes it didn't. Antonio, whose father had taken him to St. Andrews to play as a boy, and who decorated his golf balls with a small green shamrock, was only a stroke over par at that point. A small-built, elegantly dressed, handsome young man of twenty, with wavy, black hair and dark eyes, he said that at one time he had played a lot of golf. He had the swing to prove it. "But then," he told me in English, with a dimpled smile, "the soccer, the girls . . ."

Now that these other priorities had interfered with his golfing life, he'd developed putting troubles. So many putting troubles that he was using a grip I've never seen: he took hold of the putter shaft with his left hand low and wrapped the fingers of his right hand around his left forearm, pinching the shaft between. Even this didn't help. The yips. The pushes. The yanks. After stumbling a bit on the sixth, seventh, and eighth, he would finish the front with a score of 39, but could easily have sliced five shots off that number with respectable putting.

For me, after the disastrous start, there was one bright spot, and it came in an unlikely place. The par-four ninth might have been the most difficult hole to par that I have ever played. It was 375 meters, or 410 yards, so steeply uphill that Francisco and I were huffing from about the ladies' tee onward, wishing we were a few years older and had qualified for senior status and a cart. But it wasn't so much the steepness or the length that made it so difficult, it was the incredible narrowness. The hole climbed through a V-shaped valley between banks of deep rough and trees to either side, and at eighteen paces wide, there was almost no room for error until you reached the landing area, at about the 235-yard mark, where it opened up just a bit. The only club I can fly 235 yards uphill is the driver, on a good day, and the driver is not my club of choice when faced with a fairway that looks as wide as the back of a snake. So I hit my only hybrid, a two-iron-equivalent Hogan sixteen degrees with a metal shaft. The good news was that the ball stayed on the fairway; the bad news, that I had 220 yards remaining to the green, all of it sharply uphill. As if to add insult to injury, the second half of the hole was even narrower than the first, and the green had three levels and was steeply canted back in the direction of the tee.

But at that point I had nothing to lose: any hopes of Jack Merullo placing in the Advice Cup had been lost somewhere on the fifth hole, as he was helping the maintenance crew trim the rough with his seven iron. Once, twice, three times, *bravo!* So on the wicked ninth on that day I hit a vicious, anger-propelled rocket of a three wood that flirted with the right-hand tree line, curled leftward as gracefully as the calf of a female gymnast on the balance beam, then bounced once onto the green and skipped up to the back level. *"Bellissimo!"* Francisco called over. Antonio had a smile on his face and was looking at me as if I'd merely been pretending to be a mediocre player for those first eight holes and was only now showing my true American mastery of the game.

That shot made the second half of the climb more enjoyable than the first, though by that point in the round, having forgotten to bring along a bottle of water, and forgotten that the M&C had no drinking stops, I was starting to feel a little dry.

In any case, I was overjoyed to two-putt from fifty feet above the hole, and pleased with a par. But 45 on the par-34 front side, for a 10-handicap golfer, is not exactly a score to carry home and brag to the girls about.

That is the best and the worst part of the handicap system. You know exactly how good you are, or should be. Forty-five is a dream score for some players, an absolute nightmare for others. For me, it just leaves a sour taste.

I parred the equally narrow, slightly less uphill par-three tenth, and then slaked my thirst and soothed my wounds at the stone cottage behind the tenth green, where they served a dessert called *torta di nocciole,* or sweet hazelnut pie, and where I bought two bottles of the Italian equivalent of POWERade. No credit cards were accepted there, either, and no cash: you signed for your food. It's the kind of arrangement usually reserved for members at private clubs. When I wrote my name on a slip of paper, reminding her that I wasn't a member, or *socio,* the woman at the little stone house assured me I would be billed, at some point, somewhere in the future. That never happened. (My guilt about never paying for that food is somewhat tempered by the fact that the stone snack bar was closed about seven-eighths of the times I played at M&C, so my debt is small.)

"Is it customary to tip the attendant?" I asked my partners, as we sat at a metal table on the stone patio and ate and drank in a relaxed fashion that would have shocked my American tournament-playing friends. We were between holes, after all, groups on all the holes behind us. Antonio and Francisco shook their heads no, never.

From the eleventh tee, the course moved steeply downhill, with mountain views that would have distracted the most focused golfer and comforted the most disappointed. We were in a high valley, with six-thousand-foot peaks all around. And as we headed down and to the west, each hole opened onto a new vista of jagged rock faces and alpine forests, of valleys and tile-roofed settlements, of sunlight and shadow. It was almost enough to make up for the pain of our high scores. On thirteen and fourteen, the back-to-back, reachable par-fives, Antonio carded a pair of double bogeys that crushed whatever hopes he'd been cherishing; Francisco hacked his way through the rough as if his ability to find the fairway had been left at the snack bar; and though my fortunes had seen a small resurrection at the turn, it was a temporary resurrection, and too little, too late, in any case. In the middle of that scenic back nine, a familiar gloomy silence fell over the three of us. We had all reached that point in a tournament when you give up hope. Even after a 45 on the front, you can still tell yourself you'll come roaring back with a 35 on the back and maybe win one of the bottom prizes for net score. But we were past that now, all of us. The mourning lasted a few holes, then we revived. Antonio finally sank a couple of putts, and that lifted him out of his sour silence and returned the smile to his face. I asked him what he planned to do with his life and he said, "My father is a lawyer, and so I must, *must,* become a lawyer, too, even though I don't want to."

"What would you like to do?"

"I don't know." He shrugged, as if the question did not particularly worry him.

I told him that, when I had been about his age, my father, a midlevel state employee, had wanted me to be a doctor, but that it would have been a disaster. I would have made a miserable doctor, would have hated having to schedule my vacations months in advance, the malpractice worries, the parade of sorrow on the daily schedule. It was a good career, but one I just wasn't made for, and I was glad I'd resisted the parental pressure. Half my age, Antonio beamed his magnificent smile back at me and shrugged again, but the gesture had a tinge of pity, or perhaps condescension. You don't understand, he seemed to be telling me. You have never played St. Andrews. You have never belonged to a club like this. Your life, your father, your expectations—all must have been different.

Francisco avoided the rough for two holes in a row, a kind of miracle, and having abandoned all hope for success in the tournament, we all fell back on our enjoyment of the game, on the ego boost of an occasional good shot. When I finished with a six on the short, narrow par-four eighteenth, Francisco said, in Italian, without malice, "Six is a big number—*un numero grande*—for this hole." He was smiling ruefully, a fellow sufferer. He came in at 94, Jack Merullo at 90, the young Antonio at 85. On that day, Menaggio and Cadenabbia had knocked all of us down.

"I never shoot my handicap here," the young law student complained. "Never on this course do I shoot my handicap."

Before the round, I'd joked with Amanda, saying that, if I didn't at least break 90, I wouldn't be coming home. So, after we'd shaken hands and walked off the eighteenth green, I called her from the patio, sweaty and tired and troubled by watching the electronic scoreboard flashing JACK MERULLO not far from the bottom of the first flight. She said, "So, how'd you do? Can you come home?"

And I said, "No, not exactly."

But I was only temporarily discouraged. Every dedicated golfer is a compulsive optimist. He or she has to be. Deep down inside you have to believe that you are good, or at least that you have the capacity to one day be good, or at least that you might someday improve. The new clubs, the next lesson, a tip you read in your golf magazine or heard from a playing partner—somehow things will turn around and you will be good. I had been stranded near the 10 handicap mark for the past four years, after working my way down from the low 20s and into the teens. It's not a bad number. There are worse numbers. But somewhere inside myself I thought, I could be a 5. Really I could. And as I returned my *carrello* to The Smiling Matteo and lugged my heavy bag down to the gravel lot to wait for Amanda and the girls, I thought: I could break 80 on this course without much trouble. I'm going to do that before we head home. I am going to have my revenge.

4

BELLAGIO, PEARL
OF COMO

If you examine a map of northern Italy, you will see that Lake Como looks something like an armless figure from a Dr. Seuss book high-stepping in hilarious good humor through the mountains north of Milano. The character has a stick torso from the waist up, but no head. And two caterpillar legs that wobble down between the high peaks and end in medium-size cities: Como on the west and Lecco to the east. The town of Bellagio occupies the point of land where these two legs intersect, and since it has the reputation of being one of the glitziest resorts in the world (the Rockefellers had a summerhouse there; it is now the Bellagio-Serbelloni artists' colony. Napoléon lived in Villa Melzi, a short walk from downtown. Famous visitors have included Pliny the Younger in Roman times, and Franklin Roosevelt, Churchill, JFK, and Al Pacino in more modern ones).

We decided, on the day before the Fourth of July, that we should go there and eat pizza.

We had a breakfast of cereal and fruit on our patio—from which we could see the ocher-, pumpkin-, and lemon-colored fin de siècle buildings of Bellagio across the water and a bit to the northCthen headed into Menaggio, intending to park at the embarcadero and take the boat across. But the parking spots at the boat dock were all filled, and the spaces along the lake road leading into downtown were filled, and we ended up driving all the way to the north end of the town and squeezing into a place that might have been legal but probably wasn't, behind a little chapel next to a cemetery, then trotting all the way back through town and along the *statale,* and catching the steamboat with thirty seconds to spare.

Eleven minutes and four or five versions of the spectacular view later (as the boat churned across the Como leg of the lake, the mountains offered themselves from a slightly different angle every few hundred meters, like a lineup of experienced models showing off designer dresses in shades of green and gray, first this hip, then that, shoulders swinging, hems flipping up as they turned), we were spilling down the gangway in a crowd of other visitors. Not surprisingly, the main commercial street of the famous town—(no cars allowed)—runs close to the shoreline, and there you can find shops selling silk, ceramics, hand-tailored shirts, olive-oil dispensers, miniature brass Ferris wheels, watercolors of the view you can turn around and look at, watches, earrings, ice cream, towels, shoes, socks, and $20 bowls of soup. Steep, narrow stairways, or *scaline,* run like bumpy stone streams down the hillside behind and between these shops, and it is common to hear the *bellagini* use them in their directions: Go to the fourth *scalino,* then it's the second shop after that. But it is not easy to find the *bellagini* because the town is flooded with visitors speaking in twenty different languages. They prowl the promenade licking colorful globes of gelati, they peruse the merchandise. Or they sit in the shaded cafés drinking high-priced coffee concoctions and writing postcards to those left at home. *They say it is the prettiest town in Italy, and I think they're right!*

Ordinarily, Amanda and I avoid the most popular tourist spots, at least in high season. We do not like to be in crowds of people who all seem to be looking for the same thing and not quite finding it, who all seem to have read the same guidebook. But even to our sensibilities, there was something strangely inoffensive about Bellagio. I don't know what it was. "Tourist trap but nicer than that," I wrote in my notes that night, and it may simply have been the elegance of the stucco houses lined up along the quay, their flower boxes and concrete window trim with scrolls cut into it, their shutters in various greens. Or the couples of various ages holding hands, as if they'd carried the dream of peace and togetherness like a bouquet of flowers from the rainy fields of Ireland or the baking streets of Bombay and had at last found a suitable landscape in which to set it down. It might have been the air—sunny and lake-cooled. Or the dancing surface of the lake itself with the sun glinting off it like a million tiny flashbulbs going off in an endless sequence.

We strolled and window-shopped until it was time for lunch. We like to avoid the crowds at mealtime, too, especially at mealtime, and so we fell back on a strategy we'd devised on a visit to Venice years before. After a few hours of strolling and window-shopping in that other magical and tourist-choked place, we noticed that everyone was walking along the same streets, standing before the menus of the same cafés, and sitting in those cafés having the same meals. And that if you took a right turn when the crowd went left, more often than not you'd end up on a street that was just as beautiful and a tenth as crowded, and eating at a café with a more original menu offered at a third the price.

So, when we reached the lunch hour in Bellagio, we picked one of the *scaline* at random and climbed to the top. There, parallel to the shoreline boulevard and 150 feet higher, we found another lane that was good for strolling, but where we could have counted the tourists on the fingers of two hands. And then because someone—me probably—was making noises about lunch, we fell back on another old strategy and went into a clothing shop to ask for recommendations. I don't know why this works so well. There may be some connection between good taste in food and retail clothiers. Maybe, since they spend so much of their day sitting around waiting for customers, they have hours to think about food, and then, on their breaks, they seek out only the best restaurants. In any case, the two women in this fancy dress shop, one fifty and the other half that age, seemed surprised to see me. I immediately apologized for not coming in to purchase a $400 dress, told them I was there with my family, and that we wanted to have lunch in a place that maybe wasn't just for the tourists. After a minute or so of sincere consultation, they both said at once, "Baba Yagar." I thought, for a moment, that they were calling down some vengeful female spirit of the hills upon me for interrupting their midday reveries, for ignoring their silk and satin, but they gave directions happily enough, and after a short walk we became the only patrons on a covered porch that held twenty tables. Soon we were sharing a salad of arugula, lettuce, shaved carrots, and red peppers that tasted as if they had been picked eight minutes before. The second we left the clothing store, the women had gotten on the phone ("They're Americans. They look like salad people. He didn't buy any of the dresses, but, even so, we recommended you highly, so offer your best") and the waiter at Baba Yagar had ducked out into a backyard garden and started picking. Toward the tail end of the salad we were served two pizzas, one *margherita,* one *salsiccia,* which came on a wooden serving platter and were oval-shaped and unsliced, and with a half liter of dry cabernet, close to perfect.

Then it was more meandering—down to the tip of land that separates the two lower branches of the lake, and back to the busy shoreline section—ice cream, coffee, ogling of expensive shirts, watches, necklaces, earrings.

I am tired of the phrase *dolce far niente,* the sweetness of doing nothing, but what better way is there to describe that day? The entire group of tourists seemed to have been infected, and I watched them and tried to puzzle it out. What I did not understand was how the Italians, tourists and locals alike, seemed to spend so much of their time relaxing—the long lunch hours, the exorbitant amount of vacation time (an average of forty-one days compared with the average American's thirteen)—and still managed to have all the things our frantic labor enabled us to have—house, car, nice shirts, nicer shoes, good food, trips abroad. I decided, strolling along not far from the place where the Rockefellers had once set down their own hopeful bouquets, to make a study of the economics of doing nothing, the art of not worrying, the magic of eating like this and not gaining weight. I had an intuition that this sweetness, this art, this magic, could in some way be applied with positive results to my family time, my writing, my golf game. All the way across the lake I thought about that, and back at the Mezzegra house I took a nap with the bedroom windows open wide, then had a dip in the pool with my daughters, and a light supper, and sat out on the patio with a glass of Chianti and watched as a thin fog rolled lazily between the mountain peaks and brushed at the top of the dark blue water. There was such a thing, it seemed to me, as trying too hard. There was a way, even in the golf swing, in which effort had to be balanced with repose. There was a right rhythm to things, and though, for me, too many vacation days of strolling picturesque streets licking ice cream cones and ogling hand-tailored shirts would mean a kind of stultification of the soul, still, I had no doubt leaned over too far in the other direction. Who was it that said, "Swing easy and accept the extra distance"? Fred Couples? I could use more of that, I decided, on the golf course and off. I would think of it as the Bellagio lesson.

5

DOMENICO

Not long after our trip across the lake I had an extremely odd round at Menaggio and Cadenabbia, a round that would test my new Bellagio-inspired theory about playing in a more laid-back fashion (or, as I had come to think of it, the Sweetness of Golfing Slowly).

It was a Saturday morning. I'd made a nine-o'clock tee time—fairly early by Italian standards—thinking I could finish the round before the weekend crowds came up from Milan and be home to enjoy a swim with the girls in the hot afternoon. Up at seven, a stretch, a shower, the painkillers, the cereal, the water. It was a pleasure to walk out onto the patio in the morning sunlight, in golf attire, then go down the steps to the shadowy, quiet garage. As is the case with other pleasures, part of the great joy of golf comes from the anticipation of it. For me, this anticipation can be so intense that I sometimes experience a small frenzy of impatience during the forty-minute drive to the course where I'm a member. I sometimes have to force myself not to hurry the changing of shoes and the arranging of my bag on the three-wheeled golf cart. This mood, this internal sprinting, can affect the swing. My *movimento* has a naturally slow tempo, and if I rush it at all, the result is usually a piece of embarrassing ugliness: a hideous ground ball, a savage *gancio* into the maple trees.

So, as I eased the Renault out of the garage, I was simultaneously anxious to be on the first tee at M&C and trying to slow myself down. I glided along Via Pola past the Mussolini site, then stopped for a quick cappuccino (always calming) and brioche at the Bar Roma in Tremezzo, where the woman and her look-alike daughter served visitors pleasantly and endured the chattering of the old regulars with a particularly dignified patience. There was no parking directly in front of the Bar Roma. Spaces were located across the road, a row of six or seven of them set perpendicular to the lakeside railing. After the first couple of visits, I would back into these spaces—because pulling to the curb, waiting for a break in the traffic, then throwing the car into reverse and swinging it rear-end-first between the lines made me feel more Italian; and because, post-cappuccino, it was easier to pull out into the traffic lanes if you were facing forward. The tour buses, the motorcycles, the bicycle-racing teams—it was safer for all concerned if you could see them coming through the driver-side window, rather than over the shoulder.

I had a good parking *movimento* going on that morning. The right blinker and pull-over, the glance in the rearview, the shift into reverse, and the confident arc into the tight space, leaving the back bumper a foot from the rail. I walked across the busy *statale* in a happy, hopeful mood and enjoyed my ritual pre-golf snack there to the strange music of Comasco, the local dialect that bore as much resemblance to Italian as cockney does to Spanish. And then, energized by the cappuccino, I shot out of the parking space like a native and went into Menaggio and then up through the hairpin turns on a burst of positive energy. I arrived early enough to secure one of the choice parking spots and checked in at the *segreteria,* full of hopes for a bit of revenge on Menaggio and Cadenabbia.

I rented a *carrello* (though, in my haste, I mistakenly asked for a *carrollo*) from Emilio, an older caddy master who was on duty that day in place of The Smiling Matteo and whose Italian was spoken as if he were holding in his mouth some of La Baita's creamy *pasta boscaiola.* At the driving range, bathing in the glorious morning, I hit four precise sand wedges, then began to shank. These were dead shanks, as the phrase goes, the ball slanting off the clubface at a forty-five-degree angle, and shooting away to the right and over the high net that separated the range from the tenth fairway. One after the next, over the net, into the net, into the trees there. I put the sand wedge back in the bag and took out the seven iron and shanked three more. By that point the happy anticipation I'd felt had mutated into a half-astonished bitterness, a silent fury, at the club, at the ball, at the inventors of the game of golf. I tried the five iron and lined four balls absolutely sideways, a right-handed batter going opposite field. I then came to my senses and gave up and left the driving range in what can only be described as the depths of despair.

I needed to buy some tees. The sign on the store that sold golf supplies and articles of clothing indicated that it opened at eight thirty. But this must have been a Mediterranean eight thirty, because it was eight forty by then and the store was obviously closed. If I understood him correctly, Emilio said that the woman should have arrived by then, but—a shrug, a helpless raising of the eyebrows—she had not. I waited for him to ask me how my practice session had gone, but he spared me that polite curiosity.

To add another dash of Mediterranean spice to the day, Francisco, one of my partners in the tournament, had promised to join me for the round, but as it got closer to nine o'clock, there was no sign of him, either. I decided to hit some putts. The practice green had been ravaged by a week of tournaments celebrating the club's centennial, and by a period of unusually heavy rain just before we arrived, so the holes looked as if they had been torn, not cut, into the putting surface, and some burnt-out patches of the green resembled the Sahara desert in a satellite photo. It was an embarrassment for a club of that stature. And my performance on the range had been an embarrassment for a player of my modest abilities. Still, I found a section where the grass was still living, sank a few long ones, and felt some of the pain of the driving range subside.

At ten of nine the storekeeper arrived. She was a congenial woman named Sally, who spoke British English. She told me she had come to the lake to study Italian, met the man who would become her husband, and "the rest was history." We talked for a moment about the difference between Italian and English weather, which seemed to have to do, mostly, with the sun being almost always visible in the former and almost never visible in the latter— then she sold me a small packet of tees for $5.20.

Nine o'clock arrived, Francisco did not.

From the high first tee, still so traumatized by the shanking practice session that I would have done anything not to hit the ball right (which was death on that hole, in any case), I hit the ball left. Far to the left, into the high rough below the levee. It was, despite everything, a pleasant walk down the hill, with the mountain peaks catching the morning sun in front of me, and the smallest of breezes stirring the leaves of the chestnut trees to right and left. But, alas, the experience of shanking etches itself into the memory, and still traumatized after I had popped the ball safely out into the fairway, I yanked a midiron left a second time, into the trees. It bounced smartly out, as if asking me to try again. I glanced to my right, toward the second hole, and was sorry to see a couple teeing off there. Or more or less teeing off. The man hit a ground ball thirty or forty yards, and the woman followed suit, as if they were playing some game of their own in which the second golfer was obliged to imitate the first. This did not bode well for a quick round, and the first three strokes of the day did not bode well for breaking 80, and I confess to having the fleeting thought that the golfing gods were sending me a message: wheel your *carrello* back up the hill, put the clubs in the trunk, and go home. But I did not do that.

A few seconds later I glanced over at the leisurely couple again, hoping for progress, and saw an odd sight: someone, a man in a white dress shirt, was driving his golf cart down the middle of the second fairway in the wrong direction, from the green toward the tee, as if the couple were invisible. I thought, at first, that he had left a club on the tee or lost something else and was driving the course backward, looking for it. But, no, in front of the tee he made a sudden right turn, almost on two wheels, and wandered down toward the fourth green. Lost, perhaps.

My fourth shot went straight. Straight into the bunker. I began the round of revenge with a double bogey.

I arrived at the second tee, in a less than perfectly good mood, to find that the leisurely couple had not yet started up the fairway. I invited them to join me, but they declined. "We like to practice, but you go right on through," the man said with a British accent.

So I stood up beside them, confidently, with my six iron and 10-handicap swing, my Hogan sticks and Titleist driver, my bag with the USGA membership tag on it, my shined shoes that I'd won in a tournament back home. I stood up there and shanked the ball so badly that I came within three feet of ripping the roof off the English couple's golf cart, which was parked just behind the spot where they were standing. In a spasm of humiliation, I said, "That's not typical," something I don't typically say, and then, "I hope I don't hold you up," even though I knew there was not a chance in a thousand I would hold them up, once I located my shanked Titleist and brought it back into the general territory of the second hole.

"That's fine," the woman said generously, "but there is someone ahead who will probably hold *you* up."

Since the day had already taken on a full freight of negativity, I chose to ignore this remark. Thanks to a nice recovery, I made five on the par-three second and followed that with four on the par-three third. As I was finishing up there, the aforementioned fellow in the white shirt went past in his cart, just then descending from the elevated fourth tee. He appeared to have figured out the map of the holes, belatedly, and to be moving along at a reasonable pace. In any case, I was five over par after three.

The fourth hole at M&C, that short par-four that bent slightly right at the end, was a place where you had to keep your tee shot left—not a problem for me on that day. I hit a three wood over the bunker to the left side of the fairway, good position, then lofted a sand wedge a few yards short, onto the fringe. As I was walking toward the green, I again came upon the man in the white shirt. He was moving toward the next tee, and I greeted him with the traditional "*Una bella giornata.*" A nice little day. His response was extremely odd. He made a sort of growl, which, uncharitably interpreted, could have been considered lascivious. Then he said, "*Sì, una giornata superba,*" as if he were correcting me. It wasn't a *nice* day, it was a *superb* one. I nodded. All right, nice, superb, the day was fine. I noticed that he had gloves on both hands. Stocky, balding, sunglasses, loafers on his feet, the dress shirt—he cut a bizarre figure on the course, as if he were more or less familiar with the game and yet badly out of sync, as if he'd learned it from an instruction manual, or a DVD, and missed some of the lessons.

After our quick exchange of greetings, I tried to pretend he was not there and hoped against hope that he would suddenly pick up speed or let me through. From the fringe I hit a poor chip and made bogey, but the good news was that the man with the white shirt had struck a successful tee shot on five and driven his cart a couple hundred yards down the fairway. It seemed as if he would keep a good pace from that point on. I left my *carrello* on the path and climbed up to the tee. Then came the not-so-good news: the man in the white shirt was driving back toward me, the same thing he had done on the second hole. Was it some new kind of game? A kooky superstition? Hit a shot, go find where it had landed, then drive back toward the tee of each hole, make a sharp turn, nearly tip over the cart, then go on to the next tee and try it again?

As he approached the tee, perhaps to hit another ball, he waved for me to go ahead of him. I nodded, took my stance, waggled, and hit my first decent shot of the day, a hybrid two iron that drew well down into the left side of the fairway, perfect position on that uphill par five. Then, for some unknown reason, perhaps caught up in a spasm of excessive generosity after the good shot, I asked the man if he would like to join me. He paused a moment, surprised, then nodded, climbed out of the cart and up onto the tee, but *very slowly*. He was not an old man—in fact, he was probably ten years younger than I am—but he moved at the pace of a wasp on a cold New England morning. He paused there on the tee for an unconscionably long time. When I was about to ask him what was the matter, he finally took his stance, wiggled and wobbled his shoulders and hips like someone trying to shake an ice cube out of the back of his shirt, slashed his club back and down at the ball, and hit a decent fade, 175 yards.

After this shot, he asked if I wanted to put my bag on the cart and ride with him, but I said I preferred to walk. He smirked. He then asked if I was there alone, and I said no, I was staying at the lake with my wife and two daughters. He smirked again. Although my flawed Italian was better than his English, he seemed intent on conversing in English. He told me his name was Domenico; he was from Parma and didn't play much, but practiced often. "Are there a lot of courses around Parma?" I asked.

And he said, "I do not know it."

His drive had come to rest a few yards behind my two hybrid, and I noticed, as he stood over his ball and wiggled and wobbled, that he was playing blades, those unforgiving irons favored by the very best players. He hit a decent second, maybe 125 yards. I hit a three wood almost to the green. He squirted a third sideways, into the deep rough on the hillside, and required four shots to get onto the putting surface, where he did not mark his ball. The green was hard; my delicate little misplayed chip rolled all the way to the back, fifty feet from the hole. I left my first putt fifteen feet short but sank the second, at which point Domenico picked up his ball without saying a word. Not "That was a lousy first putt you had there." Not "Nice recovery." Not "Good par." Not "I've reached my limit." Nothing. He picked up his ball and got into the cart.

We went to the next tee, a downhill par four with a wide landing area, and a green that sat behind a bunker and slanted away from the fairway toward the woods behind. "Tough approach shot here," I said.

Domenico said, "Yes, a difficult hole. But is wonderful."

I like a challenge myself, and judging by that remark, Domenico seemed to have a positive attitude, so I promised myself to try harder to overlook his quirks. I pulled a driver well into the left rough, and then, after Domenico had hit, I announced that I was hitting a provisional.

The idea of the provisional ball seemed alien to him. "Why did you hit again?"

"It's a provisional," I said, making sure I used the correct word this time. "*Un provvisorio*. I'm not sure I'll find the first ball in that rough."

Domenico made a face.

As we were starting off the tee, he said in English, "I joke without limits." What this meant, I had little idea, except that it seemed to refer to my provisional. As I walked down the fairway,

I tried to puzzle it out. The Italian word *gioco* (pronounced *jocko*) means "I play," so I thought, maybe, possibly, Domenico was trying to say, "I play without limits," which might have meant he didn't abide by the rules of scoring. Which, under the circumstances, hardly mattered to me. But then why had he been driving all the way back from the middle of the fifth fairway to hit a second tee shot? Why hadn't he just dropped one out there where he was? Why had he picked up his ball after my two-putt and not holed out?

I found the first ball and made bogey out of the left rough. From the way he was asking my score and keeping his own, Domenico appeared to believe we were playing some kind of match against each other, and he seemed to be massively confused about the etiquette of golf. The English couple had caught up with us again, mainly because Domenico was lingering and dawdling and doing everything—except swinging—at half speed. They waited patiently on the fairway while I walked to the next tee . . . and Domenico waited there with them.

The par-three seventh was a tricky hole, 201 yards steeply uphill. I hit my tee shot onto the front fringe, then turned to see that Domenico was still over on the other side of the previous green, sitting in his cart. What he was doing there, I couldn't begin to imagine. I wondered if he'd decided to go back to the tee and play the hole over, or if he was resting, or if he preferred to play with the English couple instead of me but had not felt comfortable saying so. He waited until the man and then the woman hit their shots to the green, then he drove around in front of them to the seventh tee, where I was still standing, waiting for word, and he hit a ground ball maybe fifty yards into the left rough. He followed that with another bad shot, across the fairway into the right rough. As I was helping him look for it, Domenico explained that he'd had some kind of medical problem during the past year. He used a technical term, in English, I thought, though I couldn't be sure. I switched to Italian to try to clarify. He switched back to English. "Was it a stroke?" I asked, because it sounded something like a stroke, but he shook his head emphatically and used the English word again. "A blood infection?"

"No, no."

In any case, in either language, I wasn't familiar with the word (*ischemia,* it turned out to be, a localized anemia that obstructed arterial blood flow; I would find it in the dictionary much later). "I am lucky I am alive," he said. He didn't seem to have any trouble moving, but he did everything with a painfully exaggerated slowness that disappeared only when he actually swung the club. The illness seemed—and I don't mean this in a sarcastic way—to have affected that part of his brain in which consideration of others is housed. He went to his ball, hit it over the green, found it, and drilled it back forty yards down the fairway in clear view of the English couple, who had finished playing the sixth and were waiting on the tee in a posture of restrained impatience. Ignoring them, Domenico walked all the way back down to his ball and struck a nice pitch shot onto the green.

I had, by this point, chipped on. I sank a long putt for par, at which point Domenico picked up his ball. "I can't beat that par," he said. Which was fine with me, because he had left his putter in the cart.

On the right-curling, uphill eighth, after I hit my second shot and he shanked his third off into the trees, he turned to me and said, "I try another one. Have you got balls?" I tossed him one of my four-dollar Pro V1x's, hoping I would see it again. He hit it onto the green, then found his own ball and hit it up there as well, and returned my Pro V1x without thanking me. We both made bogey.

We came at last to the tee of the ninth hole, long, ridiculously narrow, straight uphill. "This is a brutal hole," I said, and Domenico nodded in his strange way, swinging his eyes to one side. The illness had cast him into another world, I thought, some other dimension of life. And then he said, again, "Yes, but is wonderful," and though it was painfully difficult for me to be going at his pace, I found that I liked his mantra. Yes, but is wonderful.

"Why don't you hit with driver?" he asked, when I took out my three wood.

"Because it doesn't go straight," I told him, and having said that, I hit the three wood into the trees on the right, very short. Domenico was kind enough to help me look, and he found the ball twenty yards from where I was searching. I popped out of the deep grass, partway up the hill, then hit a solid approach shot that bounced on the green and over it, leaving me with a tricky downhill chip out of the greenside rough. After three more shots, Domenico had a similar chip, it turned out. We both made the up-and-down and I complimented him on it. He sneered.

"What?" I said, because I was tired of all the sneering. "That was a tough chip. You did it well."

He sneered again.

I had carded a 43 on the front. After the shanking session on the range, the disastrous start, and the odd playing situation, it felt like a score that should qualify me for the Golf Hall of Fame.

After the ninth hole, at which point three hours had elapsed, despite my sympathy for Domenico, and my having said so, and despite the fact that, at moments, he was enjoyable to be around, I simply could not take the pace anymore. When he said he was going into the clubhouse to use the toilet—a fairly long ride from where we stood—I seized the opportunity. "I'll just go on ahead then," I told him. He nodded and smirked.

I walked up and over the hill to the tenth tee caught up in a small sizzle of confusion. Having endured more than my share of physical ailments, I have what I've always thought of as a deep well of compassion for the less than perfectly healthy. And, as mentioned, I had been hoping on that day to turn down the interior tick-tick-tick that often has me doing things faster than I really want to, hurrying through this to get to that, cramming pleasures, errands and work into a day as if I might stretch it to twenty-five or twenty-six hours. So I felt disappointed in myself for not being able to play at the pace the day dictated, and guilty for not wanting to keep an infirm golfer company for another nine holes; at the same time, I felt as if my soul had been bound in barbed wire for the previous three and suddenly set free.

Maybe it was a kind of divine punishment for my unwillingness to stay with Domenico: once leaving him, I began to play poorly. In fact, after making a straightforward par on the tenth, I spent the whole back nine wading through a frustrating mush of scrambling pars and sloppy double bogeys. As if it were a sound track for my bad play, the odd music of that day danced on and on. On the thirteenth, someone on the hole beside me cracked his drive off one of the old stone houses there, and the sound echoed around the course like a gunshot. On the fourteenth, two golfers came trotting toward me, moving from green to tee. "Lost a phone!" one of them called as he went past. I found the phone, a BlackBerry actually, a little ways farther up the hole and left it beside one of the golf bags that had been abandoned there, then called over to them as they were trotting up the neighboring fairway.

As I was walking up the seventeenth, I saw Domenico wiggling and waggling on the tee of the thirteenth. I tried to catch his eye and say hello, but he was otherwise occupied, or offended, and kept his back turned.

Missed birdie there, missed par with a bad chip on eighteen, returned my *carrello* to the smiling caddy master, and went home to recuperate.

6

FOOD, GOLF, ATTITUDE

I came early to good food and late to good golf. For my first twenty years—minus time away at school—I lived in the same house as, or next door to, my father's mother, Eleonora, a woman known for her sunny disposition, fondness for prayer, and fabulous abilities in the kitchen. There was nothing gourmet about her. She came from ordinary southern-Italian country stock, was raised in a tiny hilltown thirty miles east of Naples, and like millions of other women and men made the transatlantic trip around the turn of the century, hoping for an easier life.

As far as I was concerned, my grandmother's kitchen on Essex Street was the culinary center of the universe. There were thick veal cutlets, pounded by hand until tender and then panfried in a light batter and served with fried potatoes. There were fluffy omelets accompanied by endless rounds of toasted Italian bread—

soft, nutritionally useless, dusted with sesame seeds. There was escarole soup with sweet broth, a little cheese, and marble-size balls of meat; chicken soup with stars of pasta; a meatless Lenten stew called *ciambotta*, which involved a thick tomato base in which onion, zucchini, pepper, and potatoes were cooked, the bowls wiped clean with fistfuls of bread; Easter desserts such as *strufoli*—small spheres of dough that were quick-fried, drenched in honey, and dusted with powdered sugar; artery-choking holiday pies made mostly with ricotta and sugar and going by the names *pizza dolce* and *pizza gaina* (*pizza chena,* or "full pie" is the proper spelling but we never said it that way). And, like the central altar around which all these secondary rituals took place, there was the Sunday meal, a multi-course, many-hour, weekly feast that went from antipasto and heavy red wine, through a pasta dish (home-made ravioli, often enough), meatballs, sausage, and the rolled, spiced beef called *bracciola,* loaves of bread and pounds of butter, vinegar peppers, roasted stuffed peppers, then salad, dessert, coffee with anisette. After one of these eating marathons, my twenty-four Merullo cousins and two brothers and I would go out in the yard and run around for a couple of hours, then return to a table reset with sandwiches and soda, éclairs and cookies and cakes.

Eleonora's three daughters, my aunts, all lived within walking distance of us. Visits to their homes meant two-course "snacks" ("coffee and," as my father called them) or four-course lunches—tripe or chicken cacciatore or cold-cut sandwiches, spaghetti with clam sauce, thin-sliced eggplant baked in gravy, a salad of peppers, tomatoes, greens from the backyard garden. Balanced against my own mother's solid English-American cuisine—lamb, roast beef, pot roast, beef stew, baked beans, steak, pork chops, fish on Fridays, molasses cookies—it would have been enough to send us to the obesity clinic, except that my brothers and I would routinely spend four or five straight hours playing in the street—stickball, football, street hockey, basketball, kick the can, bike races, footraces, snowball fights, long chases over the neighbors' fences and serious fisticuffs in their small front yards.

It was not a country-club environment. My father and his four brothers—and the men on my mother's side—relaxed with candlepin bowling and games of whist, and then, later in life, when their children were mostly grown and their work lives mostly determined, weekend rounds of golf on inexpensive nine-hole courses.

I was fifteen when my dad and uncles first invited me to go along with them. Those invitations were acts of almost heroic generosity—middle-aged guys sharing their small amount of downtime with a know-it-all teenager who could not play the game they, themselves, struggled with. (My mother, better than all of them, gave up golf after I was born, started playing again in her fifties, and could still occasionally break 40 for nine holes into her early eighties.) In later years, two of my uncles would become fairly accomplished players—working their handicaps down into the low teens at a small private club just north of Boston, buying a good set of sticks, taking a few lessons, gaining an understanding of the mechanics of the swing. But in those days they were the purest of hackers.

In spite of their high scores, they enjoyed the game the way they enjoyed the food in their mother's kitchen, with an unpretentious, unabashed, laughter-laced enthusiasm you encounter only rarely at the finer private clubs. My father and his brothers and friends yelled and cursed, they smoked cigars and cigarettes, they sometimes used the toe of their golf shoe to nudge a ball out of a difficult lie in the rough, failed to count the first of two bad drives, or "gave themselves" a missed short putt. They played with clubs they'd bought used or on sale, and with balls they'd found during their many excursions into the woods or along the shores of small, dirty ponds. In an old-fashioned, working-class world of neat yards and regular church, they loosened up on those Saturday afternoons, told jokes they wouldn't tell at home, said words—in two languages and one little-known Neapolitan dialect—they wouldn't say in front of their wives. I cherish an enduring image of my father, ample belly, gray hair, pipe stem clenched between his teeth, grunting as he banged his old Hogan three wood into the turf of a hilly, unirrigated fairway, throwing up a divot ("veal *cotoletta*," he called it), and holding the finish as his ball went screaming away, tailed off to the right, and bounded along close enough to the green that he turned to me proudly and grinned.

I am the product of that rich table, and those scraggly fairways. Playing now at courses such as Pinehurst, Doral, and the Greenbrier's Old White, and eating at restaurants where dinner costs, literally, what my father and his brothers used to earn in a week, I often think of them and try to keep hold of their ability to be happy with simple pleasures, to live in the moment, to set aside the burden of financial or family concerns and laugh at themselves.

Amid my own modern whirl of domestic duties and career demands, I hold tight to those same inoffensive pleasures—golf and eating—as if they were two small rafts roped together in a roiling sea. Add some family time, some travel, and you have, in my opinion, all the treasure you are entitled to expect on this suffering planet.

I have always liked a good meal, but golf, real golf, became a passion for me only after I'd exhausted, or been exhausted by, other sports: the street games, then baseball and running, then rowing and hockey and karate. Because of serious back injuries and a lack of money and time, between the ages of twenty and the day Alexandra was born—a few months after I turned forty-five—I played maybe five or six rounds of golf a summer, on mediocre courses, with my dad's old set of Hogan blades, with scuffed-up balls and a made-up swing, and no understanding, really, of the game's finer points. But fatherhood seemed to magically turn some dial in me, as if I were a radio being tuned, finally, after being scanned through a lot of static and rock and roll, to the golf station.

I joined a nine-hole club up in the hills of western Massachusetts and played every chance I got. I took lessons, joined the men's league, read books by PGA stars, watched tournaments on TV. Thanks to an editor named Kate Meyers, who read a long proposal I sent to her, cold, without introduction, and gave me an assignment, I started to write about golf for national magazines, then published a book on my love of the game, then, a few years later, a golf novel. I became, in other words, against long odds, a certified fanatic.

These days I am enough of a fanatic to enjoy being surrounded by the greens and fairways, the pro-shop merchandise, the neatly printed numbers on a tournament scoreboard, and the clacking of shafts in a bag even if I'm not there to play. At home, if the afternoon has taken on a stressful shade, I'll sometimes drive up to the place where I'm a member (the Crumpin-Fox Club, an hour-and-a-half round-trip) and spend some time chipping and putting, then a few minutes sitting at a table on the back porch, nursing an iced coffee and watching players struggle with the daunting eighteenth. It is good medicine for almost anything that ails me. In the depth of winter I've been known to hike along a course in knee-deep snow, just to make contact again with the land and the memories, or I'll shovel off a patch of lawn, jam a tee in the frozen earth, and hit a few cold seven irons over the country road that runs in front of our house. On Mother's Day, I sometimes take my mother-in-law to a favorite nine-hole course in the hills for their buffet. She doesn't play, and I'm not planning to. It's just a quiet thrill to look out at the tee boxes and fairways.

DINING AT A GOLF CLUB—WHETHER THE meal is tuna on rye with a beer or Delmonico steak with an old bottle of wine—is a way of multiplying the pleasure of being in the presence of the game. I knew, even before setting foot on Menaggio and Cadenabbia's hallowed soil, that I'd be eating in the restaurant there: at home, I'd studied the pictures on the Web site, imagined a menu. So it was with some enthusiasm that we made reservations there on what we hoped would be a quiet weeknight, put on our "fancy-restaurant clothes," as the girls call them, and headed up the lake. "When I finished my round the other day," I told Amanda, as a way of whetting her appetite for an enjoyable dinner, "I could hear the kitchen staff singing as I walked past the back door."

We arrived at seven thirty, a reasonable hour, I believe, by American standards, especially where young children are involved. The place was deserted. Covered in white linen cloths, laden with heavy silver cutlery, and set close together on the old, spike-scarred floorboards, a dozen tables faced out through floor-to-ceiling windows upon stunning views. You could stand on two-person balconies for an unobstructed vista: the first tee, then the wooded hillside sloping sharply away, and in the soft air beyond it a piece of the lake caught between mountainsides, then the shadowed gray faces of the Alps in the northern distance. You could not get tired of a view like that . . . even if you stood around in a deserted dining room with restless children and empty stomachs.

Though it seemed a bit of a chore for him to summon the energies required to serve, it really wasn't long before Alessandro—barman, host, and waiter—came to give us the night's choices in lightning-fast Italian. I had seen Alessandro behind the bar—the shaven head, the excellent posture, the *Vanity Fair* coolness—and thought he was the perfect fit for M&C, where sometimes you felt welcome, and at other times you were made to feel, well, that you were wearing the wrong style of shoes.

I have nothing against people with money. Several of our closest friends have trust funds and impressive second homes, beautiful cars decorated with decals of the country's premier colleges.

Like almost everyone I know, I hope to have a lot of money myself one day, and in the meantime I try to remember how rich I am already compared to most of the rest of the world: golf, restaurant meals, trips to Italy—these are not the hallmarks of poverty.

But in people of wealth, at golf clubs and resorts frequented by people of wealth, I have occasionally encountered an attitude that makes me wonder if there is something to be said, after all, for a little credit-card debt, old banged-up irons, a car with some scratches and dents. It is not an attitude you find very often in Italy, though I remember being told at the Acquasanta Golf Club in Rome that children were not ever allowed in the clubhouse.

At Menaggio and Cadenabbia—a nice old course but not exactly the Augusta National of Europe—whether or not you encountered this attitude seemed to depend on which way the wind was blowing. Some days the bar and patio rang with laughter and golf camaraderie: I remember a friendly conversation with Nando, the head pro. We were sitting at the six-seat bar, he was shaking his head in a humble, likable way, talking about the toughest holes on his course as if they were eccentric relatives. I remember Francisco's big smile lighting up the *segretario*'s office, and Doris's soft-spoken kindness. Then at other times I felt that some poisonous sense of superiority had been passed down from the British founders to present-day Milanese industrialists, had spilled over to the waiters and caddy master, and had pulled the air of the clubhouse so tight that a child's voice, a dropped spoon, or a small grammatical error would echo against the old silver trophies and glassed library shelves like the notes of a blasphemous sermon.

This was one of those times. The girls had pasta with tomato sauce, Amanda a nice cut of meat, and I went with what turned out to be a superb dish of spaghetti with mussels and clams. Good glass of wine. Great view, also, which must have been included in the tab, because, at the end of the meal, I was presented with a folded *conto* on which had been written a sum that translated, at that summer's exchange rate, to a round of golf at the most expensive daily-fee course in New England. During the meal, all of us feeling less than welcome, we'd had a memorable, if somewhat strained, conversation that began with Alexandra saying she thought the pasta was undercooked, and my telling her it was perfectly al dente, and that, in Italy, what the girls referred to as "too chewy" pasta was actually the sign of an excellent chef. "The better the restaurant, the less they cook the pasta," I told my girls, who at times can seem older than their years.

Alexandra came back with "So at the best restaurant in Italy they don't cook it at all, right?"

"Exactly," I said. "They dump it out of the box onto the plate."

"Really, Dad?" Juliana asked.

"It's just your father's way of talking," Amanda said. "He doesn't mean it literally."

And I said, "Let's go someplace else for dessert."

After paying the tab at M&C, we went into Menaggio and had ice cream at a place called Edo. There, the serving girls were friendly, the prices *normale,* and the gelato top-shelf.

7

THE INTERNATIONALS

Golf reveals character; every golfer knows this. Do the people you are playing with cheat? Do they care about their score so much that a bad hole drives them into spasms of anger? Are they considerate of their fellow players? Are they obsessed with the idea of breaking 80, 90, or 125? How do they handle failure? Embarrassment? Success? Defeat and victory and intense competition? Negative thinkers, positive thinkers, excuse-makers—it all comes out so quickly on a golf course, as if it were a hidden rule of the game that we be required to play psychologically naked.

Not long after our less-than-pleasant dinner there, I had a day at Menaggio and Cadenabbia, a fine, hot, cloudless midsummer day that seemed as if it had been specially designed to provide a view of a wide span on the spectrum of humanity. It actually began the evening before, when, at a birthday party for our young

Juliana, I ate and drank with too much gusto and ended up getting an insufficient amount of sleep. I had made a tee time for ten thirty, and Harold Lubberdink—who had brought his family to the party and who had been eating and drinking with me—was supposed to meet me there at that hour.

We had a bit of golf history, Harold and I. In the early days of our stay he had done us so many favors, and had heard me talking about golf so often, and had confessed so sorrowfully to being a not-very-good player, that I'd half seriously suggested I give him a lesson or two as a way of repaying him for his generosity.

Offering to help someone with his or her golf game is a tricky business. I observe a strict policy of never giving advice unless a playing partner specifically asks for it. For one thing, I'm far from an expert and usually have my own troubles to figure out; for another, even good advice from certified PGA professionals sometimes works like a bite of an excellent meal, well prepared, offered with warm affection, that goes down the wrong way. Advice given to a spouse or lover can be particularly risky, but it seems to me a dangerous enterprise in general (you are, after all, speaking to a person who is playing a maddening game with a metal stick in his hand), and so I do my best to maintain a respectful silence, even when my playing partner is chopping foot-long clods of earth out of manicured fairways or, on the downswing, stepping forward with his left foot, like a center fielder at the plate.

In this instance, to make matters more complicated, Harold had a lively sense of humor: about half of what he said was meant, in one way or another, as a joke. So, though he'd sounded receptive to a little help on the driving range, I couldn't really be sure.

Our history consisted of this: One day early in the summer when Menaggio and Cadenabbia was closed for a tournament, Harold and I had agreed to meet at the next-closest course, a nine-hole place called Golf Club Lanzo, high up in the Intelvi Valley, right next to the Swiss-Italian border. The drive to Golf Club

Lanzo made the zigzag climb to M&C look like a bicycle ride along the beach. We made the mistake of trying to make it into a sort of family outing. Up and up and up and up we went, the children complaining of car sickness in the backseat, big trucks and crazy bicyclists zipping down past us, the engine of the Renault straining in first gear, tiny hamlets populated by men and women in shorts and hiking boots passing in a blink, brief, spectacular views of the lake and the Alps appearing for a few seconds like mirages . . . and then the road would swing away from them, and the signs would stubbornly insist that a place called Lanzo was not an imaginary town, but an actual one, just a few kilometers farther up the road.

At a certain point—and perhaps we shouldn't have been surprised—the signs simply ceased. Or perhaps we missed one. We seemed to be at the summit, or one of the summits, and so we stopped and asked a man with no teeth in his lower jaw, who was selling watermelons from a wagon by the side of the road, where we might find the famous golf course that was said to exist in these parts. He was a large man, with a friendly face and a few days' growth of dark beard, and I was tempted to buy one of his fine-looking watermelons, but didn't want to be late for the tee time. This fruit seller spoke a quick, slurred Italian. He gave us the route in great detail, moving his hands this way and that, a right here, a left there, a landmark, a warning. I listened attentively and understood almost none of it. The longer he went on, the more lost I became in the murky waters of his diction, in the fog of my grammatical weaknesses, though all the while I nodded and repeated a word occasionally to make it seem as though his generosity was not falling, like pearls before swine, on the ears of unappreciative foreigners in a blue car with French license plates.

In the end, all I managed to glean from his minute-long explanation was that we should turn around and take the first right. So we waved and thanked him, turned around, and headed right. "I think he said something about not going to Switzerland," Amanda suggested. A kilometer or so farther down the road, once we were out of sight of the fruit seller, we asked someone else, who gave us much briefer and more easily understood instructions that ended in the Italian equivalent of "Take the next left and you can't miss it." A minute after that we turned onto a road lined with parked cars whose owners were playing golf.

Harold was already there, hoisting his bag out of the trunk of the Audi, with a big, devilish grin on his face and the sun shining off his shaved head. He hugged Amanda, lifted the girls off the ground, gave me a big happy smile. "This area," he told me as we were walking toward the pro shop, "used to be very nice, very up-market. But now not so much."

Despite its outstanding ham-and-cheese sandwich, served on lavash bread by welcoming people in the upstairs restaurant, and despite a classy, friendly caddy master, Golf Club Lanzo, I am sorry to report, was a disappointment. It had all the trappings of a first-rate course, but wasn't. It proved, in fact, to be something like certain kinds of Italian pastries, all cream and fluff and pleasant-looking, but not really satisfying. The people at the check-in desk had attitude. The prices were on the high side. There were expensive cars in the lot, and well-dressed men on the driving range. But the golf itself was second-rate. Later, when I would tell Italian golfers that I'd gone up to Lanzo to play, they would make a face, a certain kind of Italian face—cheeks pinched up, forehead pinched down, eyes squinting sideways as if they'd just hit their thumb with a hammer—that is at once dismissive and touched by revulsion.

Lanzo's driving range was composed of eight or ten positions, set up high so that you had the illusion of hitting the ball farther than you actually did. I liked that, of course; everyone likes it. But if you shanked a shot there, you had a good chance of killing somebody on the third hole. And if you planned on hitting a driver, you had to wait to be sure no golfers were coming up the fourth—which ran perpendicular to the end of the range. The sign didn't say NO DRIVERS, which might have been the more sensible thing. It said something like WAIT TO HIT DRIVER UNTIL YOU ARE SURE NO ONE IS COMING UP THE FOURTH FAIRWAY.

Standing near him at one of the driving-range positions, I watched Harold swing. It was a strongman's swing, heavy on arm and shoulder action and accompanied by a full-body twist at the end, almost a dance move from the midseventies, as if both shoes were simultaneously extinguishing small fires. Based on this initial observation, I offered a piece of advice, I forget what it was, and Harold said, "I'm just stretching," which was another way of saying my advice wasn't really wanted. Which was fine.

The first hole was straight, bland, and slightly uphill. A simple hole. Harold and I both made sevens. "My hole," he said.

"What?"

"Well, I'm a thirty-six handicap, so I get some strokes."

"All right. I didn't realize we were playing a match."

What followed was a series of holes without much character: fair conditions, hills, woods, wide and tree-lined fairways. Perhaps I am being too harsh on the course. It almost could have been a good course. Maybe, at one time, it had been a good course. And surely, sitting so high up in the mountains as it did, Lanzo faced certain weather-related difficulties that would excuse its lack of perfection.

In any case, after the troublesome start, I carded six straight pars and there was no more talk of playing a match. My friend Harold struggled, swinging mightily off his back foot and drilling ground balls along Lanzo's spotty fairways. But he played, as he did everything else, with a persistent good humor and infectious enthusiasm.

I remember taking a divot with my sand wedge on the slightly more interesting eighth, and Harold asking if I'd taken up the dirt on purpose or if it had been a mistake. "On purpose," I said. "With the shorter clubs especially, that's usually the way you try to hit it."

He nodded, as if filing the information away. He putted remarkably well, I will say that, and when he connected with a solid stroke, the ball went a long way, but he was always swinging off his back foot, so always topping the ball, and finally, late in the front nine I tried again, in as inoffensive a way as I could manage. "Mind if I make one suggestion?"

"No, of course not. I want to learn."

"You should try to shift your weight onto the front foot as you hit the ball. Try that and see what happens."

He tried it; it didn't help. In spite of his struggles, however, it was easy to envision a bright golf future for the guy. To begin with, he adored the game—always the first step in becoming a player. He was obviously a good athlete, strong, and if he ever had time to devote himself to playing the way he and Sara were devoting themselves to building up their business, then, before long, he would be taking money out of the pockets of golfers like me.

It was the first year of his business, and prime season, too, and he had a hundred phone calls to answer, and so, after nine holes, we shook hands, he drove back down the mountain, and I had a ruinous, shank-infested backside that did nothing to improve my opinion of the place. I lost two headcovers there, as well.

During our stay at the lake, I never made the arduous trip back to Golf Club Lanzo to play a second round (though I did make the arduous drive back to retrieve one of the two lost headcovers that had been turned in), but I will remember for a long time the expression on the face of another golfer there. This man was in his late sixties or early seventies, and playing just behind us. At one point, early in the front nine, Harold and I had invited him to join us, and he'd declined. He was a poor player, no doubt a complete beginner, but as we were on the seventh tee, he came over to us from the sixth hole and said he had a question. The question, which Harold translated to be sure I understood correctly, had to do with the rules of golf: If a ball goes under a tree and you have to take it out to hit it, is there a penalty? Here was a man with probably a 50 handicap, playing alone, absolutely determined to abide by the rules, to put in a correct score at the end of his round, to learn the game. It reminded me of Domenico at M&C and his "Yes, but is wonderful" mantra. Yes, I'm struggling. Yes, the ball went under a tree and I had to move it. Yes, I've gotten a late start at the game. But I want to play it the way it's supposed to be played.

THAT WAS MY GOLFING HISTORY WITH Harold, and I was pleased that he'd be joining me for my ten-thirty round at M&C. Fueled by a cappuccino and brioche at the Bar Roma, and despite the lack of sleep, I made the drive along the *statale* in a happy mood, with motorcycles buzzing past the Renault's fenders, and the lake glinting and sparkling in the sun.

At ten o'clock, I drove through M&C's grand gates (where the motto of the English founders, Far and Sure, is still visible on the coat of arms) and checked in with Doris, who had the shadow over her on that morning, and who made me feel as welcome as a hemorrhoid. This might have been because, two days earlier, I'd mentioned that I wanted to have a short, informal interview with the club's president. That information had been received in something like the way a cool, deep body of water receives a thrown stone. For a second or two, a ripple of doubt crossed her face. She said, in an unconvincing tone, that she'd look into the possibility. On this morning I reminded her of my request. "Oh, he is here only on the weekend," Doris said.

"I wish I had known. I would have made an appointment for yesterday."

"He is very busy."

"Of course. I understand."

"Perhaps next weekend," Doris said, and I thanked her and headed out of the small office and around the corner to the caddy master's shop. It was Monday, The Smiling Matteo's day off, apparently. His place had been taken by The Smiling Emilio, older, smaller, harder-boiled, but with a sparkle of the potential for friendliness beneath his features. At the moment I arrived, Emilio was being besieged by an Englishman in his early sixties—white hair, jowls, a belly, maroon pants—who was accompanied by a pretty Asian woman less than half his age. He was with two friends and their young female guests, a sixsome, and he was badgering Emilio in loud English about carts and had a list of other questions, which Emilio answered, it seemed to me, with a beautifully balanced mixture of patience and disdain.

In a moment, several moments actually, the sixsome moved off in the direction of the driving range, which brought me to the happy conclusion that they would be teeing off after us and I would never see them again for as long as I lived. Emilio ducked into the caddy master's shop and brought me out a *carrello*. As he'd done on previous occasions, he strapped my bag to it with a bungee cord in such a way that the putter, in its separate tube, was wrapped so tightly against the top of the bag that it could not be removed. "Busy this morning," I remarked as I was freeing my Bettinardi and retying the cord.

"All the other courses—*tutti gli altri campi*—around here are closed on Monday," Emilio said, though which courses he was referring to, I didn't know. Golf Club Lanzo, maybe.

I was waiting for Harold. Ten fifteen. Ten twenty. I was hoping against hope that the sixsome were going to spend half an hour on the driving range, so we could tee off before them.

At 10:26 Harold came into view, the top down on his Audi, the driveway gravel snapping beneath the tires, his face shining in the sun. I was amused but not surprised to see that he was talking animatedly on the phone. Another few seconds and he was bounding up the steps saying, "Sorry, sorry, was halfway up the hill when I realized I had to get petrol."

"It's all right," I said. "We have two minutes."

"Need tees."

"I can give you—"

He ducked into the little shop and started chatting with the woman there and their conversation went on a bit, and it was discouragingly late by the time we headed down to the first tee (*partenza*, it is called in Italian—"departure"). As I had feared, there was the sixsome, loudly trying to figure out who would ride with whom. "We are the ten forty, aren't we?" one of them said loudly. And then: "Doug, you ride with the girls, and then with me later, if that's acceptable."

Doug was not pleased. I wasn't either.

While all this was going on, Harold and I could only wait. We waited a good long while as the six of them figured out their transportation arrangements and then, at last, teed up their balls and slapped them down into the woods. In the interim, I'd had time to make small talk with one of the Englishman's friends, who lived half the year in Miami, it turned out. "Not Miami, really," he said, when I told him I knew that city a bit. "Fisher Island. Do you know it?"

"No. We go to Miami Beach in the winter sometimes. One of our daughters—"

"Well, this isn't Miami, really. It's Fisher Island."

"Sounds good."

Eventually, all six of them had departed. Harold and I climbed up onto the *partenza* and made some desultory practice swings, from time to time casting our eyes down toward the slanting fairway, where all kinds of things were going on, none of them promising. Beneath my breath I said a quiet prayer for patience. As we waited, a young couple came walking down from the parking lot, the man of slight build, with short hair, and the woman wearing dark glasses and a black dress. He was carrying clubs; she was just along for the walk. We invited them to join us. They introduced themselves as Karl and Sandra. "It seems ve vill haff a slow day today," he said, in solid, German-accented English.

We were still waiting for the fairway to clear when, five minutes later, a deeply tanned man of middle age came striding down the path accompanied by his young caddy. This man was Rudy, "From Philly!" he told us exuberantly, and his caddy and friend was Ricardo, who taught tennis in Bellagio. Rudy asked if he could join us, and, of course, we all agreed. We now had a sixsome of our own, though two of them were not playing. Rudy asked if I was at the lake alone—this seemed to be the mandatory introductory remark—and I said no, I was there with my family. He did not smirk, at least.

At long last, there seemed to be no further evidence of the sixsome on the short grass below, so I stood up on the tee and hit a two hybrid that sailed up into the morning sun, high over the trees on the right side of the fairway, then began to curl gently left. Just as the ball reached its apex, two of the women members of the sixsome came walking out of the woods into the landing area. What they had been doing there all that time I cannot speculate. Looking for truffles, maybe. "Fore!" we yelled in chorus. They heard us and, strangely, started to run from the edge of the fairway toward the middle of the landing area—as if the chances of a ball having been hit well were so slim that the fairway was the wisest place of refuge. My ball came hurtling down with the force of a meteorite—having been launched from a point fifty or sixty feet higher than the women's heads—and bounced hard onto the short grass three yards behind them, exactly where they had been a second earlier. We were glad, naturally, that no one was injured. But I have to report that there were various half-serious comments made among us to the general opinion that we were as glad some members of the slow sixsome weren't hit as we were that they had almost been hit.

They were out of range now, really. Karl was next on the tee. He went up on his toes before starting his swing. It was a nice, tight *movimento,* and he lined a decent drive down the left side of the fairway. Harold grounded one into the trees. Rudy hit one into the trees on the right, too, and immediately gave us to understand that he was playing with rental clubs.

We made a pleasant, upbeat group. Sandra seemed shy and said almost nothing, and Ricardo kept a quiet smile on his face while Rudy talked about how much he loved it near the lake—he had come to Bellagio every year for the past decade. He tended to speak in exclamations, but if one place on earth deserved exclamations, I thought, it was Lake Como. Isn't it spectacular! Isn't it wonderful here! I can't think of anyplace on earth that's better!

Harold dropped a ball and hit a hard grounder out of the nasty rough at the edge of the trees. Rudy couldn't find his ball and dropped one also. Karl blasted a long iron to the green, and I hit a seven iron to the front fringe, chipped on, and sank the putt.

When Karl's second putt lipped out, Rudy yelled, "Call the sheriff!" and I wasn't sure Karl understood.

We had to wait a long time to step onto the second tee, and when we finally arrived there—at the start of the uphill par-three where going too far left is death—I hit into the left bunker, Harold hit two balls well left beyond the steep drop-off, Karl hit one to follow him, and Rudy drilled a nice four wood, of which he was justifiably proud—more exclamation points; and this with rented clubs!—to the front fringe.

I bogeyed from the trap, a fairly typical scenario for me as I had been having trouble with sand shots for several years and had done nothing about it. Harold and Karl found their balls down in the shaggy valley, and it took them several more shots before the putters came out of their bags. Rudy three-putted.

On the downhill, par-three third I hit to the front fringe of the green, as did Karl. We walked down together, and as we got to our balls, he said, "Zo, now ve can be happy, uh?" We were moving at a snail's pace, so there was plenty of time for conversation. Karl was thirty-eight and already retired from a business he and a friend had started when they were in their midtwenties. Video surveillance cameras, for casinos, mostly. They'd worked hard for ten years, traveled a lot, built up their business to the point where they had thirty employees, then sold it to a competitor and would, it seemed, never have to worry about money for the rest of their lives. Karl wanted to work again, though, and was "looking for the purpose in my life," taking psychology courses with the thought of going into motivational speaking. All this was said modestly, as if he were neither embarrassed by nor particularly proud of his accomplishments and his wealth. German by birth, he'd moved to Switzerland to avoid the 25 percent tax on selling a business, and there he'd met Sandra, his lovely, quiet friend, who worked with children and who was going to Lake Garda the following week to a golf school. What I liked about him, right from the first, was his obvious passion for golf. You can't hide something like that, and you can't fake it. He was infected, addicted, obsessed in the best possible way—and he had taken Sandra along with him so she could become addicted, too.

Another long wait on the elevated fourth tee. Rudy talked about the course conditions, which were "much, much worse last year. You would have hated it. Dry as a bone. I think they sank some money into it for the hundredth anniversary this year, and they've had some rain. But something's not right. It's not managed the way it should be. It's private, you know, owned by a family, but something's not right."

I said I was hoping to have an interview with the president

soon, and that I would try to figure out the situation behind the situation, and Rudy wished me luck.

When Harold hit another poor tee shot on the downhill par-three third, Rudy, who was not timid about offering advice, suggested Harold not swing so hard, and this resulted in his blasting three beautiful drives in a row, on four, five, and six, long and dead center. But the unofficial mayor of the Tremezzino enjoyed his success only briefly because his cell phone kept going off. He answered it in German or Dutch or English or Italian and sometimes fell behind the rest of us to convince a visitor of the pleasant view from a particular apartment, to give an address for the deposit check, or, he later told us, to smooth over the feelings of a fussy American client whose vacation had been tarnished by the sight of a construction crane in the near distance. "When we signed the contract, there was no crane in the picture on the Internet," the American had complained over the phone, while Harold was trying to concentrate on swinging easy.

Rudy kept up an enthusiastic line of conversation: how much he liked Bellagio, and Philadelphia, how he was leaving that afternoon to be a guest at the British Open, escorting the widow of a friend of his who'd passed on two years earlier, how the R&A tent was always full of people all dressed up but wearing golf shoes—that's the tradition—how he'd bumped into Justin Leonard at the airport after Leonard had won the Open at Troon, and how no one else had recognized him, how Boston was a great town, too, and so on. Several times amid this happy chatter he made fun of—or perhaps *acknowledged* is a better word—my accent, which people tell me is strong. When I said, "You don't want to go too far left," Rudy would repeat, in a loud voice, "Fah! Fah! Too fah! Left!" When I used the word *corner*, he said, "Cohnah! Cohnah!" And so on.

On the fifth, thanks to a ninety-yard sand wedge to three feet, I made birdie ("We're going to make you putt that one, hah!" Rudy said, then congratulated me profusely when the ball dropped in), while he and Harold struggled in the deep rough to the left side of the green, and Karl, who had been playing along at a steady bogey pace, carded an unfortunate eight from the bunker. And then, though it was just noon, Rudy said he had to leave because Ricardo had a one-thirty boat to catch.

The group in front of us seemed, by then, to have separated itself into two threesomes and to be moving along at a brisker pace. We weren't exactly tearing up the fairways ourselves, though things picked up once Rudy and Ricardo headed off. Harold had answered eleven or twelve phone calls in the first six holes. His phone rang again on the seventh green, just as Karl was trying to make a four-foot putt for par. The putt went wide; Harold apologized. "I guess I will put it on vibrate now," he said. No one objected. I suggested Karl take the putt over again but he shook his head.

On the eighth, Harold and I started talking about food, for some reason. Hunger pangs, maybe. We had eaten together several times by that point, including the night before, and our shared appreciation for the game of golf seemed to have found its equal in our shared appreciation for the joy of eating well. He knew his wines, knew the best places around the lake for lunch and dinner, fish and pizza and steak, and for dining with children. "Yes, you must pay attention to food," he said, as we climbed. "Food runs everything."

"Which is something the Italians understand."

"Yes, definitely. Absolutely."

I hit a running, hooking three iron that reached the green, then three-putted from twenty feet, running the first putt too far left and over Harold's coin.

On the wicked ninth, Harold yanked his drive dead left into deep rough. When Karl and Sandra set off to look for it, he said, "Watch the snakes," and did not seem to be joking.

"Are there snakes here, really?"

"Yes. Vipers."

Karl found the ball without getting snakebit. Harold slashed around there for a minute, then picked up. I managed a three wood to the plateau, then another three wood to the back of the slanting, three-tiered green, and two-putted for par and a frontside score of 38.

Harold had to go back to work, so we shook hands all around. "Let's have dinner at the Barcola," he said.

Let me dwell on this remark because it is an excellent excuse: When Harold pronounced the name Barcola there next to the ninth green on that hot afternoon, I believe it set off a series of chemical reactions in my brain that made golf success, or further golf success, however modest, unlikely. On our first or second afternoon at Lake Como, Harold and Sara had taken us to the Barcola for lunch, and it had been such a memorable lunch, and I was getting so hungry now, that my center of mental focus shifted from golf to food, hands to belly. I was still suffering a bit from the night before, and the sustenance from the Bar Roma was wearing off, and what with the two-hour-and-forty-minute frontside, the heat, the comments on my accent, the ringing phone, the various personalities, well, it was probably too much to ask to break 80 on that day.

Karl and Sandra and I made our way up the asphalt path and then over a small rise and down to the tenth tee, which sits hard by the driving range. In a foolish gesture of excessive caution, a net had been hung up there to protect golfers on the tee from shankers on the range. On this most sociable of all golf days, we encountered a trim woman standing near the net, waiting for the remains of the noxious sixsome to finish playing the tenth. This was Heidi, who, it turned out, had the good fortune to live in St.-Moritz during ski season, and Menaggio in golf season. Somewhere in the second half of middle age, Heidi was a nice woman, a good athlete just becoming familiar with the game of golf, and so of course we invited her to join us. Just as we were about to hit, two members of the maintenance staff zoomed up on their cart. On that sunny day they were dressed in the customary maintenance-staff attire—bathing suits and work boots, nothing else—and went riding along with such pleasure that it seemed they were, like the happy kitchen workers, about to burst into song. When they got out of the cart, took the back tee markers, and moved them thirty yards forward on the long, skinny tee box, neither Karl nor I voiced a syllable of complaint.

The tenth at M&C is another punishingly narrow hole, 171 meters, or 187 yards, from where we would have been playing without the unexpected assistance from the maintenance staff. (I believe that the narrowness of the course can be attributed to the Englishmen who laid it out. No doubt they were trying to compensate for the lack of gorse and stiff ocean winds and didn't want friends visiting from Glasgow or Avon to belittle them for making it too easy. *First, you come down here in summer because you can't take the real weather; second, you design a golf links on which anyone can shoot par.*) The hole climbs steeply tee to green, with trees close in on both sides. It is a straight-hitters' hole, and I tend to hit largish draws, which means, standing on this tee, that I always had to try to find the courage to aim at the hillside of trees to the right of the green and hope I made good enough contact to work the ball back toward the flagstick.

On that day I hit a decent middle iron but pushed it right. It did not draw much, but took an undeservedly fortunate bounce off the hillside just inside the trees and ended up twelve feet from the hole. I was beginning to think the golfing gods were with me on that day. I had been kind and generous, had curbed my impatience, invited half the world to play the round with me—a Dutchman, a Swiss woman, a German millionaire and his pretty friend, a loquacious Philadelphian—and here was my reward, bounces like this.

I sank the putt.

But, alas, the golf gods despise hubris. And while *hubris* might not be precisely the right word for what I was feeling after my birdie on ten, it was true that Heidi, the beginner, was already lavishing me with compliments, marveling at how far I hit the ball with my irons, how easily I'd knocked in the tough twelve-footer. Later she would say, "I learned a lot from you today about how not to make worry when you play." It is nice to be on the receiving end of such flattery, even if you know, in your heart, that it's only half true. Heidi had reached the green after bouncing the ball along the fairway a few times, but, like Harold, she had such an upbeat attitude and knew the etiquette of the game well enough that Karl and I were glad we'd invited her to join us. The other factor in all this was that the two threesomes seemed to have lost what little speed they'd picked up and were now making us wait again. Never a backward glance.

"Do you have sheriffs on courses in the U.S.?" Karl asked, as we all stood on the eleventh tee, performing the small housekeeping tasks golfers like to perform when they have to wait—marking a fresh ball, taking out a few more tees, going over the scorecard, rearranging the bungee cord yet again so that the bag sat properly on its *carrello* and the shaft of the expensive putter wasn't made crooked, offering sarcastic remarks about the people holding us up.

"On some courses, yes. We call them marshals."

"They have them here, too," Heidi put in. "Sometimes."

"And do they control the pace of play?"

"A little bit," she said, then, in a gently sardonic way, "Italian control."

I would like to blame the long wait for the next shot I hit, but I won't do that. It would be like blaming thoughts of food, or rental clubs, bad luck, the distractions of an insensitive companion, punched greens, the wind, the temperature, business or marital concerns, insufficient sleep, a sore finger or back, the lie, a clump of mud on the ball, and so on. There is no shortage of excuses for a bad golf shot, but the truth is I hit a bad golf shot, that's all.

The eleventh is a 409-yard par four, played out of a chute, with trees on both sides of the fairway and a large bunker, unreachable for most players even with the elevation change that cuts perpendicularly across the fairway at about the three-hundred-yard mark. I surveyed this pretty scene for a moment, appreciating yet again the vista of the mountains rising around us on three sides. Then I yanked my tee shot deep and left, into the woods. We searched and searched there and Sandra found it, beyond the trees at the edge of the sixteenth fairway. I hit what would have been a nice recovery shot, had it not struck the middle of a thick oak branch and flown back over my head, still farther into the sixteenth. Drilled the next one through the trees all the way across into the rough on the other side. Limpid gap wedge into the greenside rough. A chip and a putt and a nice triple bogey. The little cushion I'd built up was sliced in half. These things happen so quickly. Foot by foot, handhold by handhold, you make your careful, painstaking ascent toward a good score. And then one small carelessness, a momentary lapse, and you slide a hundred feet back down the slope.

The downhill twelfth was an easier, shorter version of the eleventh, and I made par there. Karl played along steadily. Heidi started to hit some good shots. Sandra watched us, studied us, without saying a word.

The par-five thirteenth, still descending the long slope away from the clubhouse, asks for another tee shot out of a chute, but this is complicated by a tree in the middle of the fairway, and a bunker just beyond it. A few yards past the bunker, the fairway makes a sharp left turn and drops to a shallow green, set at a thirty-degree angle to the fairway. Over the green is a steep drop-off and out-of-bounds.

Karl hit two career shots on that hole, which left him looking at a forty-yard pitch to be on in regulation and have a rare try at birdie. Those first two shots had given him great pleasure; you could see it on his face, and hear it in the surprised way he said, "I am here at this place in two hits." He may have said something else, in his quiet, modest manner, about never having been that close to the green in two. And then, having offended the fairway gods, he stood up to his ball and drilled it over the OB stakes back of the green and down into the overgrown valley. *Golf,* I wanted to tell him, *is the cruelest game,* but it is best not to say anything in a situation like that. My cousin and regular playing partner Joe Bones has a good way of doing it. He'll wait until we finish the hole, then he'll come up and say, "You're pissed as hell, aren't you?" Which sometimes works. Another playing acquaintance takes the opposite approach, which I don't like nearly as much, and says things like "One of the worst shots I've ever seen." Or, "Now that's something to be ashamed of."

I made par and remained silent. "Now I vill play not for score," Karl said in a voice full of disappointment. He dropped a ball, chipped it close, and sank the putt. Naturally.

On the fourteenth, another short—495-yard—par five, I was on again in regulation and missed the birdie putt by an inch left. From there, you have to cross the twelfth fairway to get to the next tee, and Heidi said, "Nice pair," to me, as we were walking, meaning that my score had fallen into the territory between birdie and bogey. Same to you, I thought of replying, but that would have been either misunderstood or inappropriate, or both.

Even after a bogey on the short, uphill, par-three fifteenth, I arrived at the sixteenth tee seven over par. Menaggio and Cadenabbia is a par 70, which meant that I had a two-stroke cushion, still, if I hoped to break 80. But at a slight 368 yards, the sixteenth is a nasty hole. Standing on the tee, blinded from the landing area by a low hill in front of you, you feel as if you have a ten-yard-wide tunnel to hit into. In fact, once your ball actually gets out to the landing area, things widen up in a reasonable way. But that's not the information your eyes are providing to your mind, and your mind to your body. You know that if you push the tee shot slightly to the right, there is a sharp drop-off there and out-of-bounds stakes. Too far left and you can end up blocked out by the trees, or up against the chain-link fence that protects golfers on the eleventh tee. To further complicate matters, if people are playing in front of you, you have to wait an extra few minutes to be sure they're out of range because you can't see them, or the green.

So, after another wait, I went with the two hybrid, made a tentative swing, lost the ball deep right, and ended up with a tap-in for a triple-bogey seven. Ten over par all of a sudden. Ten over par at M&C equals an even 80.

But one of the things I loved about the course was that the two finishing holes were very short and devilishly tricky, classic risk rewards. The seventeenth (which my friend Andrus thought was the only bad hole of the eighteen) was only 257 yards long, drivable for the longest hitters. The trick of it was that the fairway bent a few degrees to the right at about one hundred yards from the tee, and there were tall trees growing on both sides, so that the airspace between them was only about ten yards. To make the driver option even less appealing, a pond stood just in front of the green, the only water on the course. If you went with driver, you had to hit a fade that flew 250 yards or so, cleared the water, and stopped dead. Beyond my abilities.

By that point, the groups in front of us had kept us waiting so long that a foursome that had started probably half an hour behind us was coming up the sixteenth fairway on our heels. Since we couldn't see the people up ahead, we invited Heidi, the shortest hitter, to go first, and though she'd really been playing along well, she must have felt the pressure of the group behind us, because she hit an awful dribbler to the left that bumped against the hillside there and rolled sideways and backward onto the sixteenth green. Sandra went to fetch it, but she walked onto the green just as the group on sixteen was about to hit. They whistled at her. She waved a hand in apology and hurried off. Karl hit a five wood between the trees, I hit six iron, and we were both safe. Heidi struggled and struggled, running little twenty-yarders left and right, but it didn't matter anymore, timewise. It was a five-hour-plus round and we'd just have to grind it out to its finish.

As we were waiting to hit our approaches, the folks in front of us, considerate to the last, strolled right across our green after hitting their tee shots on eighteen. I just watched them. Karl watched them. We looked at each other, waited, waited some more, then I hit a partial sand wedge just a bit too far and ended up on the top tier, with a bending, downhill, fifteen-foot birdie putt that I would miss by three inches. Heidi finished with what must have been a twelve or fourteen, but the last of those strokes was a thirty-foot putt from the back fringe that plunged hard into the middle of the cup, so she was happy and we were happy for her. "That is the life of golf," she exclaimed.

At 255 yards, eighteen is another wonderful hole. In match play, I imagine, it would be spectacular. Its narrow fairway has woods on a hillside to the left, and a line of trees and then the clubhouse patio to the right. The green is canted toward the tee, elevated just a bit, with a bunker in front and thick rough all around. You can hit everything from eight iron to driver and make par, but I needed a birdie to break 80. I took out the long stick, made a bad swing, and was saved from injuring someone on the patio by the trunk of a tree. It was a great piece of luck—not only was no one hurt, but the ball bounced out to where I had a look at the green, maybe sixty-five yards away. From the forward tees, Heidi hit two awful shots that didn't even clear the driveway forty yards in front of us. She hiked down there to look for her ball anyway and forgot her cart. Karl went to help her. I pulled her cart over so she wouldn't have to walk all the way back for it, and after she'd hunted for a while, in vain, and climbed back up onto the fairway, she saw her cart sitting there and delivered what I thought was a classic line: "Out I vass," she said to me. "Thank you. You are goot boy."

The bunker in front of the eighteenth made even a good boy want to play it safe and go long with his approach, which I did, but only a bit long. I was fifteen feet past the pin in the left fringe, facing, for 79, a downhill birdie putt that might or might not break a few inches. I waited for my playing partners to hit onto the green, then surveyed the putt, stood up to it, made a good stroke. The ball came out of the fringe clean, tracked at the hole with ample speed, then, about three feet from its target, it moved an inch left and skidded past the edge and six feet down the slope. Missed the comebacker; 81.

Afterward, Karl, Sandra, Heidi, and I enjoyed a drink and a snack on the shaded patio. Our talk wandered from the unification of Germany, to the war in Iraq, to Mussolini and the complications of modern Italian history, at which point Karl delivered another memorable line: "Ve didn't have any complications in Chermany. It was just all bad there for one period." While we were talking, a golf ball came bouncing hard off the fairway, smacked onto the patio stones, and missed our table by a few feet. I thought, There but for the grace of the tree trunk go I, and when a woman walked up to retrieve it, smiling sheepishly, I told her, "You weren't the first and you won't be the last," and she seemed to appreciate that.

"Those people in front of us," Karl said. "I saw them at the secretary's office when they were checking in. The man was asking her about fifteen questions."

"Not a nice group."

"No, not nice at all. Not my kind of golf players."

8

CRUISING THE LAKE

Amanda is a photographer by profession—museum work, portraits, travel essays—and though she has worked only a few dozen days since Alexandra's birth, she has not lost her love of wandering around in someone else's country with a camera in her hands. At home and when we travel, she is gracious about my golf addiction, and I tried to return that graciousness, while we were at Lake Como, by making a side trip with the girls now and again so she could spend that time pursuing good pictures.

On this day, she dropped us at the embarcadero in Cadenabbia, ten minutes down the road from our house, and went off in the Renault for territories unknown.

I had told the girls we'd be taking a boat ride up to the top part of the lake, to a town called Gravedona. They were not overly excited. Though I had never been to Gravedona, I'd developed a mild fascination with the place. This happens to me. I love to look at maps and often imagine whole worlds based on nothing more than a name or a route number. Gravedona was a place like that.

"What's there, Dad?"

"A very old church, it says in the guidebook. We'll have a nice ride on the boat, find a good place to have lunch, and come back. Sound okay?"

"An old *church*?"

But it was more than the church. I liked the idea of cruising the lake in the cooler air, being presented with different views of the mountainous shoreline and the various towns, doing something with my daughters that was unlike the kinds of things we did at home. According to what I'd read, Gravedona did have an interesting church, and a history of difficult relations with church figures, and Wordsworth had spent time in the town, once setting off for a hike and getting so lost he'd had to spend the night in the wilds. That was enough reason to go.

As we were waiting for our boat, we were entertained by the arrival of another ferry, this one headed south toward the city of Como. I watched the captain as he brought his big white craft to the dock. Up there on his glassed-in bridge, holding a cell phone to his ear with one hand, he aimed his vessel toward us at a fast clip—almost too fast, it seemed. At the last instant, he spun the wheel and cut the engines so that the stern end came swinging around in a perfect half circle and the boat bellied up to the pier. A small audience was waiting. I almost expected them to break into applause.

Our boat—it arrived a few minutes after the Como-bound ferry had made a somewhat less spectacular departure—was smaller and slower, with a noisy engine. But it carried us across the lake without any apparent difficulty. We stopped first at Varenna, neat as a watercolor, where a cluster of lemon- and pumpkin-colored houses stood as background to the humble curve of waterfront. After taking on and discharging a handful of passengers, we headed north to Bellano, with its small silk mills and terraced hillsides above; and then Dervio, perched out on a flat spit of sand; and then we started back across the lake again, angling northwest, toward Pianello.

"Those are skyscraper mountains," Juliana said of the rock faces that came into view to our north. We passed a lone windsurfer and settled into the slow pace of things, staring out at the water, dark, green, and rumpled as the skin of an avocado, and the groups of houses here and there along the shore.

I was thinking, naturally enough, about food and golf and things Italian, the trio of pleasures that had brought us to this place. I knew that writing about the culinary delights of Italy would be a dangerous enterprise, akin to choosing the cold of Russia or the hilarity of *carnevale* as a topic. Everyone knows about the food in Italy, even if all they've actually experienced is the diluted version—a supermarket's frozen pizza or canned tomato sauce. Gourmet American chefs steal recipes from peasant women in the Sicilian countryside; famous food writers make tours of Tuscan kitchens. I was aware of that. And yet, I knew this, too: each meal, like each lovemaking, each reading of a new novel, every twilight swim in the ocean, has the potential for a washing clean of the memory and the imposing of a fresh stamp upon the senses. It doesn't matter that you have made love with the same person for twenty years: there is still the possibility of surprise—not the surprise of some new maneuver, but an interior astonishment, the opening of a door onto some landscape you have never visited. The trick is, after a thousand lovemakings and fifty thousand meals, to keep your mind open to the miracle of it, to make the world fresh for another hour.

It is that way with the food in Italy, for me at least. Even allowing for regional differences, restaurant menus are often similar from one place to the next—*panini*, antipasto, spaghetti, a cut of *vitello,* a bowl of gnocchi, a plate of chicken parmigiana. But in that country, eating has about it the sense that you are participating in some familiar yet sacred act that might lead to a sudden enlightenment. Food is not trifled with there. Freshness and wholesomeness matter more than they matter in America—in my extensive experience of eating in American restaurants—and the Italian chefs and waitstaff take things with a seriousness that has the pride of thirty generations to it, something inextricably linked with the idea of being Italian.

I take my food seriously, too, and come, as mentioned, from a line of people who made food—and physical warmth—the center of their relationships with relatives and friends. They would no more neglect to offer you something to eat within thirty seconds of your stepping into their house than they'd forget to shake your hand or embrace you when they hadn't seen you since the week before.

I am still linked to this chain of souls, fond of all my numerous cousins; really, many of them are more like brothers and sisters to me. The cousin I see most often is named Joe and sometimes still called by his childhood nickname, Joe Bones, though he is now a sixty-six-year-old retired schoolteacher who still lives a few miles from where we both grew up. (I have another cousin named Joe, and one surviving uncle named Joe, and three cousins once removed named Joe, and my paternal grandfather and mother's brother were both Joes. We keep them separate in various ways: for instance, we'll say, "Cousin Joe, you know, Uncle Joe's Joey"; we'll call one of them Joe Bones, another Young Joe; or we'll say, "Joe, you know, Joe and Susan Joe"; or "Joe, you know, Peggy and Joe's son"; or, "Jackie and Lori's boy.") About half of my cousins went to college, but Joe Bones and I were two of a much smaller number that went away to college—he to the University of Michigan in the 1960s, and me to Brown in the 1970s—and I think this has aligned us in a certain way, within the tightly knit tapestry of the family. We both have a passion for the game of golf; we both married "outside the Church"; we both like to read; and we both have an interest in spiritual subjects, though neither of us associates himself with a particular church or discusses such things in the company of most of our golfing friends.

"He's like the older brother you never had," Amanda said to me once, and I think that's true. But the reason I bring him into the story here is because of another of those strands that link us: a love of food that borders on the pathological. When we speak on the phone, it is not unusual for one of us to mention, in passing, that he went out to dinner the night before. At which point the other will interrupt the main thrust of the conversation and say, "What'd you have?" The answer is never a simple "pasta" or "lobster" or "just a salad." "Susan and I went to Rino's," Joe Bones will say—a restaurant in East Boston that we both like. "And when we got there, Tony called me into the kitchen. 'Joey, look at this,' he said. And he had these unbelievable pieces of pork. I'm telling you, Rollie, they were as thick as two hands on top of each other and tender as—"

"How did he cook them?"

"Wait a minute. So he calls me into the kitchen, and he shows me the pork, which he just had delivered that afternoon. And he says, 'Let me make them up for you my special way. I put them in the pan with onion and garlic and oil, and I cook them a little bit, and then I take and I bake them with vinegar peppers, and at the end I put a little gravy over them.'"

"How many did you have?"

"I had three. My two, plus one of Susan's. Plus the salad, the bread, wine."

And so on. Tony's New Zealand cockles, or frutti di mare, or calves' brains. Sometimes we will return to the main topic of the call and sometimes not. Over the years, both of us have exercised a great deal—in part because we were athletes in college, but mainly because we want to be able to eat the way we eat, to love food the way we love it, without gaining so much weight that it will adversely affect our golf swing.

In one memorable conversation, Joe Bones told me about a neighbor of his, a guy he's done a few favors for over the years. One day this guy knocks on his door and says, "Come over to my house, Joey, I just bought eight pounds of squid at the fish market and I don't need it all. I'll give you three or four pounds." And then, to my great pleasure, my cousin went into a long narrative about how he learned to clean the squid under this man's tutelage, exactly how you wash them, how you cut them and take the eyes out, and the ink, and then how you bring them home and prepare them, with this or that seasoning, cooking them for this amount of time, serving them with a "nice dish of hot peppers and garlic. You should see the way Susan makes it."

Fortunately for all of us, Susan, his wife, is a cook of world-class abilities. It's an interesting tale, their marriage. In the city where we grew up, the Revere, Massachusetts, of the 1950s and '60s, a mostly Italian-American Revere, there were some Irish, English, French Canadian, and Eastern European families, and a whole neighborhood of Jews. This neighborhood was always referred to by the name of its main street, Shirley Avenue, which ran for half a mile or so from Bell Circle (which had the state record for the most auto insurance claims) to Revere Beach (which was America's first public beach, a lesser version of Coney Island in those days). I remember, as a boy, how exotic the shops with Hebrew letters in the window seemed, and how the smells and names and sights of Shirley Avenue always made me feel as if that right turn off Bell Circle had transported me into a different world. I remember, too, how there seemed to be only a thin line distinguishing the Jewish and Christian populations in that city: among my father's closest friends was an exceedingly gentle man named Dave Calichman, and I knew he was Jewish the way I knew that my mother's family was English, or that Sokolowski was a Russian name and Masse a French one. On the one hand, this distinction was worth mentioning; on the other, it never seemed to matter much. Generally speaking, the Jews liked one end of Revere Beach, and the Christians liked the middle, but with so many friendships across that imaginary border it was all but meaningless.

But when Joe Bones—who is one of two people ever to hit a baseball out of Glendale Park in Everett, Massachusetts, dead center field (the other was Babe Ruth); who was the starting catcher on the Michigan team that won the NCAA national championship in 1962; who was signed by the San Francisco Giants while still in college, shortly before his career was ended by a freak auto accident; and who was already a kind of family hero by the time he turned sixteen—decided he wanted to marry a Jewish girl, suddenly the distinction between Christian and non-Christian mattered. I was only twelve at the time, but I remember the stir this engagement caused in our family. One of the priests at St. Anthony's had announced that if Joey and Susan went ahead with their wedding, Joey would be excommunicated, and excommunication, of course, meant he would suffer forever in the fires of hell when he died. I think my uncles and aunts held about a three percent belief in this particular Vatican dictum; still, the wedding caused a ripple of trouble. Inside them, if I can presume to know, a battle was being fought between two armies: family loyalty and allegiance to the Church, and those were extraordinarily powerful armies in our place and time. But this was Joe Bones, Cammy and Josie's kid, Lennie and Stephen's brother, our nephew, our cousin. What kind of church would condemn a person like that to hell?

The priest went further: if any of the aunts and uncles attended the service or brought a gift, they would be excommunicated, too. I have vague memories of conversations about this dilemma, carried on above my head, or on the telephone while I was in the next room. Should we go? How can we not go? My grandmother was by a good measure the most devoted of a devout bunch: church every Sunday and on holy days, confession, the rosary several times a day. It was she who tended the flower garden around the statue of the Virgin in our backyard. And it was she, alone among the relatives, who ended up attending the wedding ceremony of Joe Merullo and Susan Schwartz. My parents and our aunts and uncles went to the reception. No doubt they carried gifts, in spite of the priest's made-up rule, because not bringing a gift would have been a sin of a different kind, against a different code, the code of southern-Italian generosity.

It is an irony probably lost on the priest at St. Anthony's that Joe and Susan's marriage has proven more resilient and happier than some of the Catholic-Catholic marriages of family members and friends. And another irony, perhaps, is that our Jewish cousin-by-marriage has turned out to be the premier cook among an impressive pantheon of family cooks from her generation. A beautiful woman, then and now, daughter of a general practitioner who volunteered to serve—as a psychiatrist—in World War II, she is unfailingly modest about her culinary abilities. "It could have used a little more salt, don't you think?" she'll say. "I could have cooked it another few minutes." Or, "It might have been better with green peppers instead." While everyone at the table shakes his head, no way, and chews.

Joe and I live a hundred miles apart, and so, typically, on the night before one of our Boston-area golf matches, I'll drive down and spend the night at his house, arriving in time for dinner if it is at all possible. I'll bring along something they don't need—another bottle of wine or a jug of maple syrup—and take my place at the kitchen table, where Susan has the seat of honor. Joey will get a particular look on his face, a mischievous glimmer of ecstasy, as if we're about to embark on a secret voyage, half illicit. He'll take out a bottle of the only wine he buys for himself, something called Fortissimo (in Italian this word means "strongest"), which is closer to some kind of 60-proof red whiskey than a real wine, but which I like very much. It comes in one-gallon jugs. We'll sip the wine and talk while Susan works at the stove a few feet away, then brings over an appetizer of roasted red peppers and fresh Italian bread and sits down to nibble at it and sip from a glass. Often, if there is any advance notice to be had, Cousin Joe will ask me what I'd like the meal to be—meat, fish, pasta, all of the above? Susan knows I have a special place on my palate for chicken cacciatore (hunter's-style chicken) so it will often happen that, after the red peppers have been eaten, she'll bring a huge platter to the table: chicken pieces, peppers, onions, mushrooms, all in a strong gravy, accompanied by a side dish of broccoli rabe or escarole.

We will then begin to eat in earnest, Joey and I, Susan sitting between us taking small bites and looking dubious, as if the cacciatore had turned out reasonably well, but not really the way she'd envisioned. The conversation will spin from our children to books to sports to something one of our long-ago-deceased relatives said or did, but it will always circle back to the meal, as if the mechanics of eating were the gravity of our solar system. There are the tastes, of course, but the smells, sounds, and textures should not be discounted: the gurgle of Fortissimo as it is poured into a glass; the slight crunch of the onions; the dusting of sesame seeds on the bread we use—Joey and I use, at least—to sponge up the last of the succulent gravy.

In my own house I like to do dishes by hand after a meal like that, but Joe and Susan will not allow this, and it would feel, somehow, like invading a surgeon's operating theater or the station of an air-traffic controller if I were to step too close to the stove. So, after the meal, I bring a couple of dishes to the sink, then my cousin and I sit opposite each other in a posture that signals something has been accomplished. It is like the feeling I remember when I walked out of church after the Sunday services of my youth: you have attached yourself once again to the ancient ritual;

you've performed that ritual with people who are close to you; and you've done something to sustain yourself—body or spirit. Sometimes the meal will have been so remarkable that we already know, even as it is being digested, that it will be material for a phone conversation in the coming months. "Remember that fish Susan cooked on the night before we played Ferncroft in the rain?" Joey will ask. And I'll say, "Yes, sure, of course I remember." And I do. And the next day we'll head off, in the company of our golfing *amici,* A.J. and Ronnie, and play a fine or not-so-fine golf course in the Greater Boston area, Joe Bones and I competing as a team, fueled by the repast of the previous evening, soaking up the day as if it were the last day like that we will ever have, the last family memory, the last bit of tomato gravy on a plate, the last small sip of Fortissimo. "It goes so fast," he will often lament, after we've played five or six holes. "I want the day to slow down."

By the time we reached the northern end of the lake, the girls were restless, I had emerged from my reverie, and it was as if the mountains had stepped back from the shoreline. In contrast to the middle of the lake, where the shores were steep and sometimes rocky, Como's northernmost terrain was more placid, the land flat, or almost flat for a few kilometers before the hills rose and then turned from rounded to sharp, from green to gray. It was hot in Gravedona. The girls wanted pizza again. I didn't care. In the shadow of the hills, within sight of the lake, we walked along the main road until we came to a restaurant that said PIZZERIA, and we went in and found a table and sat there hopefully until the waitress came and informed us that they served pizza only for dinner. We got up and walked to the next place on the road—no pizza there either, something about a lack of dough or oil or the right cook. We headed back into town and heard the same sad tale at the third restaurant we tried—a two-table café near the waterfront. Gravedona was bereft of pizza, a disappointment, an affront. I thought of the words of the Emperor Barbarossa: "Clemency for everyone except the perfidious people of Gravedona."

We stayed at the café and settled for salads and bread, a ham and cheese crepe, and a short lecture from Dad on the unpredictability of the traveler's life. The girls had ice cream for dessert; I drank a small glass of beer.

After paying the *conto,* we walked to the south end of town and found there the church of Santa Maria del Tiglio, which dated back to the twelfth century and was made of dark gray stone. Small, square, cool, the nave with its high, timbered ceiling was empty save for a lectern, an enormous iron bell sitting on the floor, a roped-off area where a tile mosaic had survived since the fifth century, and an unusual crucifix on the north wall. "I don't think Jesus looks like that," Juliana said. "He's a small angel with wings. . . . And why does he always have a beard?"

The Jesus of Santa Maria del Tiglio was thin and thin-faced, his feet supported by a small shelf, as if the sculptor could not bear the idea of the weight of his body pulling down on his nailed hands. A sort of wooden skirt covered his thighs and hips. Juliana stared with a critical expression. Alexandra, usually the one more interested in things religious, set her new Harry Potter book on the lectern and read like that, unself-conscious as the stones themselves, a silent priestess.

After walking back through the town, we waited at the dock with a family—grandparents, a young boy and girl—who seemed to have emerged from the backcountry for a rare outing. Curious to see what Alexandra was reading, the boy, who must have been twelve or thirteen, pawed roughly at the book in her hands, frightening her. Then, as if she had known me all my life, the grandmother took my arm as we were walking down the gangway toward the boat and told me, *"Ho paura. Ho grande paura!"*

"I'm afraid, too," I said, though it wasn't true. She squeezed my arm and wouldn't let go until we were safely aboard.

We sat behind them on the long trip home, and I watched the grandfather pointing out things on either shore, giving the boy and the girl a guided tour in the dialect of Comasco. It was the language of the lake, so they must have lived nearby. Yet it was as if they had never been out on the water, never seen anything beyond their little village, tucked back in the hills beyond Gravedona, perhaps, down one of those guardrail-less, two-track roads where tourists got lost. I wondered if the boy and the girl might be cousins, and if they would someday get married outside the church, to spouses who did not speak Comasco, but who were wonderful cooks, and if they would come together again in twenty, thirty, or forty years, drawn by a midlife passion, a round of golf, say, at Menaggio and Cadenabbia, and a home-cooked meal the night before. I thought about how families open themselves to include outsiders or have difficulty doing that; how the bonds that link them are stretched and broken by distances and politics and faith and time, or reinforced by regular meals and a shared passion. I watched my daughters watching a solitary sailboat traverse the lake.

9

VILLA D'ESTE

From time to time—either because of scheduled tournaments that I could not play in, or because I wanted a change from the narrow fairways, steep hills, and elegantly slow pace of play at Menaggio and Cadenabbia—I would sample some of the other courses within a reasonable driving distance of the lake. Getting to those courses was as much of an adventure as playing them, and I believe that is a basic and unchangeable aspect of Italian golf. If you live a few doors down from the course, maybe driving there won't offer much in the way of entertainment. If you know the roads because you play the same course time after time, as I did at M&C, or if you have an Italian friend who is familiar with the area, then driving will be an issue only insofar as you will be dodging the usual assortment of oncoming Mercedeses and Fiats, and watching young men on motorcycles fly past a few inches from your fenders. But if you are on your way to an unfamiliar course that is a fair distance from the place you are staying, and especially if you are getting your directions from someone at the pro shop or *segreteria*, then (a) you should allow an extra hour for getting lost/stopping to ask directions/treating yourself to a cappuccino to calm down, and (b) you should, despite the cappuccino, plan to arrive in a state of agitation, unless you are someone not at all like me—that is, someone who remains calm when he is lost and late for a tee time and eager to play.

Years before, in Rome, where I was writing about golfing and eating for an American magazine, I would often find myself caught in the frenzy of the deadly five-lane Raccordo Annulare, or Ring Road, a superspeed, demolition-derby ribbon of hot tar that runs in a rough circle around the Eternal City. I would have a paper cup of coffee balanced somewhere beside me, and a map or scribbled directions spread out across the steering wheel between my hands, and I would be careening along in the vehicular Roller Derby, glancing up at the road and down at the map, and fretting about exactly which exit was supposed to lead to the golf course where I had made an appointment to play. At last, agitated almost to desperation by the traffic, the road signs or lack of road signs, the small print of the map, or the imperfect directions in my hands, I would just take whatever exit came next and plunge into a side-street melee of cars, Vespas, trucks, and motorcycles, and I would have been told that the golf course was just straight ahead from that point, *sempre diritto,* I couldn't possibly miss it, right there on the road. After trying to sort things out on my own for another half hour, I would toss away my pride, stop and ask, and understand half of what was said to me. Half the time what was said would turn out to be accurate and half the time not, so that I had roughly a 25 percent chance of actually finding the course. But that would be true only if I asked once. Often, I would have to ask half a dozen times, which would mean that my chances reduced themselves, stop by stop, to .25 x .25 x .25 x .25 x .25 x .25, or .000244 chances out of a million.

Of course I am exaggerating. But not by much. In Rome, in northern Italy, I always eventually found the course I was looking for, and though I sometimes didn't arrive until after my tee time, this was never a problem. Never a problem, that is, until the very last round of the summer. But I digress.

On the morning I was to play Villa d'Este, I left two hours early for what I had been assured was a forty-five-minute drive. An hour at most, if the traffic was bad. Reserving the tee time over the telephone, I had asked for directions, twice, and these were the directions I had been given, and this is not an exaggeration: Go to Como. In Como, follow signs for Bergamo/Lecco. At Lipomo, turn toward Montorfano, and the course will be right on that road.

No distances, no landmarks. In American terms, this might be roughly similar to directions like these: go into Des Moines. Once you get into Des Moines, follow signs for Iowa City. In Lafayette turn toward St. Louis. And the course will be right there.

But, with all the enthusiasm of a golfer heading out to play, and all the optimism of someone who has found his way around the world several times over, I rose early without an alarm, stretched, dressed, drank some water, left the sleeping threesome of females in the night-cooled house in Mezzegra, and headed south for my game. As far as the city of Como, at the southernmost end of the lake, all went well. I stopped on the outskirts of the city to buy gas and have a cappuccino and a brioche, standing up, in the gas station snack bar. Outside again, I told the stocky, friendly, overalled attendant (a gruff, good man, who assured me, after three words, that I spoke Italian beautifully) that I was headed to Montorfano and asked if he could help me find the correct road.

"You're going to play golf," he said, a quick assessment that might have had something to do with the fact that I was wearing short pants, a striped jersey, and little socks, but which struck me as a good sign anyway.

"Yes, at Villa d'Este."

"Of course, of course. *Certo, certo. E' semplice.* It's simple. You just go up here, straight ahead—see that road?—and look for the signs for Bergamo."

When I thanked him, he added the comforting phrase, "It's all one road."

It may well have been all one road, but, if so, I somehow managed to meander off it. This might have been because I was looking for what proved to be a nonexistent sign for Bergamo/Lecco, I don't recall, but in any case I missed a key turn, soon realized my mistake, made a risky U-turn through the parking lot of another gas station, and headed off in what seemed to be the right direction. It was true, of course, that the route to Villa d'Este consisted of only one road, in something like the way that, for rain falling in Minnesota, the route to the Gulf of Mexico consists of only one stream. But there are innumerable rivulets, oxbows, puddles, currents, and there are innumerable side roads, lights, stop signs, intersections, forks, and yields, and so it is not really such a simple voyage. I made the U-turn and quickly found the right road, and everything went perfectly well—there was Lipomo, there was a sign pointing to Montorfano—until I came to a pair of orange sawhorses set across the road, and handwritten placards on the sawhorses indicating that both lanes of the two-lane highway were under construction and absolutely closed. Not closed to all but local traffic. Closed. Period.

There was no one in the vicinity of whom I might ask help. No detour/*deviazione* signs pointing out the alternative route. Nothing to do but turn around and head back along the one road until something happened.

As luck would have it, I soon saw two men walking on the shoulder. I pulled over and asked them how I could get to Villa d'Este, since the road behind me was not open. "Just circle up over this hill," one of them said, pointing over the roof of the Renault. "Keep taking rights, and you'll come back down to this road again. Take another right and you'll see it."

So I circled up over the hill, took the first right, and all was going well. I didn't see a golf course, but felt as if I would see one soon. I took the second right. After a hundred yards, this road turned into a steep dirt track leading up through a weedy field and into the driveway of a private house. I made the third in that morning's series of creative U-turns, backtracked, tried the next right, which seemed wrong, and pulled up beside a man pruning roses. "No, you should have gone left at the last intersection," he said, with some authority, and from what seemed to me a place of deep calm. The relaxed quality of his voice, contrasting as it did to my own mood, made me wonder if I would have been better off spending the day in the garden. "I don't know where the golf course is, exactly," he admitted, "but if you go back and take that left, you'll get into the center of Montorfano, and I know you'll be close."

The road he had pointed to did, in fact, lead into the center of Montorfano, a tiny, busy little place, where I stopped to ask the first people I saw—two older women—if they knew how I might get to the famous golf course called Villa d'Este. They had heard of the course—or seemed to have heard of it. Shopping bags in hand, they conferred. Cars were damming up behind me, then pulling around as I edged two wheels up onto the sidewalk. The women went on conferring. At last, to their great credit, they said, "You really should ask at that bar." There were no parking spaces near the bar, and none on the narrow square in front of it, so I pulled into the end of an alley, a few feet from the outdoor tables, and speaking out the car window, disturbed two gentlemen at their morning espresso. They stood up and walked over to me, one of them pounding on his chest when he heard the name of the course and saying, "I live there." A brief disagreement ensued:

they were competing for the title of The One Who Knows. The second man, who didn't live at Villa d'Este, and who seemed if not the more intelligent then at least the more sober of the pair, had the final word.

Five minutes later I was pulling up to a set of ten-foot-high wrought-iron gates beside an intercom and a sign saying the course did not open until eight thirty (in midsummer!). It was, according to the clock in the Renault, 8:31. I identified myself, stated my purpose, and the gates swung open. Past the gates, at the end of a long, tree-lined drive, stood a grand stucco clubhouse, lemon-colored, with a patio, a series of a dozen arched doorways on the ground floor, and more windows, awnings, and a stately veranda above. Villa d'Este, named for a famous villa half an hour to the north, had been designed in 1926 by Peter Gannon, the British Amateur champion, and had hosted the Italian Open in 1972. Clark Gable, Bing Crosby, and King Leopold of Belgium had all graced its fairways, and according to one ranking, it was the twenty-eighth best course in continental Europe. Inside, a friendly *segretaria* named Andrea found my name on the tee time list.

"When I called," I told Andrea in careful Italian, "I said I hoped I could play with someone who knows the course well. A member, possibly."

A shrug, a smile. Andrea was sorry, but that had not been arranged.

Everything else was in order, however. My bag was taken into the building and carried downstairs to the caddy master, a portly, white-haired fellow. This man welcomed me warmly, said I was sure to enjoy the course, and pointed me in the direction of the driving range.

As is the case on many Italian courses, the range at Villa d'Este consisted of a linked series of private wooden enclosures with mats on the floor. You can't see the other players on the range, and they can't see you. You can't hit them with an errant shot, and they can't hit you. You can swear or sing or shank or weep or pray or change your pants standing next to your bucket of balls and no one will be the wiser. It was as calm as a confessional in that ten-foot-square booth, with the range, and the day, spread out in front of me. And I hit the golf ball beautifully, perfectly, wonderfully, working my way up through the bag with a series of gentle draws and long drives. It was the kind of practice session that makes you believe you are someone you are not, that all your golfing sins have magically been forgiven, that somehow, in your sleep, or over dinner the night before, or by pondering things on a long boat ride with your children, you have unlocked the vault in which Ben Hogan and Sam Snead kept the secret of their swings and now you have the password that will admit you to the exclusive club of those who play golf as well as they want to.

After finishing with several long, straight drives, I carried the last few balls up to the short-game practice area, dumped them into the sand, and knocked every one of them out of the bunker and up near the pin. This, for a player with a lengthy history of sand troubles, was unheard of. I had tried one small new thing—shifting my knees forward on the downswing—and by some Villa d'Estian magic, I was now a force to be reckoned with from the bunker. (This technique has continued to work, I should mention, to the present day. No Paul Azinger from the beach, I am now at least moderately confident of getting the ball onto the green in one swing.) Once I mastered the sand shots, I practiced chipping from the fringe, putting over mounds, knocking in those deadly three-footers. Success everywhere. Then, full of hope, I walked up onto the tee of the first hole, a gorgeous, left-sweeping par five, and hit a perfect three wood that swept in from the right edge of the fairway and bounced happily along in the short grass there, like a puppy running onto its own lawn after a week spent wandering the alleys of the city, hungry and wet. It was all so easy, so simple. It was all one road.

Of course, it is not that simple. If it were that simple, golf would have all the appeal and challenge of eating a bowl of oatmeal. From the perfect lie on the Villa d'Este's well-groomed first fairway, I hit a shot I had not managed to hit on the range that morning, a severely yanked ground ball that bounced and skittered and then tumbled sideways into the rough, side hill. Then another similar shot that might have been its demonic twin. Then, of course, a soaring four iron that stopped just short of the green. A fine pitch, or what I thought was a fine pitch. The green was shaded and damp, and the ball stopped dead, twenty feet short of its target. Two putts. Double bogey.

I followed this display with a resounding seven on the simple, uphill, par-four second.

Then bogey on the long par-three third.

But, despite this awful start, I was appreciating Villa d'Este, a famous tournament course at one time, which had fallen from grace, like so many other famous tournament venues, due to a lack of length. One nice touch was the tee-box markers, which provided a diagram of the hole using trees as measuring points. It was, for example, exactly 140 meters from the oak tree on the right to the front of the green; 230 meters from the tee to the big chestnut on the left, and so on. One of the pleasures of the course was the variety of foliage by the sides of the fairways—birch, oak, chestnut, pine. A member told me, later in the day, that in the fall Villa d'Este was so littered with chestnuts the maintenance crew had fits keeping it playable.

On the fourth, you had to hit your tee shot out of a chute of trees to a fairly small landing area. I slapped a nice two hybrid onto the short grass, then, to avoid a sucker left pin placed a few paces from a severe drop-off, I hit a sand wedge to the middle of the green. When I drained the twenty-five-foot putt for birdie, all the extravagant hopes fanned on the driving range burst into flame again. I could play. I could play well. Perhaps very well. I could break 80 without breaking a sweat.

It was, however, not to be. Bogeys and double bogeys on the rest of the way out, a parade of happy sloppiness, and I finished the front side in a dispiriting 44.

On the tenth tee—after a quick drink in the clubhouse, served by a friendly fellow who admitted to having zero interest in golf—I came upon a pleasant woman named Sylvia, a Villa d'Este member, and we played the back nine together. Tall, trim, dark-haired, she had worked as a medical editor but "now I let my husband earn the money." Sylvia made four on the simple par-three tenth, to my hideous five, but then began to struggle, her smooth swing resulting, by some evil physics, in ground balls that squirted left and right. I hit approaches into bunkers on three holes in a row, but made two par saves, an unheard-of percentage for me.

One of the things I liked about Sylvia was that, though she spoke excellent English, she appreciated my desire to improve my Italian, kept the conversation going in that tongue, and suffered through my grammatical lapses with only the politest of corrections. On the left-breaking, par-five thirteenth, after a particularly frustrating midiron from the fairway, she let out what sounded like an epithet. I asked for a translation. "It just means 'Madonna in the sky,'" she said sheepishly. Then added, after a moment: "But I think the Madonna has more important things to help people with than their golf games, yes?"

Sylvia did not need any help in shushing a pair of men talking loudly on the fifteenth, as we were teeing off nearby on the pretty, downhill par-three fourteenth. *"Scusa, scusa,"* they said, hunching their shoulders like scolded boys.

But then her cell phone rang, and she stepped a few paces to one side. "I can't talk, I'm sorry, I'm playing golf," she said, and went on for another five minutes, and this happened as I was addressing my ball, which I hit into the trees on the right. I was enjoying Villa d'Este all the same. Nestled in gently rolling hills that occasionally offered views of the old city of Bergamo in the distance, the course was a much easier walk and had more breathing room off the tee than Menaggio and Cadenabbia, though it was still mostly a three-wood, short-iron type of layout, with long par-threes making up some of the distance. The exception to this pattern was the par-four fifteenth, played into the wind on that day, 442 yards for the men, the number one handicap hole on the course. I hit a long, straight drive, then a two hybrid that bounced on the green and over into deep rough behind. Fifteen over par at that point, nothing to lose, I flopped one up onto the putting surface with all the confidence of Phil Mickelson, then drained the putt.

But it was a short-lived triumph. Even a textbook par on the uphill eighteenth, with the glamorous clubhouse sitting off to the right like an observation post from which members could evaluate the suffering of their peers, even a lively conversation with Sylvia—which took us from cystic fibrosis to Italian politics ("The coalition is crippled by the extreme left"), to maternity leave ("It's a generous policy we have, but those women are rendering an important service"), to the retirement age ("Too young here; it's putting a strain on the economy"), to my work ("Give me your name so I can tell my friends I played with a writer")—couldn't leave me with much optimism. An 85, on a course where I should have shot a leisurely 77. So it was. Friendlier than my home course by the lake, beautiful in a less spectacular way, Villa d'Este was, for me, like spending a few hours with a former movie star who was past the prime of her career. She had accepted the end of her days in the spotlight with an infectious grace, had welcomed you into her home for tea and cakes, then touched you once on the shoulder as you said good-bye. You would not forget her.

By THE TIME I FINISHED MY round and drove down the tree-lined drive and out through the gates, a few *deviazione* signs had been scattered about. Guided by them, I found it a simple matter to find the way back. Before long I was slipping through the familiar outskirts of Como, with the lake looming off to the north. Two-thirds of the way from Como to Mezzegra the little town of Argegno crouched against the *statale* with its back to the hills. With an array of colorful awnings above its bars and trattorias, the curving road, and the way the green mountainsides sloped to the water and folded in behind each other, Argegno was another course in Lake Como's visual feast. I found a parking space there and, thirsty and hungry from the hot trek at Villa d'Este, stopped into one of the bars on the western side of the shore road and ordered something called a *snello,* which turned out to be an excellent grilled prosciutto and mozzarella sandwich on a soft roll.

Bar is not really the right word for these establishments, though it is the word Italians themselves use. In America, the word brings to mind a place where people go to drink alcohol, and that's pretty much the long and short of it. Yes, in some cases food is served—pig's feet, beef jerky, maybe a hot dog on a bun. And there might be televisions hanging near the ceiling showing NFL games or NASCAR races, a pool table or two, a dartboard or pinball game, possibly a jukebox. For the most part, though, when we think of a bar we think of a dimly lit place on a side street, the air touched with the yeasty stink of old beer, a few regulars slumped over their damp glasses, and, in the old days, the twirl of cigarette smoke in a band of sunlight.

The bars near Lake Como, and the bars in other parts of Italy, don't have much in common with that scene. Often they are well-lit places where children are welcome, where the walls are decorated with framed pictures of soccer teams or American movie stars, with statues of the Madonna or a patron saint, where food is an important part of the experience, where people often go for breakfast, though that meal usually consists only of a pastry and coffee. It is common enough to see regulars with a glass in front of them, but alcoholism has a disgraceful color to it among most Italians; or perhaps it's truer to say almost the opposite: that growing up with alcohol as they do, drinking wine at the table from a young age, watching their parents entertain friends with a shot of grappa or limoncello, Italians have made alcohol into something so ordinary that the lure of the forbidden has been siphoned away. There is some alcoholism, of course. But in all the months I've spent in Italy—eight long visits over fifteen years—I can't honestly remember seeing one drunk staggering down the street.

So, though you'll see men drinking wine or a liqueur at breakfast time, they are usually in the company of pals, rarely turn their eyes away from the families that come in for a pastry, and almost always, after a game of cards or two, will stand up and head off to work, or home to trim the hedge or cultivate the tomatoes. Later in the evening the scene changes. At times at the Bar Tre Archi in Mezzegra, for example, the sidewalk porch had a more raucous air. But even then the surliness and anger seemed to be missing, as if they were eddies of litter the warm Mediterranean air had blown off into the distance.

In much the same way that you'll see three or four friends standing at a pub rail in London or Dublin carrying on a pleasant conversation over their afternoon pint, in Italy you will come upon three or four men, and sometimes a couple of women, standing at the bar just long enough to finish their second or third espresso of the day while exchanging a few words about the fortunes of AC Milan and Juventus. I have had a number of these conversations myself, though usually not about soccer teams. Down south, people remember the American army working its way up from Sicily, or talk about grandparents who moved to America. In the north, sometimes, they complain about doing all the work, while the southerners, those dark, lazy southerners—your people aren't from there, are they?—live off the excessive generosity of the state.

But it was quiet in the bar in Argegno on that afternoon, and

I stood at the rail alone, eating my *snello* and drinking my decaffeinated *macchiato*. In those solitary moments, one's eyes tend to wander, and after a while, my wandering eyes fell upon a small display of postcards set up on a shelf behind the bar. There was a view of the Manhattan skyline, and there, front and center, stood a postcard of Mussolini at strict attention, giving the Fascist salute. It made me think of a comment made to me in a pro shop in western Massachusetts. "He did some good things at first," the assistant pro said about Hitler. And it made me think of a time long before, at a seacoast resort in what was then the Soviet republic of Georgia, when I'd stopped into a stand-up snack bar for a *khachapuri* and a cup of Turkish coffee and seen a brass-framed photo of Joseph Stalin displayed proudly on the counter. And it made me think of a conversation I'd had at the pool behind the Mezzegra house, with a friendly martial artist named Ronaldo. "Ten years ago they said it happened this way," he told me. "Last year they discovered new documents and said it happened that way. In my opinion, *secondo me,* there is no history."

But there is history, of course—Italy is soaked in it—and you could often feel it around the lake. Friends told us that a house we walked by several times a week on the stone-paved path down into Lenno had been headquarters for Nazi officers during the war, and that some people still believed it to be haunted, or cursed, and would make a wide detour to avoid going past it. One morning we walked into town for breakfast and saw that someone had spray-painted graffiti on the wall of Villa Belmonte, where the black cross was fixed near the spot where Il Duce had been shot. NON VI RISPETTO NEMMENO DA MORTE it read. "We don't respect you even in death." And then, as if to underscore the remaining ambiguity about Mussolini's legacy, someone else had come by with a different-colored spray paint and tried to obliterate that message.

Despite all the atrocities of the Fascist regime, for some Italians

Mussolini's name continues to have positive associations, and it wasn't particularly rare to see his face on posters in gift shops. We had come upon such a display weeks earlier, on our quest for the great northern-Italian pizza. On that evening we'd been directed to a place called Il Cris, a ten-minute drive south of where we were living. Il Cris was said to be inexpensive and first-rate, popular with locals more than tourists, in part because it was in a residential neighborhood, well off the tourist route . . . and perhaps for other reasons.

We arrived at seven thirty and were greeted by a not particularly friendly host, who asked, though every table in the place was empty, if we had reservations. No, no reservations, we said, and with what seemed to us a shadow of reluctance we were led past a small bar and into a room that looked out on a patio where six or eight tables had been set. Our waiter was a young black man—a rarity: the black faces you see in Italy tend to belong to poor Africans walking the streets and beaches selling cheap toys, gum, leather goods, or dresses. As the tables around us quickly filled, he brought our salads and then the usual pizzas—one plain cheese, and one more adventurous. In our quest for the perfect pizza, we'd developed an expression that the girls liked to use. "Dad," one of them would say, "does this place make the cut?" Il Cris did not. The edge of the pizza crust was crisp, even burnt in a couple of places the way I like it. But the tomatoes had soaked through the dough beneath it so that when you lifted up a soggy slice, the cheese and tomato slid back onto the plate. This wasn't as much of an issue for the locals, I would guess, since northern-Italian pizzas come to the table unsliced, and most people eat them with knife and fork. For us, though, it was a sloppy, unsatisfying meal, 43 euros (about $60) with the ice cream and *panna cotta* desserts, and one good draft beer.

On the way out I stopped at the bar to pay and, waiting there, noticed something we'd missed on the way in: a corkboard hung with framed quotations in large letters. These were things like WHEN THE GOING GETS TOUGH, THE TOUGH GET GOING, accompanied by a date. It took me a few seconds to figure out that these were the framed words of Il Duce himself, and that the dates referred to particular speeches he had given. There was a picture or two of the not-so-great man, the steel-spined posture and lantern jaw, the wide lips and sorrowful eyes, as if he were still a little boy, trying again and again the same cute trick that had made his mother smile . . . and ready to beat her to death if she didn't. Beneath the quotations was a framed document that listed his accomplishments:

1927—Institutes an insurance program for widows and orphans.

1933—Builds aqueducts bringing fresh water to Perugia and Orvieto.

Then a large gap during the war years, where what might have been inscribed but wasn't would have been things like:

1938—Passes anti-Semitic laws that will result in seven thousand Italian Jews being sent to the death camps.

1939—Forms defensive alliance with Adolf Hitler, leading Italy into a disastrous war in which half a million Italians will die.

1945—Attempts to flee the country with his mistress and a million dollars in cash.

THAT SAME NIGHT AFTER OUR UNSATISFYING dinner at Il Cris, we drove down into Mezzegra, parked near the Bar Tre Archi, crossed the *statale* toward the lake, and walked along an ancient alleyway that turned into a dirt track that led to an abandoned church. "I expect to see syringes here," Amanda said, and that was the feeling: cut off from the tourist hotels and grand villas, it was a strip of roughness and sorrow in the shadows. On the way back, we found a place where the alleyway opened into a cobblestone square. A 250-year-old magnolia tree spread its branches over a part of the square, its trunk so large that the four of us could barely stretch our arms around it. There was a restaurant nearby, with a few loud drinkers, then more alleyways that led through tiny courtyards and past uneven stone houses—their windows shuttered, laundry hanging on lines—where people had lived for a millennium, through invasions and wars and periods of grandeur and peace, through the likes of Mussolini, with his big words and big gestures, and empty soul.

I finished my *snello* and *macchiato,* left a small tip, and on the way home went past the place on Via Pola where Mussolini had staged his last performance. According to some reports, he had faced his executioners bravely, with one final grandiose line: "Shoot me in the chest."

IO

MONTICELLO

All the golfing people I spoke with at the lake told me that
the two courses at Monticello—an hour to the south—were
"American-style courses." What this meant I wasn't sure, since
the United States has parkland, mountain, desert, and links-style
courses, but I was curious. Not long after my solitary trip to Villa
d'Este, I made plans to travel to Monticello with Harold's friend
Alberto, a champion skier and restaurant owner with whom I'd
played one round at M&C. But Alberto had to cancel at the last
moment, so I ended up making the trip solo. To reduce the risk,
I had called the course twice for directions, and this was what I
heard, both times, from two different employees: go toward Fino
Mornasco.

"How should I go? Through Como?"

"Yes, through Como, and then head toward Fino Mornasco."

"And then what?"

"Then you will find the course."

Like a reporter trying to squeeze hard information from a reluctant politician, I pressed for details, but the details were not forthcoming. Head toward Fino Mornasco.

So there seemed to be no option but to drive into Como and go toward Fino Mornasco, whatever or wherever that was. As a backup strategy, I'd planned on stopping at the service station on the outskirts of Como and asking my gruff overalled friend there. But when I approached the station on that morning, I noticed a sign on it saying CLOSED FOR REPAIRS, so I just pressed on, watching for FINO MORNASCO signs and trying to maintain a positive attitude. I saw one such sign and made the appropriate turn, but soon I was lost in a wilderness of apartment houses, shops, and signless intersections. On the left, two workmen were getting into their truck. Though it was a bad place to stop, an uphill, two-lane road with fast traffic, I pulled over near the sidewalk opposite them, rolled down the window, and asked for help.

"Oof, Fino Mornasco," one of them said. He made the kind of face you would make if someone had just hit you in the nose with a small pie. *Oof.* Eyes closed, head tilted back, lips turned down. Fino Mornasco. He shook one hand loosely from the wrist. He turned to his friend. "Fino Mornasco, he's trying to get to," he said, as if Fino Mornasco were a field of ice on Saturn.

The friend made the same face, then lifted his jaw up the way a horse does and raised his eyebrows. Ey, Fino Mornasco.

I was waiting by the side of the road, cars going past, horns, squealing tires, a muffled epithet.

"Listen," the first man said after a few seconds of contemplation. "See that green sign up ahead. The autostrada? *Segui quelle insegne verdi.* Follow those green signs, get on the autostrada, and you'll see the exit. It's not the fastest way, but the other way you could get lost."

I nodded, sent a *grazie mille* across the road, then followed the green signs with great care. It took ten minutes of city driving, but they led me, at last, to the entrance to the superhighway. I sped south along it, behind schedule at this point, hoping against hope that the first exit would say FINO MORNASCO. It did. The exit ramp curled me down into another busy little city in which there were no signs for a golf course. So I just drove along until I came to a bar with a parking space out front. Inside, an attractive woman with a half-unbuttoned shirt made me a cappuccino with whipped cream on top, served me a brioche, and provided, as a sort of bonus, excellent directions to Golf Club Monticello—go back past the autostrada entrance, take a right at the second rotary, you can't miss it.

En route, I called the golf clubs to say I was *in ritardo,* which was, a friendly woman told me, absolutely not a problem. I found the appropriate right at the third rotary, not the second, but there was a sign, and soon I ended up at the gated entrance to Monticello's two courses and drove up a long lane to a pleasant stucco clubhouse. Nothing on the order of the grand structures at M&C or Villa d'Este, but the place had a quiet, well-organized, uncrowded feel that could be termed American. The check-in went well, someone at the driving range provided change for the *gettone* machine, and at the fifty- and seventy-five-meter marks were net baskets that you could try to hit into—another unique touch. I did put a couple of balls into the seventy-five-meter basket, which seemed a good omen. And I didn't shank, which seemed like good omen *numero due.* I hit a few sand shots and putts and strolled contentedly up to the first tee.

There was a short wait, time enough to read a sort of educational billboard, something I had never seen on any course, Italian or otherwise. A series of colored drawings illustrated the rules of golf and demonstrated good etiquette: a player fixing his ball mark, people letting a faster group play through. In frustrated foursomes, I've more than once heard the suggestion that there be a licensing procedure for people who want to be admitted to a golf course. It should be like driving a car: before you step onto the course, you'd have to prove you know how to play at a reasonable speed and be considerate of the group behind you. Not the best idea, probably; the billboard was a more practical choice.

Though I started out with a double bogey from deep greenside rough, then a bogey on the second, also out of deep greenside rough, I liked Monticello. I was playing the Red Course, a flat but not featureless layout that offered a mixture of short and long, curling and straight holes, all well maintained.

On the fourth, I was amused by the sight of a young woman walking her dog, just on the other side of a row of moguls that marked the edge of the fairway. She was riding in a golf cart, the dog trotting on a leash beside her.

On the fifth, I sank a twenty-foot putt for birdie, and playing the sixth, became aware of a man with an odd swing, playing alone two holes behind. We hooked up on the eleventh, where he drove up in his cart and said, "I saw there is a little traffic ahead." Paolo was his name, and he had one of the strangest golf swings I've ever seen, an extremely deliberate three-part takeaway with pauses between—to the knees, to the shoulder, to parallel. But he brought the club back down with all the fluidity that it had lacked on the backswing and made unfailingly excellent contact. We carried on a friendly conversation in two languages, during which he talked about how fine it was to play golf with his son, "an excuse to spend five hours together," and told me, "It would be paradise here in Italy if there were no politics." When he learned I was from New England, he mentioned an autumn trip he'd taken there a few years earlier, then phoned his wife to ask what foliage season was called in Maine. "Boo-Boo," he said, standing on the fifteenth tee with the cell phone to his ear, "I'm here with a *ragazzo* from Massachusetts. What is that word they use in Maine when the leaves turn?"

But Boo-Boo didn't know, and we played another level, pretty par four, complimenting each other as we went. "You turn very well the shoulder," he said, but, for me, it was a day of fifteen-, twenty-, and twenty-five-foot putts rescuing me from so-so ball-striking. I finished 42-41–83, and Paolo treated me to a quick lunch of pasta in the clubhouse. "Could you explain to me," he said, as we ate and he smoked, "what happened in Florida during the election in 2000?"

II

AGRITURISMI

Just when you think you are making progress in the language of your father's father, someone asks you for an explanation of the presidential vote count in 2000 in Florida, and you realize how much territory you still have to cover in your quest to master Italian.

And just when you are starting to feel that you have made a thorough exploration of the cuisine of the *bel paese,* you find yourself at a table at an *agriturismo* and realize that there are layers upon layers to Italian food, whole sections of the cookbook you haven't opened yet.

Agriturismi are not restaurants, exactly, and not country inns, but an arrangement by which the owners of small agricultural properties can supplement their income by feeding lunch and dinner guests and housing overnight visitors, as long as at least half their annual income is derived from the production of some foodstuff—olive oil is a popular choice. (Of course, in the traditional Italian way, a variety of strategies enable the owners to get around the noisome technicalities of the 50 percent rule.) The food at *agriturismi,* in our experience, is universally excellent, and the hospitality particularly warm.

When our older daughter, Alexandra, was four months old, and Amanda and I were flush with the joys of new parenthood, we decided we should make another trip to Italy. Friends counseled against this. But working to subvert their sensible advice was the long New England winter, our love of travel in general and Italy in particular, and our proud insistence on proving incorrect those people who told us our traveling days would end somewhere in the third trimester and not begin again until the child had earned her college diploma. So we decided to spend the month of March in Lucca, a charming old walled city less than an hour north of Pisa.

Crossing the Atlantic, none of us slept well. By the time we retrieved our bags at Rome's Fiumicino Airport and started up the coast in a rented car, we were all exhausted. It was a cold, blustery day. We stopped in Viterbo for lunch, and the waitress lifted Alexandra out of her mother's arms and brought her into the kitchen so she could meet the cooks. In the hilltop city of Montefiascone, we pulled over and slept, with the engine running to keep us warm, Amanda and I waking periodically to check on the sleeping infant in back. After our nap we made it only another hour up the road, still a long ways short of Lucca. Darkness was falling, our exhaustion was regrouping and making another assault, and it seemed the wise thing to look for a place to stay before we found ourselves deep in the Tuscan countryside, and deep into the Italian night, with an unhappy baby in the backseat.

On a curve in a two-lane highway we saw a sign for an *agriturismo* and turned into a gravel parking lot beside a stone farmhouse, pale brown, that looked as if it dated back three or four hundred years and had been renovated the previous summer. We were greeted there by a man named Giampietro Rosati, his sister Alba, and her husband, Paolo, and later that evening, in a partly subterranean room lined with wine bottles, we were fed a meal so unforgettable that we were instantly converted to the religion of the *agriturismo*. Pasta, pork, roasted vegetables, local Tuscan wine with the richness of the soil in it, then a piece of fruit *torta,* and a limoncello to finish. But those words can't begin to describe the freshness of the food, the simple ingenuity of its preparation, and the obvious good feeling with which it was brought to the table.

The next morning, still adjusting to this new world, Alexandra threw up all over herself and her mother. Giampietro was standing nearby at the time. He laughed in a gentle, sympathetic way, and in a tone of bemused appreciation spoke the line that has become legend in our family: *"È regurgitata tutto!"* She threw up everything! Then he helped clean up.

We've been to Locanda Rosati twice more in the intervening years, once calling, with no advance notice, on a day when the inn was open but the restaurant closed. "Can you recommend a place to eat nearby?" I asked Giampietro over the phone.

"No, listen," he said, after considering the question for two seconds. *Ascolta.* "Just come by. We'll whip up some little something for you. Don't worry about it."

The little something turned out to be a mini-feast of pasta with cherry tomatoes followed by a rabbit, potato, and pepper stew.

Just south of the small city of Orvieto, and just north of a golf course called Le Querce (which has been the site of several European-tour events, houses the headquarters of the Italian Golf Association, and has the fastest greens I've ever played on), Locanda Rosati is a kind of precinct of paradise to which we hope to return in this life as many times as possible.

Since that serendipitous left turn, Amanda and I have made a point of seeking out *agriturismi* whenever we find ourselves reservationless and on the Italian road. We have enjoyed memorable multicourse meals and warm hospitality near Florence, Rome, and Naples. Not just the to-be-expected pasta and tomatoes, or pizza and a salad, but inventive combinations of pork and eggplant and beef and spiced potatoes and garlic and hearty bean soup, all of it cooked on the premises and most of it grown there as well.

To those landmarks in our geography of eating well, we must now add the Barcola, just up the hill from Menaggio, a mile or so past the turn to M&C.

We'd been living in Mezzegra only three days when we had our first lunch at Barcola. Harold took us there, of course. You reach it by turning north off the difficult-to-find-at-night highway that connects Lake Como with Switzerland, then guiding your vehicle down a steep road composed of dust and stones. You will know you are on the right road if it seems to be leading into a pasture. Beyond the pasture, tucked in a small, sharp valley, sits a stone building with a stone porch linking it to a parking area that holds seven cars (if the people parking them are Italian; otherwise there is room for three).

Inside, seated at a long table with Harold, Sara, and Dalila, we had salad and bread, then two pasta dishes—a simple bow tie dusted in a light tomato sauce, and a more complicated penne in a creamy curry sauce with morsels of the Barcola's own sausage mixed in. This was followed by pork cutlets served with cooked spinach and tender potatoes, and a dry house red wine I loved, and finished with a *macchiato* and a smile on the face of my wife. Ten euro per person. Harold's treat.

We would return to the Barcola twice more—including a raucous final dinner at the lake with Harold and part of his family. On that infamous night we would arrive an hour and a half late, thanks to protracted hors d'oeuvres served at Harold and Sara's place and a fair amount of wine drunk there to celebrate the end of our vacation. At the house, while the adults were having their olives, nuts, cheese, pizza, and champagne, Harold's barefoot, rambunctious son, Kevin, made the mistake of getting on the bad side of my daughters, who took their revenge by hiding his shoes and not telling us until we had driven up the hill and turned onto Barcola's dusty entrance road. "I thought Harold was going to be right behind us," I said to Amanda, as the pasture came into view. There was, at first, a silence in the backseat. Then someone there said, "Uh, Dad?" Soon, one of our well-behaved daughters suggested that Harold might be delayed because he was looking for Kevin's shoes.

"Why would he be looking for Kevin's shoes?" Amanda asked.

A silence. I asked the same question in a somewhat different tone. And then: "Well, because we hid them on him. He was being fresh."

We called Harold to tell him where the shoes were hidden and a few minutes later saw his Audi coming down the drive, Kevin following on a skateboard—though the road was not exactly skateboard-friendly, what with the stones and steep drop-offs to either side. The bushy-eyebrowed owner was upset at our late arrival, tapped his watch and shook his head, moved us from a table out front to one in the back, brought bread and wine. I asked for butter. The waiter misunderstood and brought more bread. The food was long in coming, so the girls, apparently having reached some sort of rapprochement, went outside to try the skateboard, which worried me. Juliana knocked over the basket of bread before she left, rolls on the floor. Alexandra came in crying, saying that Kevin had pushed her. I went out to make Kevin aware that high on my never-to-allow list was a boy hitting one of my girls. Harold was oblivious. His dog—he'd practically thrown her out of the Audi on the way in—was snarling at the Barcola's dog, teeth bared, saliva dripping. The girls returned to the table red-faced and upset. Amanda and I had a small moment. The waiter told us that *cavallo* was an option for that night's meal, and when I translated it for Alexandra, our horse-loving daughter, she started to cry. I went into the bathroom to wash my hands and take a few calming breaths. Back at the table, we started to talk politics, which turned out to be a mistake. But the food, at least, was good: two dishes of pasta, both gnocchi, one with *funghi porcini con bresaola,* and the other *al pesto;* then pork and beef with arugula and melted cheese; a bit of grilled eggplant and pepper; more wine—a cool bottle of Trento white.

The *agriturismo* experience—real, if nothing else.

12

TO DOLCEACQUA

Once we had been at Lake Como for a while, enjoyed a second meal at Barcola, sampled other eating places and golf courses and had a swim or two in the lake, it seemed a good idea to make a drive to the seacoast—the road trip Harold and Sara had been recommending almost since the day we arrived. We settled on a date, Harold provided directions, Harold-style, and a booklet he'd put together on their Dolceacqua apartment: fifteen or twenty bound pages of text and photos, in well-meaning English, that offered suggestions for dining, swimming, and low-key excursions.

That summer, it always seemed impossible to get ourselves up and out of the house at a decent hour (though rising for an early-morning tee time was never a problem). Accustomed to getting to bed at eight thirty or nine of a summer evening, earlier on school nights, our daughters had quickly fallen into the European way of things and didn't hit the pillow until ten o'clock or later. This new habit could be blamed on the fact that it stayed light around the lake until after ten, and the fireworks displays started, usually, at quarter to eleven, and Luca and Pietro, the cute young boys next door, were often up late themselves, kicking a ball in the yard, or bringing over a croquet set and trying to puzzle out the rules without accepting offers of advice (Pietro, the elder, would not allow any of the wickets to be placed in the ground and would become upset if anyone tried to do so), or entertaining us by dressing up in bathing suits and their mother's leather boots, plastic cowboy hats, a pair of plastic holsters, and strutting around waving toy pistols, while Alexandra and Juliana hugged them and lectured them, guided them away from real and perceived danger, and generally used them to make up for their not having any brothers.

Late nights meant relatively late mornings (though Juliana would often come into our room at seven, stand next to the bed for a few seconds, and then inquire, in an energetic voice, which of us was interested in walking into town for fresh pastries), so it was not surprising that our plans for an early departure for the coast withered beneath the reality of life at the lake. On the morning we left on the Dolceacqua excursion, Juliana and I walked into town for brioches, Amanda cut up strawberries and melon, and out on the patio we made a feast of the creamy Sterzing yogurt we all liked, strong coffee for the adults, brioches with chocolate, jelly, or a lemony cream filling, and glasses of pineapple juice poured from a box with the ingredients printed in twelve languages.

It was midmorning, dry and hot again, before we packed up and headed out. As far south as the city of Como, all went well. Then, twenty miles beyond Como, following Harold's directions for a shortcut between two autostradas, we lost an hour in an exurban wilderness of car dealerships and masonry yards, at last finding the right person, who gave us the right directions that led us to A-26 and south toward the sea.

The area west and southwest of Milan is one of the few parts of Italy almost completely lacking in any aesthetic appeal, a kind of agricultural/industrial wasteland made for driving through as quickly as possible. "There will be no one on A-26," Harold had predicted. "You'll be able to go as fast as you want." And we did, ignoring the 78 mph speed limit as did the few other cars and trucks we saw. In early afternoon, having failed to see any signs advertising *agriturismi,* and anxious to get to the coast, we stopped for lunch in an Autogrill, a roadside rest area where the food resembles the food at rest areas on American interstates in somewhat the same way that the *Mona Lisa* resembles the paintings you see on towels and carpets hung up for sale on ropes strung between telephone poles at an intersection outside of town. I had penne carbonara cooked to order, a good salad of radicchio and watercress with decent tomatoes and onions, half a loaf of soft bread, a cappuccino, and finished it off with some prosciutto and melon stolen from Alexandra's plate. With its portable toilets and big rigs in the lot, the rest area had a rough two-day-growth-of-beard-and-spit ambience, a kind of Wild West of the Italian road peopled by characters who looked unhappy and rootless. It made you beep the car twice to make sure it was locked. It made you keep an extra eye on the whereabouts of the girls. But the food was good.

A-26 ended at the engineering miracle called A-10, a highway on stilts that winds, via tunnel after tunnel, through the arid hills of Liguria ("You expect to see cactus here," Amanda said), and on which you should not be surprised to pay tolls roughly equal to the monthly income of a first-year schoolteacher. On the slopes to either side of the highway we saw scores of greenhouses, a few hundred hectares planted in grapevines, and off to our left the flat expanse of blue-green sea.

According to Harold's directions we were to take exit 2 just before we came into the city of Ventimiglia, turn right at a rotary, and just keep going until we saw something called the Ancient Bridge. At the Ancient Bridge we were to drive across what seemed to be a sidewalk but really wasn't, then squeeze between two buildings and find our way down into the town parking lot. From there we could walk over the bridge and into the old section of Dolceacqua, where the apartment occupied Number X Castello Street. We couldn't miss it.

The exit ramp off A-10 spilled us smoothly onto a road that curlicued down and down, through a Mediterranean arboretum of palm, plane, pine, cypress, and olive trees, and roadside gardens of oleander, hibiscus, orchid, and bougainvillea. We'd spent time along this coast on earlier trips and remembered it as a place where fresh air from the sea brushes up against the hillsides, mingles there with the scent of the greenery and flowers, and creates a kind of salubrious perfume. Liguria, this section of Italy is called, but it is also sometimes referred to as the Italian Riviera, and though it has a more tattered feel than the French Riviera, the food and wine are wonderful, and the warm ocean and mild air have, for centuries, attracted travelers—everyone from Russian royalty to famous British literary figures.

Hot and road-weary, we bypassed the historical center of the city of Bordighera in favor of its beach. Like almost all the swimming spots thereabouts, Bordighera's shoreline was carpeted in sea-smoothed stones. We found a place to park and wandered down onto the beach. The surf was mild, the sun strong. It took a few minutes, and the asking of advice from a couple of bathers, before we understood the system: you went up to a man with a ponytail and a shirt that read LIFEGUARD, and you asked him the price for wooden lounge chairs and umbrellas. No official tariffs were listed. The lifeguard, if that's what he was, seemed to me a rough-looking, unsmiling, unsavory sort, and he inspected me from head to toe before announcing his price. Ten euro.

Fair enough. We rented two lounge chairs and an umbrella and plunged into the sea.

We spent two hours there—lying on the chairs and soaking up the sun and warm, salty air, then hobbling across the hot stones and diving into the water. Walking out dripping, and diving in again, floating, swimming out, watching the kids in over their heads and paddling around. Getting out to dry in the sun and admire the tanned bodies (Amanda noted that just about every woman we saw in Italy, young and old, thin and not so thin and eight months pregnant, wore a two-piece bathing suit. It seemed part of a general corporeal shamelessness, an acceptance of the appetites and their results, a comfortable unself-consciousness), lying down for a half snooze, a piece of dream, only to be called back into the water by the happy voice of one of the girls. The sun had apparently stalled in mid-sky and was baking the hundred or so beachgoers into a peaceful stupor. It seemed to me that we could just have stayed there, on the beach at Bordighera, for two days, then gone back and told Harold we'd had the perfect vacation from our vacation.

But eventually it was time to move on. We showered, changed out of our suits, found the broiling Renault, and drove farther down the coast, traveling on a lively road that ran through every seaside town and was chockablock, as Harold would have put it, with pastel-colored three- and four-story buildings. Apartments above, shops on the street floor, balconies with elaborate wrought-iron railings everywhere, this route was a visual feast of colors, textures, and shapes. This was city life in all its multiplicity, each small, individual enterprise sporting its own awning, its unique sign, its personally decorated windows, with proprietors sweeping up out front, or standing in the doorway with an apron on, or taking the time to explain their wares to customers with shopping bags over their arms and a fistful of euros clutched in one old hand.

We were, by this point, starting to see signs for France—the border was only a few kilometers up the road—and there was a distinctly French feel to the life of the street. It was something palpable but indefinable—a mix of faces, of foods for sale, even of driving style, that gave a certain accent to this Italy, in the same way that Switzerland gave an accent to the Italy where we'd awakened that morning. We found the rotary that was mentioned in Harold's directions. We turned right onto a two-lane road that led alongside a river, between ranges of dry hills. We had a moment of concern about the directions: What was an Ancient Bridge, after all? And what if there were more than one of them? But then, off to the right, arcing up sharply over the stony riverbed, we saw a rickety-looking, somewhat asymmetrical stone bridge with a tall arch beneath it, as if it had been built in the long-ago days when the parched riverbed was filled with water and traversed by boats with twenty-foot masts.

As instructed, just beyond the town piazza, we drove across the sidewalk, within inches of a display of homemade ceramics, through a narrow opening between buildings, and down into the municipal lot. The parking lot was an Italianesque festival of creative vehicle placement. Cars and small trucks were tucked into every open corner and along every unoccupied edge, whether those places were marked as official parking spaces or not. This was done expertly, so that each individual vehicle had the necessary maneuvering space . . . but barely. By some miracle, we arrived just as a legal spot was being liberated. We left the Renault there, then rolled our suitcase over the steeply arched, cobbled bridge and into the distant past.

On other trips to Europe we had of course walked through town centers that had narrow streets and stone buildings, but stepping into La Terra (c. 1100), as Dolceacqua's old town was called, on the west bank of the Nervia River, just at the far end of the Ancient Bridge, was like parting the thick veil of years that stands between the world we know and the world we sometimes read about. The three- and four-story houses, crafted of a million small stones, seemed to stand on each other's shoulders, or thigh to thigh, creating between and around them a warren of living spaces that resembled some kind of stone hive more than any human community. A few meters from the end of the bridge (Monet had painted it in 1884 in a canvas called *The Château at Dolceacqua*), you stepped into what almost seemed like a tunnel. This tunnel turned out to be a street, the buildings rising straight up from the cobblestones and almost touching above, the air dank and dim, the windows shuttered. One or two shops selling olive oil had been carved into the street-level stone, but the feel was almost purely residential: cool-faced, gray houses, closed off from the sun. Voices echoed from window to window above us; the sound of our suitcase wheels rumbled up into thousand-year-old rooms; and various other tunnels/streets angled off to the right and left.

We soon found Castello Street, and the girls counted down the numbers. Only when we reached the doorway did we realize Harold hadn't told us exactly how we would gain entrance. We stood there, next to a man and a woman having a friendly conversation, and we looked at the door, the doorbell, the list of names. "How do we get in?" one of us said aloud, and the woman standing a few feet away interrupted her conversation, reached across in front of me, turned the handle, pushed the door open, and smiled.

"Cosi," she said. Like that.

Harold and Sara's apartment had recently been renovated, with tile floors and tile walls, a new shower and sink, a fully fitted-out kitchen that had modern cabinets, countertops, and stove. There were only two windows in the four rooms, one in the second bedroom, one in the kitchen. The first of these looked out above the street to another house, ten feet away. The second opened into a courtyard where you could see eight other windows, laundry hanging there, potted plants, shutters, a thin shaft of light angling down from two stories farther up. I stood on the balcony for a moment and thought: not much was private here.

For dinner that night we went across the Ancient Bridge, across the road, and onto a central square that belonged to a slightly newer Dolceacqua called Borgo (c. 1400). A dozen or so shops and restaurants opened onto this square, and again at Harold's recommendation, we ended up at a place called La Rampa, eating in the open air. Since arriving in Italy, we had been on a quest to find the best pizza. In the northern part of the country, pizzas are made on a thin crust—it resembles matzo more than anything else—with a sometimes watery paste of fresh tomatoes and mozzarella. It's a recipe that falls somewhere between the thick-crusted, rather doughy, cheese-heavy pizzas, made mostly by Greeks, in rural New England, and the oily, bubble-crusted, truly Neapolitan variety of a place such as Pizzeria Regina in Boston's North End or Sally's in New Haven. For the northern-Italian version to work, it has to be cooked perfectly, the dough not so thin that it crackles when you chew it, and not so under-cooked that it has a pasty quality. La Rampa got it just right. The mixed salad was good and fresh, and even though the bottle of Ligurian wine I chose tasted weak and too light, the evening air held a perfect texture, and it seemed to me that the past was leaking out of the pumpkin and tangerine buildings behind us, and from the gray mass of the old city across the way.

It is foolish to romanticize that past. Most likely, the stone al-leyways outside the apartment—they seemed so charming—were at one time a septic mess of horse droppings and the contents of chamber pots, the air fetid with disease, the whole closed-in-upon-itself city and the ruined castle above bearing witness to centuries of invading armies of this or that municipality or nation-state. No doubt the small-town gossip could be savage, the familial rivalries eternal, and no doubt the bitter political winds of the thirties and forties had blown across this piazza, too: sweet air and proximity to the ocean have never rendered any place immune to power madness. It was not hard to imagine Nazi officers drinking and carousing in the square on a summer night like this, or Mussolini's Blackshirts wringing confessions out of unionists in the nearby countryside. You can make a fetish of the past, setting it up against the strains and blemishes of the present in something like the same way an old lover can be set up against a real-time spouse, all of his or her annoying quirks and bad behavior rinsed clean by the wash of time.

Still, the visual parade of the past is part of why so many people come to Italy. It soothes us in some inexplicable way. It holds lessons, and we try to read those lessons in the cracks in the church walls and hear them in the music of an a cappella choir. The world was slower then, certainly. And there is a way in which our speed has a note of violence in it, as if we are racing to wrest something from life that it ought to be allowed to give us only slowly, uncoerced.

There's more to it than that, though; there is, in old places, the sense that you can take hold of things. Without being a mason or a woodworker, you can understand how the buildings and furniture were made—from stones and trees, not chemical compounds put together in some factory or laboratory. You can feel and taste that the food comes from gardens and small farms, not megaacreage and meatpacking plants. Yes, it's not as neat: there are halves of pigs hanging in store windows instead of shrink-wrapped chops lying in a row in a supermarket cooler. Occasionally a tomato might have, God forbid, the mark of an insect, a bruise, a scar. We want the sterile, packaged neatness, of course we do. But a part of us responds to the handmade and hand-grown the way the human ear responds to a language it understands. The words sink into us, the shapes and colors and textures and tastes sink into us. In some mysterious way, the past lives in our cells. Like so many other visitors, Amanda and I go to Italy and love places such as Dolceacqua because they remind us of all that.

HAVING FINISHED OUR MEAL AT LA Rampa, we walked back across the river and listened to an open-air concert given by the City of Hull (England) Youth Symphonic Wind Band. The buildings enclosing the square where the stage had been set up all had a slow-built sense of beauty to them. In that place, in the time when they'd been erected, it appeared not to have been enough to simply build a warm house. The lintels of the doorways, the spacing of the windows and slant of the roof, the elaborate facade of the church of San Antonio Abate at the east end of the square, even the intricate diagonal patterns in the stone and brick pavement, a Ligurian specialty—all of it staked a claim to some aesthetic priority. We have to live with this, the builders must have thought. We'll have to look at these houses and walk on these bricks until we die. Let us make them as attractive as we can.

The attitude was similar, in my mind, to that of Italians toward eating. The modern slow-food movement started here, but it had its roots centuries in the past. Little by little that attitude is being eroded by the armies of the gods of convenience. There are prepackaged meals in the supermarkets now, imported tomatoes. Some people complain about the quality and flavor of the bread. In places, the traditional two- or three-hour lunch break has been shaved down to something approaching the twenty-minute gulp-fest you find in the typical American office, each unit of labor consuming its food alone in a sterile cubicle, instead of with family at a table covered by handmade cloth.

Sitting on a low stone wall, waiting for the music to start, we struck up a conversation with an American woman who was in Italy on a short vacation from her native North Carolina. "The beaches all have stones here, and we have those beautiful sandy beaches on the Outer Banks," she said, starting off the conversation. "Sometimes I wonder why we even leave home."

Politeness kept me from telling her that we had left home exactly to experience this scent of a different way of living, the inlaid marble floors and altars of the church, a hundred years in the making, these flower boxes on small balconies against a pumpkin-colored stucco wall, these salads with hand-sliced, homegrown tomatoes, these pizzas cooked on a wood fire. Stony beaches seemed a small price to pay for that. When the music started—the orchestra composed of sixty young Englishmen and Englishwomen wearing identical white shirts—it seemed perfectly fitting to hear such sounds in the summer air, and to see people on their sixth-floor balcony, arms on the railing, taking in the show while swallows swooped and glided overhead. No amplifiers, no electricity—we might have been there listening to people play music hundreds of years before.

Amanda and I and the girls were sitting at the back of the square. In a while an old man sat down beside me. Shortly after he'd settled himself, he motioned to two passing teenagers who were in a hurry to be off somewhere. One of them seemed to be his granddaughter. "Sit, listen," he said to them, in a mock-stern voice. "I'm telling you." (*"Siedete, ascoltate. Io dico."*) But of course they didn't want to. The light, happy music and the magic of the past held little interest for them. They shook their heads no. He insisted. They kissed him, carelessly, and hurried away, and the old man turned to me and raised his eyebrows in a gesture of comic helplessness. Where are they hurrying to? he seemed to be wondering. Toward what are they hurrying?

AFTER A GOOD NIGHT OF SLEEP in the dark and quiet apartment, we walked across the bridge again the next morning and had breakfast in a downstairs bar on the piazza. I ordered two *spremuta d'arancia* for the girls, coffees for Amanda and me, and while we were waiting at the table, we saw the young owner of the place hurry outside and then return a minute later with four oranges, bought from a vendor in the square. He sliced the oranges in half and squeezed the juice into tall glasses for us. Which took some time.

13

DROPPING SOME CASH IN MONTE CARLO

I had planned to play golf on our second day near the coast, but when I examined the map more closely, I saw that the course I wanted to play, Golf Club Garlenda, was more than an hour to the east, back in the direction of Lake Como. So I wandered through the subterranean streets of Dolceacqua to a place where the cell phone worked, called, apologized for the late notice, and canceled the tee time. It hurt to do this, I have to admit. I had gotten up early, showered, and dressed for golf (the shorts, the little white socks, the collared jersey—these are not things I wear every day). I was suffused with the particular feeling of happiness that precedes a round, the anticipation of being out on the course, of making a good shot. It is like being very young again, taking a shower, dressing a certain way, heading off toward a party where you know that good things might happen, that you might meet a wonderful young woman, dance, drink, have the conversation of your life, walk out in the sweet darkness with her and take her hand, or take her home. It's like that for a lot of golfers. It's like having a bank account of pleasure, and you're heading out to make a withdrawal.

Standing on the ancient square with the cell phone to my ear, I felt a small sting of disappointment. The party had been canceled, or put off. Or the young woman had not come or did not want to dance.

There were, of course, compensations. It was market day, for one thing, and the pleasant bustle caught all of us up in a wave of optimism. After finishing our glasses of fresh-squeezed orange juice and cups of strong coffee in the half-subterranean bar, we made a short tour of the stalls that had been set up in front of La Rampa—vendors selling fruits and vegetables, scarves, dresses, books, toys, boots. In a sort of movable butcher shop housed in a trailer, there were skinned rabbits set out beside the cheeses and salamis, their thin, pink heads and glazed eyes shocking sights for modern American girls. There were peaches, grapes, strawberries, raspberries, apricots, cherries; each of us chose a piece of fruit to balance out the sugary pastries we'd had in the bar. As we walked to the parking lot, we passed the dry riverbed near the Ancient Bridge. Three backhoes were at work there, one of them operated by a boy who could not have been older than twelve. There he was, perched in the seat and working the levers and shifts like a master, calmly raking piles of stones out of the river channel, scooping them into the bucket, and swinging the arm around.

We consulted the pages Harold had given us. I suggested to Amanda that we make an excursion in the direction of Monte Carlo. If there happened to be a course along that route, I had my clubs in the back, and I'd jump onto the first tee and play eighteen while the females checked out the beach options. If not, we'd have a family day. We headed down the river valley and turned west toward Ventimiglia.

On the map, Ventimiglia is a dot on the coast of southern Europe, a sleepy border town with a long name. In fact, it is a visual and auditory phantasmagoria, traffic-choked streets lined with every imaginable type of shop, and wild rotaries navigated by careening Peugeots and girls on bicycles. During the go part of our stop-and-go trans-Ventimiglia passage, we spotted a tourist information office on the right-hand side. No parking places nearby, but I had been in Italy long enough by then to understand that a real driver, a true artist of the roadways, makes his own parking space, using for his material a few feet of illegal curb, the generosity of the law enforcement powers that be, and the understanding of his fellow motorists. I parked exactly at a corner, fender sticking out into traffic, waited for a police car to slip past, and then, as Amanda counseled caution, opened the door and stepped out, with a delivery truck literally three inches from my shoulder. There was a certain thrill in doing this, maybe just the thrill of an ordinarily law-abiding citizen walking an inch or two on the wild side. I felt unfettered, creative, free, and I knew that the Italians around me—*polizia* included—understood this feeling, and respected it, and would never try to dampen it by the enforcement of petty laws. There would be no ticket for illegal standing, no warning, no lecture, not even a lingering glance. I went down the sidewalk with a certain shoulders-back swagger, passed an old church in a happy stride, confident, ebullient, but still secretly holding to a thin hope that some golf might be ahead of me in the beautiful, warm day.

Helpful as she was, the friendly French-speaking woman at the information office lacked an appreciation for a golfer's needs. No, she did not know of any courses along the road to Monte Carlo. She wasn't a golfer herself, couldn't offer any brochures, didn't get many requests. But she was kind enough to give me the number of another office, across the French border, that might be of some help.

Crossing that border, you feel as if the lens of the camera has been cleaned. Everything from the sidewalk edges to the royal palms in the median strip is one notch more orderly than it was in Italy, cleaner, half a decibel quieter. I'm not sure I liked it. We were attuned to Italy, to the happy disorder, to the vocabulary of the road: *bivio, parcheggio, sosta vietata, senso unico.*

Passing the old city of Menton, with the sparkling Ligurian Sea to our left, I spoke by phone with a friendly fellow in a French information office, and he guessed that the nearest golf courses were all the way west in Nice. So, because that ruled out any hope of golf, and because in his homemade booklet on the Dolceacqua apartment Harold had mentioned that "the charming touristic town of Eze Villages is an absolutely must-see," we stopped in Monte Carlo only long enough to have a stroll and a snack, to see that there was a big municipal swimming pool there with a waterslide, to deflect the girls' pleas that we use the pool, to get some money from the bank machine, and then we headed up the mountain.

Wreathed in a steam of humidity and perched on a hilltop with an impressive view of the sea, Eze Village turned out to be a kind of Dolceacqua gone bad. To begin with, now that we were in France, the park-wherever-your-car-fits idea had gone out of favor: one was required to actually obey the rules. After a quarter of an hour of prowling various lots, we finally spotted a car with its backing lights on, pushed in close so no one else would steal the space, parked, paid, and stepped out into a town that was crawling with tourists and pocked with overpriced eateries. In some vague hope of finding a decent and affordable lunch we dragged the girls up the spiraling paths in the heat.

One possibility was the restaurant X, where the luncheon menu was posted beneath glass outside. At the bottom of the impressive display of culinary excellence was the price: 97 euros. Roughly $135. Per person.

"Aren't we going to eat here, Dad?"

There were little shops selling olive oil and handmade scented soap, little shops selling postcards and flavored grappa, little shops selling little flags and baskets and napkins and tablecloths. Hungry by then, surprised at the power of the sun at that altitude, we were tormented by the sound of clinking utensils from outdoor patios, where masses of German, Dutch, French, and American tourists—wealthier than us, no doubt—sat in precious patches of shade. The whole scene just made me want to get back in the car and drive away. And it made me hungry.

Back at the base of the hill we found an open-air restaurant called du Cheval Blanc. There, the girls had pizza, Amanda ordered *poulet et frites,* and I opted for the perfectly good and reasonably priced menu: Caprese salad with cool lumps of mozzarella topped with a basil leaf, followed by a thin slice of salmon in a cream sauce. And too much of the house white wine. Early on in this meal, we noticed that the bread was better in France, but, presented with a basket of it, realized that we would still have to ask for butter. Amanda and I put our heads together, reached back into the dim past of junior high school language classes, and seemed to recall that the word for butter was *beurre.* I was designated to be the one who would actually pronounce the word in the presence of our no-nonsense waitress. Once that was done, followed by a capable *s'il vous plaît,* we waited in suspense to see if the owner of the place would arrive with the local magistrate, come to arrest me for having called into question the waitress's honor, or with a doctor intent on removing something sharp from the foot of the stoic *américain. Mais non,* the linguistic experiment proved successful, butter was brought to our table, and the girls, at least, were impressed. We ate and drank. And drank. Surrounded by chocolate mousse and various ice creams, I opted for a selection of cheese with which to finish my wine and enjoyed a wonderful plate of Brie, Swiss, and blue.

Du Cheval Blanc was almost enough to take away the taste of Eze Village, and of the fact that the British Open was being played and there was nowhere to watch it.

To be fair to the girls, who were, by that point, not particularly happy with the day's hot adventure, we returned to Monte Carlo with the intention of checking out the municipal pool. Strolling around there, we encountered an unexpected bit of entertainment. We saw an armored car stop in front of a bank, and two uniformed men wearing flak jackets get out and, one by one, unload bags of coins from the truck's side door. The bags were heavy—sixty or seventy pounds each, I'd guess—and the shortest route between the door of the armored car and the door of the bank took the guards up and over a waist-high concrete flower box. No sense in using the sidewalk when that option was available. Struggling with his load, the first one climbed up, stepped between the flowering plants, and accidentally dropped his bag of coins in the petunias. He laughed. His friend took the same route, with the same result, except that he nearly fell on his face and then dropped the heavy bag in the petunias. With the armed driver standing guard, and the flak jackets, and the sheepish look on the faces of the two uniformed money-carriers, it was a kind of Monte Carlo slapstick.

Once this show was over, we made our way toward the harbor, where a row of $100 million yachts were anchored, and there we found the entrance to the swimming complex. Named for Princess Grace and Prince Rainier, it was as clean as just-washed silverware, with a spiral waterslide and a diving platform. The water was ocean water, salty and cool. The girls were excited, for a variety of reasons ("Mom, that woman isn't wearing a top to her bathing suit!"), and waterslides always make me feel young, so we lounged away the rest of the afternoon there, spiraling down into a salty splash, practicing our dives, baking in the sun, then we showered and drove into Ventimiglia for a Chinese dinner.

IT IS INAPPROPRIATE, PERHAPS, BUT WHAT I feel for the owners of Chinese restaurants in Italy is something akin to pity. Once, sitting by the pool behind our house in Mezzegra, I was audience to an animated conversation held mainly by two of our neighbors. The subject was food, not an uncommon subject for Italian conversations. "The French," one of our neighbors said with a perfectly straight face, "the French prepare duck well, and they have good cheese, there's no question about that. And good wines. Red wines, at least. And the bread is acceptable. But the cuisine itself, well, there's something insubstantial about it. The dishes they prepare are not bad, in themselves, but they leave you hollow. There's no weight to them. Pasta, for example, is almost unheard of. No pasta, no polenta."

It is not news, of course, to claim that the Italians have a good national cuisine, or that they care about food, or even that they insist on a level of freshness as a point of national pride in something like the way that Germans insist on a certain measure of efficiency, or the British on being polite. But I don't think there is a full understanding in the rest of the world as to the actual place food occupies in the Italian national consciousness. I'm not sure even the Italians themselves have a perspective on it.

Once, years before, on assignment for a golf magazine, I had dinner with Amanda at a pricey restaurant in the heart of Rome's historical district. The restaurant was located on a tilting alleyway, you had to ring a doorbell to be admitted, and the waiters placed small, upholstered footstools beside the women's chairs so that they could rest their purses there and not have to hang them awkwardly from the back of their seat, set them on the floor, or leave them in the coat check. The meal itself—pasta, meat, wine, salad—was first-class, but what I recall most vividly about that night was a conversation with the owner. Young, broad-faced, black-haired, happy, he made the rounds of the tables as many restaurateurs do, inquiring as to the comfort and satisfaction of his guests. When I complimented him on the meal in general and on the tasty gravy that had been ladled across our rotelli Bolognese in particular, his face took on an expression akin to the one you see on the faces of new parents when they begin to speak of their child. He moved a few inches closer. He began to tell us how the sauce was made. They used pork in their Bolognese, he told us, because pork gave more flavor to the sauce than beef or veal. But it was not enough to use any part of the animal, one had to use the meat of the *guancie,* the cheeks. While not the best for eating, the cheek flesh of the pig was ideal for making gravy. He went on and on, talking about the history of the use of pork in that part of Rome, then about creating an atmosphere conducive to good eating.

I've encountered this on numerous occasions in Italy, and almost as often among Italian-Americans. Food as sacrament. Like so many aspects of Italian culture, this one is easy to mock. Italians as buffoons; look at how they go on and on about a meatball sandwich, a slice of pizza, the meat of the cheek of a pig, the preparation and cooking of squid. But what's lost in this discussion, I think, is something more profound and mysterious. "Everything starts with food," Harold had said as we walked the fairways at M&C. He was right. By beginning with food, by caring about it as much as they do—to the point where the great cuisine of the French can be called insubstantial—the Italians have burrowed down into the essence of being human. Good food, for them, is like the laying of a foundation for a cathedral. Get that part right—level, even, solid—and the rest has a chance at greatness.

Having said this, I would never intimate that other cultures' culinary achievements are suspect. Certainly I would not disparage the French. And certainly, back home, we get as much pleasure from a night out at the local Chinese place as we do from any of our other dining options. But on those occasions when I have tried Chinese food in Italy, I have come away with what can only be described as a small fever of dissatisfaction, an *agita,* an all-body ache that has the scent of defeat to it.

I remember, for example, a particularly bland dish of duck with vegetables in a restaurant in the Monteverde Nuovo section of Rome. It was like eating water. When we tried the local Chinese restaurant in Mezzegra one night, not long after our arrival, well . . . we never returned. The place was set right on the *statale,* and the owners, a young couple, greeted us with what almost seemed gratitude. There was plenty of space at the tables in the open-air patio, and a foosball game there, which thrilled our daughters. I accompanied them to the foosball table, because next to it sat a pair of thirtysomething, German-speaking men. They had that look some drunks get when they are at the stage of their drunkenness where all the pain and resentment in their lives has been stirred to the surface and is bubbling and snapping there. On the table between them stood a bottle of sake. They were smoking like chimneys.

Nothing happened, at first. Though they cast their mean, watery gazes at my daughters, they soon went back to their loud laughter and cigarettes, and we soon went back to our table. The first course was a plate of stringy, dry, almost fluffy seaweed—an experiment for us—with a wonderful salty crunchiness. And then the dumplings arrived, and these, too, were quite good. At some point between the dumplings and the chicken dishes—washed in soy sauce and poorly spiced—the two drunks picked up the bottle of sake, ducked into the alleyway that ran beside the patio, and hurried off. In a few minutes the young owner came out and saw that they had absconded with his bottle and without paying the *conto*. He smiled helplessly, ruefully, and looked around. His wife was furious. She made him hustle this way and that along the alley in a vain attempt to recover the sake and perhaps convince the good fellows that they should pay their check. But in a few minutes he returned empty-handed.

This incident stands out in my mind as a symbol of the fate of the owners of Chinese restaurants in Italy. Stepping through the door into a room of perfectly set, empty tables, you can almost hear the scorn of the society that surrounds them. If French food is considered insubstantial, what must the Italians make of Chinese? And not even good Chinese, the restaurants supplied with the freshest, most authentic ingredients by graffiti-covered trucks from Chinatown. How do the owners of these places survive?

We had pretty much given up on the idea of eating Chinese in Italy, but when, on the way back from Monte Carlo, we passed a sign in Ventimiglia that advertised Chinese and Tibetan cuisine, I said to Amanda, "We'll give it one more shot." And we did. And it was about the same. The beautifully set and mostly unoccupied tables, the friendly staff, the decent dumplings and bland chicken and beef dishes (though I did like the Cantonese rice, with ham, egg, and peas mixed in). It made me sad, somehow; I can't explain it.

Back in Dolceacqua, while Amanda meandered with her camera in the older section, I took the girls for an evening stroll through the newer part of town. Holding hands, we prowled the narrow streets above the piazza where most tourists never ventured. We petted the dogs and wished *buona sera* to the women standing in doorways; on the other side of the river we sat and watched eight men, no longer young, who were playing an animated soccer game on a half-size, fenced-in field; and we stepped into the church to listen to the choir practicing, and to light a candle for an older friend of mine named Anthony, who'd given me my first golf lesson, who'd encouraged me to go out and see the world, and who'd had a stroke that spring.

14

GARLENDA

Unless you are staying at a hotel, where buffet breakfasts often include cold cuts and cheese, cereal and yogurt, fruit, fresh-baked goods, juice and sausage and boiled eggs, you may find that the morning dining options in Italy are somewhat monotonous—cappuccino, *macchiato*, espresso, usually a limited selection of filled pastries under glass, maybe a fresh-squeezed orange juice. Enjoyable as these are, someone accustomed to a longer list of options—pancakes, waffles, omelets, sugary cereals, corned-beef hash, granola, oatmeal, grits, finnan haddie—might find that he or she is waking up of a Mediterranean morning with more appetite than anticipation. The Italians do this to themselves on purpose. They observe a kind of partial fast in the morning, knocking back a single espresso while standing at the counter and perusing *Corriere della Sera,* allowing themselves a few bites of brioche *con marmellata,* so as to enhance the pleasure of their midday pasta and meat, their *broccoletta rabi, pollo a la cacciatore, penne amatriciana, spaghetti al mare.*

When it comes to the table, I have a painfully good memory. It seems like only yesterday that Amanda and I were walking into the breakfast room at the Hotel Europa in Merano, where long tables were covered with platters of cheeses and processed meats, where the muesli was freshly made and the milk cold, where baskets of warm bread stood beside dishes of butter and various jams. Fifteen years ago it was, in fact. And four years ago that we sat with our overflowing plates in the sunlit breakfast room of the Hotel Belvedere in the picturesque town of Portovenere and watched the waiter pouring hot milk and potent coffee from silver pitchers into our cups.

The memory of that coffee and hot milk surfaced as Alexandra, Juliana, and I walked back from watching the no-longer-young soccer players toward our Dolceacqua digs. Since our one breakfast in France on the drive from Paris to Como, we hadn't been able to find a place that served a good café au lait, and I missed it. Wandering the cool stone alleyways near Harold and Sara's apartment, we'd come upon a couple of signs for bed-and-breakfasts, so on that night I made a small detour, found one of them, and rang the doorbell. No answer. A phone number was listed on the sign. I punched it into my cell phone and we walked a little way to an open area where I had service, and I made the call. *"Buona sera,"* I said to the woman who answered. "This is an unusual request. We're from America, and we're staying here in an apartment in Dolceacqua, and we were hoping to have a full breakfast someplace. I know we're not guests at the B and B, but we'd be happy to pay for a sit-down breakfast tomorrow morning if such a thing is possible."

"You want a good breakfast?" the woman asked.

"Yes, exactly. Coffee and hot milk, maybe some eggs, if you have—"

"That's not a problem."

"No? Excellent. Wonderful. *Benissimo.* What time should we arrive? It will be my wife and our two young girls and I. Four of us."

"You should go to the Bar California," the woman said. "It's across the river, near the piazza."

"I know. We saw it there the other day." We had, in fact, walked into and out of the Bar California, unimpressed by their small selection of croissants under glass. "But I was hoping for something different. A full breakfast. A big breakfast. Coffee with hot milk, eggs, if you have—"

"My husband runs the Bar California. You can't find a better breakfast than he serves. Go there."

"Yes, all right then. Okay. *Va bene. Grazie.*"

"What did she say, Dad?" the girls asked when I hung up. I had made the mistake of describing the Italian hotel breakfasts to them in detail.

"She said we should try the Bar California, across the street."

"The place we walked out of?"

After another good night of sleep in the dark Dolceacqua apartment, we enjoyed the traditional breakfast in the Bar California. No coffee and milk poured from separate silver pitchers, no eggs, no muesli or fresh bread or jam, but the husband of the woman I'd spoken with was a kindly, hospitable man, who motioned us to a table and brought us the customary fare. The men's room was spotlessly clean. Large windows gave on a view of the street and square. On the walls hung pictures of our host as a young man in uniform, at his marriage, with his family, and the photographic display was a kind of testimony to the passage of time, the constancy gained from living in one place, with the same people . . . eating the same breakfast year after year.

❧

We brought our saucers and cups to the counter, thanked the man, and headed off toward Golf Club Garlenda. It was more convenient now: not far off the route we'd have to take on our way back to Mezzegra. I would play, Amanda and the girls would explore the coastline, looking for good swimming options and good pizza.

As if to break the pattern of my getting lost en route to golf, getting to Golf Club Garlenda proved not difficult. An hour of avoiding roaring eighteen-wheelers on A-10's elevated, high-speed curves, ten minutes on a calmer two-lane road, and we came upon the course without trouble. By M&C standards at least, Garlenda was set on a flat piece of land, fifteen minutes from the coast, surrounded by hills and stands of pine and groves of old olive trees.

You can usually tell from the first moments on the property what a golf course is going to be like. It's the small touches—the way you are greeted in the pro shop or *segreteria,* the arrangement and condition of the driving range and putting green, the quality of the turf on the fairway in front of you, the layout of the opening hole. Garlenda received high marks in all respects, with bonus points for something I'd never seen: a computer screen at the desk, facing out into the room, with slots on the screen for each tee time, and names next to the ones that had been reserved. American pro shops have the same information, but the computer faces in, and you have to wait in line to check what time you're supposed to be teeing off, and to see if there might be open spaces ahead of you.

Jack Merullo was on the screen, except this time he was Robert Merrullo. But it didn't matter. The day was sunny and mild, the girls were happy at the thought of heading off to find another beach, and the flower-lined first tee looked out on a flat opening par four that bent just far enough to the right to give it some texture.

With a German couple and the girls watching, I hit a perfect hybrid far down the left side of the fairway. Three kisses, a flutter of *I love you*s, then the exquisite feeling of walking off the first tee onto good turf and seeing a white spot there, in the distance, sitting up nicely and waiting to be hit.

I thought, for a while, that Garlenda was going to be the place where I finally broke 80 in Italy. I thought so, in fact, all the way to the first green, onto which I hit a perfect eight iron, over the wide, thin bunker in front. The ball stopped ten feet left of the front-center pin. As I rolled my *sacca* and *carrello* down the fairway, I was embraced by pleasant memories of the courses I'd played around Rome. It wasn't so much that Garlenda looked like Acquasanta, Marco Simone, Le Querce, Arco di Costantino, Fioranello, Castelgandolfo, or Olgiata. In fact, for the most part, those had been hilly tracks, and Garlenda started out as flat and neat as the slices of salami at La Baita. It had to do with the light. At Menaggio and Cadenabbia the fairways were guarded by thick stands of trees, and even in the strongest, most direct sunlight, the mountains surrounding them seemed to promise, with their cliffsides and high shadows, that cooler air was wafting and gliding just a few hundred feet above our heads. At Garlenda, there was a breeze from the direction of the ocean—you could taste the salt in it—but the sunlight was what I think of as Italian sunlight: a yellow-gold that dusts the blades of grass and glints off the bunker rakes and flagsticks and has such an intensity that it feels capable of drying a soaked shirt in thirty seconds. You can see this light in Italian paintings, in the large canvases of Bellini, for example, where the blues, greens, and reds all seem to have gold in them and the sky seems not just lit by the sun but suffused by it. Stupendous as the views were around Lake Como, the light was different there, cooler and richer but somehow not hinting at the existence of an actual paradise, the way this light did.

Or maybe I was just carried away by the pleasure of my first two shots. In all my playing in and around Rome, and in other parts of Italy, I had broken 40 for nine holes a few times, but never put two sub-40 nines together. And here I had hit the first tee shot exactly where it needed to be hit—left edge of the fairway; and followed that with a short iron that landed a pace or two beyond the trap, the only place I could have landed it and stayed anywhere near the pin. No one else seemed to be on the course—no one in front to hold me back, no one behind to push me. I was well rested, well enough fed. True, there hadn't been time to hit balls or repair my putting stroke before teeing off, but that sometimes works to my advantage: I went onto the course without any fresh bad memories.

I set the flagstick carefully on the green, took my time over the slightly downhill, ten-foot birdie opportunity . . . and left it four feet short. This is one of my worst golfing habits, and it drives my golf partner, Joe, into fits of cousinly fury that he does a good job of disguising as mild annoyance. It is as if I expect the ball to go into the hole of its own power simply because it has been touched by the blade of my Bettinardi, simply because two good shots preceded it, simply because I want it to.

I made the second putt, but was angry at myself and pretending not to be. On the down-sloping par-three second I hit a pathetic ground ball off the tee. It bounced over a rise and ended up in a greenside bunker. I fluffed it out, leaving myself with a sixty-foot, uphill par putt. Not wanting to repeat what had happened a few minutes earlier, I banged that putt six feet past the hole and missed the downhill comebacker. Two over after two: it all happened so quickly.

I love the start of a round of golf, when hopes are unblemished. Even after a bad putt and a bad hole, you can still cling tightly to those hopes. Starting a round, I sometimes have the strange image that I am carrying a beautifully decorated and delicious cake to a lover on the other side of a wide body of water, a reservoir perhaps, walking along the top of a narrow concrete dam that has no railings. It's a sunny day, just a hint of wind. I get out over the water, walking along fairly well, and the wind starts to blow harder, and I nearly slip off. In the act of catching my balance, I squeeze the cake a bit too forcefully and a small piece or two falls off. Bogey, double bogey. Still, it's a nice cake, a perfectly edible cake, and I know she is going to be pleased by it. For another little while I go along—par, par, par—without trouble, though maybe one or two bits of the frosting blow off in the wind—a missed birdie opportunity, a less than stellar drive—and it begins to seem that the top of the dam is growing even narrower. Then, sometimes, there is a big slip—a three-putt, a grounder off the tee; a chunk of the cake falls away. To prevent any further errors, I begin squeezing it tighter, mashing it into a different shape now—even if I don't break 80, I can still shoot 81 or 82 and go away happy. And then, not every time but often enough, at some point on the back nine there is a disaster—a lost ball, a flubbed chip, and a three-putt on the same hole—the cake is crushed between my fingers, shapeless, all but inedible. I throw it down into the water, all my hopes gone, but still continue to lick my fingers now and then at a good shot.

It's a peculiar and imprecise image, no doubt, but it was a little bit that way at Garlenda. As I walked to the third hole, I was only two over, after all, even though I should have been one under, but, still, the cake was more or less intact, and the third hole was a wondrous thing to look at. You stood up on the tee box, which was cut into a tunnel of pines, and looked down across the tops of smaller trees to a sweeping stretch of fairway, the grass shining in the sun, the hole curling slightly left as it climbed toward an invisible green on the top of the hill. A short par five, 510 yards.

It took me a few seconds to realize that there was a road in the foliage below the tee, the same busy, two-lane road we'd come in on. ACERTATEVI a sign posted on the nearest tree said: before you hit, *make certain* that the group in front of you is out of range, and that no cars are approaching along the road. Impossible to do the latter, of course, but I waited until things seemed quiet enough and then hit a three wood that started out over the rough and drew in beautifully to the right side of the short grass.

Somehow, from that ideal position I made double bogey.

Double again on the downhill par-four fourth, which moved between groves of olive trees on both sides, and I found myself six over par, and suddenly close on the heels of a foursome of seniors, riding in three carts. A quarter of the way over the dam, in other words, and the delicious cake was already a mashed-up mess. At home, I might have been hurrying along to the next tee, muttering a litany of self-criticism, but this was Italy, I was here to relax.

All right, I told myself, the day was still beautiful. A 78 or 79 might be out of the question—I'd have to par my way in to shoot that—but I'd paid my 60 euro ($84), and the birds and cicadas were singing and buzzing in the trees, and it wouldn't do to spoil the day because of a little thing like three consecutive double bogeys. Yes, the foursome in front—four players in three carts is always a bad sign—seemed to have gone into reverse. And, yes, I'd tweaked my back a bit on the tee shot on four, finished the hole with a poor chip from the fringe and two putts. But there was always the back nine to think of. And there was an encouraging note on the scorecard that read: *Il vostro posto sul campo è immediatamente dietro all squadra davanti è non immediatamente davanti all squadra dietro* ("Your place on the course is immediately after the group in front and not immediately before the group behind").

My type of message. I only hoped that the foursome ahead of me had read it.

Forced to slow down to about half my normal playing speed, I made a solid par on the par-five fifth and followed that with another perfectly respectable three wood that sliced the middle of the fairway on the short, flat, pretty par-four sixth. At that point, the gentlemen in front waved me on. And though I told myself not to, I hurried the swing and drilled a simple sand wedge over the back of the green. It's always a delicate dance, being a single waved through by a foursome. You suddenly have an audience, for one thing. And inevitably one member of that audience believes in the outdated idea that foursomes have the unquestionable right-of-way on a golf course, no matter at what speed they are playing, how much open space lies in front of them, or how fast the single has caught up to them, and you know he has been grumbling to his pals something like "We're playing pretty fast. I don't think we should let him go. What if there's somebody behind him, are we supposed to let them go, too?" But while I was thinking these things, making my fast chip onto the green and missing a make-able eight-foot putt for par, one of the gentlemen drove over to my *carrello* and took hold of it from the driver's seat. As I replaced the flag and mumbled some well-known American curse words, he motioned me over. It was, he indicated with one arm, a long, uphill climb to the next tee.

On the ride up the hill he said, in English, "We have to let you go, or we will be holding you a long time."

"Playing for money?"

He shook his head and laughed. "No, just for *blood*," a word he pronounced so that it rhymed with *mood*.

I liked the idea that these four guys, who could hit the ball all of 125 yards, still cared enough about the game to play against each other and have the match mean something. I switched to Italian and complimented my friend on his course.

"Ah, you speak excellent Italian!" he exclaimed. "Excellent. Excellent!"

"Yes, I do. As long as I keep the conversation to ten or twenty words."

He laughed and told me Garlenda was *normale*, not too long or too short, not too easy or too hard, not too hilly or too flat. And I thanked him and complimented the course again and wished him good luck in his match, and after I'd hit my wedge to fifteen feet on the par-three seventh, I could still hear him exclaiming to his pals about my wonderful abilities with the language.

Not so, I thought. And not so, either, my abilities with the Bettinardi on that fine day. Another shy birdie putt, another disappointing par. I finished the side bogey, bogey, for a 45, and tried my best to put it behind me.

Sometimes, halfway across the dam, you just have to toss the old cake overboard and imagine yourself a new, somewhat smaller, and less elaborate one.

It almost worked. If nothing else, carding 45 on the front leaves a 10-handicap golfer with little left to lose, and so I promised myself only that I'd putt like a grown-up on the backside—an expression I sometimes use when I'm being too timid on the greens. Funny, then, that on the downhill par-four tenth, which was made more difficult by trees pinching in from the left, I found, after I'd hit my driver to within sand-wedge distance, that I was being observed by a boy of about ten. He was well off to the right of the green—perhaps he'd walked down from one of the homes up on the hill—and was watching me as intently as if I were performing surgery on one of his parents. I waved. He did not wave back. He was studying me, watching carefully to see how grown men played the game. I hit an acceptable wedge onto the green and putted well and boldly, like an adult, the ball skidding three inches past the hole. I waved to the boy again and asked him the way to the next hole, but he seemed not to hear, or not to understand, or to be too shy to answer.

I found the eleventh and made par there. Bogeyed the nasty, dogleg twelfth, then made par again on the neat thirteenth, a 207-yard par-three with a fifty-yard-wide dry streambed cutting across it, mid-fairway. Parred the par-five fourteenth and made a fifteen-footer to save par on the par-three fifteenth. Then it was double bogey and par again, and I stood on the tee of the eighteenth needing a par to break 40 and make partial redemption for the debacle on the front side.

For a minute or so I thought I'd lost my way and was back on the third tee. There was the same ACERTATEVI sign, the same tunnel of trees, the same hidden road. But instead of curling left and up-hill, the eighteenth curved right and stayed flat. I hit a three wood over the road to the center of the fairway and, when I walked down there, discovered that the ball was not far enough left, or deep enough: a large tree blocked the line to the right-side pin. The best I could do was hit a nine iron to the left side of the green, leaving myself a long, crescent-shaped putt across that upper tier. And then, at last, I hit the putt I should have started the day with, a confident stroke that traversed the upper level from one side of the green to the other, slipping steadily right, then plopping into the hole. 45-38–83. All right. Nothing to brag about, and noth-ing, even with Garlenda's 133 slope, that was going to do great things for the handicap, but it's always fun to end with a birdie. And the 38 seemed to promise better days down the road.

Inside the cool clubhouse, with its large sitting rooms and abundance of leather-upholstered chairs, I accompanied a deli-cious prosciutto-mozzarella-and-tomato-on-baguette lunch with about sixteen glasses of ice water and POWERade to rebuild my depleted electrolytes, then one piece of apple torte. The Open was on, Garcia in the lead, Mickelson on his way to missing the cut. I sat and watched it for a while with a friendly Italian law student who told me he was off for the summer now and would be playing a lot of golf until classes started up again.

"When do they start?"

A shrug, a sheepish grin. "September. Maybe October. When-ever the professor wants them to."

Garlenda, he told me, benefited from the mild Ligurian cli-mate and stayed open year-round. The club gave its new members five years to pay off an initiation fee of roughly $6,000. As we watched, an American family wandered in, mom, dad, shy daugh-ter. They liked Italy well enough on this first visit, the dad told me—good train system, nice people—but he wished there was an Albertson's around here someplace where you could go on a Sunday and get the kind of food you wanted, rather than having to rely on what the Italians served. "It makes us appreciate what we have at home," his wife told me, twice.

The remark, the attitude reminded me of a woman, a Welsh friend of Harold's, who was spending some months at Lake Como while the pain of a recent divorce subsided. "I don't think the food here in Italy is very good," she said, as we sipped our local red wine and nibbled our grilled zucchini, sausage, and arugula paninis near the shore of the lake. "It really can't compare with English pub food."

Thinking about that remark, I find it momentarily difficult to go on. Later in the summer we would, in fact, have a chance to make a fair sampling of English pub food—fish and chips, cheeseburger, bangers and mashed, a salad, a couple of pints of ale—and while the pub atmosphere was most congenial, and the room-temperature ale absolutely superb, I would not be eager to invest in a company that had plans to open a chain of English pubs in Italy. Let me leave it at that.

From the Garlenda clubhouse we'd planned to head straight back to Lake Como, stopping for dinner en route. But we hadn't been on the autostrada very long when we started to see warnings, on the overhead electronic signs, of a big tie-up at the *bivio,* or junction, of A-10 and A-26. There is a tunnel just at that junction, and the trouble was so bad that as we approached the tunnel we saw several cars pulled over onto the shoulder. The occupants were picnicking or talking on cell phones rather than taking the risk of being stuck in the bad air for an hour or two on a hot Friday night.

Amanda was navigating, as always. Checking the map, she found an alternative route north, through Genoa and onto A-7.

"What about dinner in Genoa, then?" I said. "We'll make a little detour before getting on the highway."

She wasn't sure. It would mean a late bedtime for the girls.

"Birthplace of pesto," I said, and the clogged A-26 suddenly had no chance.

We took the right fork, away from the traffic jam, and quickly found ourselves . . . in a traffic jam. This was nothing as exotic as the huge roadblock caused by thousands of Genovese fleeing the city and heading north to the mountains and the lakes; it was just ordinary Friday-afternoon traffic, the downtown streets thick with vehicles of every description bunched up at stoplights. The trams rumbled, the buses belched, the motorcycle commuters, boots on asphalt, worked their way forward at the pace of worms through wood. It took us the better part of an hour to get from the autostrada to the Old Port, and then, in the tangle of cars there and thanks to a bit of unclear signage, we missed the Old Port altogether. When we were finally able to turn back toward the city center, we found ourselves making slow progress through a residential neighborhood with two hungry children in the backseat. We decided to save the Old Port—the gritty, smoky, ancient Genoa where we had hoped to have dinner—for another visit and parked on a street lined with eucalyptus trees, with views over a railing to rooftops and the domes of churches below.

This turned out to be a section of the city called Carignano, a fairly well-off and entirely pleasant district that might have had a number of good restaurants in Columbus's day, all of which seemed to have gone out of business in the intervening centuries. We walked a couple of blocks, past brown and gray apartment buildings with carved doors and gargoyles, telling ourselves that the next corner would reveal those places where the Carignani must go for dinner on Friday nights. But no. The next corner came and went and it was just more apartment buildings. At last, and at the urging of our hungry daughters, I stopped a man who seemed like a local. *Mi scusi, ma si potrebbe dire dove è possiamo trovare un buon ristorante?*

There is a type of Italian personality—I am sure every nation on earth has its equivalent—so good-hearted and generous, so straightforward and unarmored, so childlike and kind, that even the briefest encounter with it leaves one full of optimism about the future of the human species. This was the type of man of whom we asked about places to eat in Carignano. The first thing he did when he saw Alexandra and Juliana was to crouch down to their level and tell them what wonderful girls they were, ask their names, and then, once that introduction had been completed, stand up and cup his jaw in one hand and give the restaurant situation deep thought. After a moment, he started leading us in one direction, then changed his mind, stopped, and said, "*No, ascolta. C'è un buonissimo ristorante. . . .* No, listen, there's a great restaurant a few blocks from here. They will feed you well there, they'll feed you very well. And the girls will like it. And I think it will be open at this hour."

He gave us precise directions, walked with us a little ways to be sure we weren't going to get lost, then bade us such a sincere and affectionate *buon appetito* that I wished, afterward, we'd invited him to join us. There was something unusual about the man, almost as if he were rehearsing for a future lifetime as a saint of the lost and hungry. I would think about him, remember him, all the way back to Lago di Como and for months afterward.

The restaurant he'd recommended, a little place called Da Genio tucked on a corner beside a military compound in an out-of-the-way neighborhood of bars and shops, compensated us handsomely for the ninety minutes spent sitting in traffic fumes.

It was only six o'clock, the hour at which Italians might possibly be thinking about eating but are not, of course, actually performing the sacred act. Da Genio appeared to be empty when we walked through the door. There was a small bar hard on our right, but no one behind it. A row of unoccupied tables down the left wall, all neatly set for dinner, and in front of us, beyond an archway, more tables in a blue and white room on the walls of which hung dozens of original oil paintings placed close together. We waited a minute, then called out. The man who emerged from the kitchen was middle-aged, and somewhat beleaguered, it seemed to me. He led us to a table in the all-but-deserted back room, where the reason for his beleaguerment became apparent: a quartet of young Japanese guys who seemed to be laughing at him, at us, and at everything on the menu. They did not speak more than a few words of Italian, though they were expert at mocking the sounds of the language, pronouncing words aloud from the menu, then laughing in an unpleasant, if unthreatening, way. As we sat there perusing the dinner options, they kept calling the man out of the kitchen for this or that—bread, water—and he waited on them with lips pressed together, at one point telling them, *"Aspettate, aspettate!"*—Wait, wait!—in an angry voice that he did not use with us.

Amanda ordered the pesto lasagna, which turned out to be like no other lasagna we'd seen: no cheese, no ricotta, just wide, flat noodles on a plate, smothered in pesto sauce. But the sauce— creamy and thick in the Genovese way—brought a delighted smile to her face that I hadn't seen since we'd first tried pesto in these parts, twelve years earlier. That had been at another off-the-beaten- track place called Naomi, in Santa Margherita, an hour train ride to the south. We still talk about the way the pasta arrived, with a large dollop of the creamy, light green pesto on top, and about the locals telling us it had been invented thereabouts and had to be made with the smallest of the basil plant's leaves or it would lose its distinctive taste.

Amanda was happy, which meant I was happy. The girls had pasta al pesto, too. I went with a tender piece of steak, cut into strips and laid across a bowl of fresh greens, accompanied by a glass of light white wine (I adhere to the somewhat illogical practice of not drinking red when driving), and followed by a Genovese dessert called *scarpitantina,* a sweet vanilla cake with cream between its layers, a touch of chocolate, and powdered sugar on top.

As a way of putting a damper on their mocking laughter, I made small talk with the Japanese guys, in English. It turned out that they were some kind of superscientists, in town for a conference on ceramics and spaceships, that they'd been to America plenty of times, and that they were, once you got to know them, more nerdy than outright rude.

THE RIDE BACK TO MEZZEGRA WAS, as we used to say where I grew up, no picnic. I don't know if it was the good dinner, the wine, the hot day at Garlenda, or the small uneasiness Amanda and I always feel when we are driving away from the seacoast. When we finally pulled into our subterranean garage, it was well after midnight. We let the girls go to bed without brushing their teeth.

15

THE OPEN

On the Sunday of the British Open we headed up to Menaggio and Cadenabbia, where I expected to find the clubhouse
filled with golf fans, but found, in the cozy TV room with its pea-
nut-butter-colored leather sofas, only four men and one woman
watching. It was early afternoon, Garcia still holding on to his
lead. The five interested M&C members were lounging about in
poses of confident relaxation, their arms draped over the backs of
the sofas, or their hands holding drinks. Between the ten-minute
chunks of golf action, the TV channel kept showing a commercial for a hair-trimming product designed to reach those difficult
places—eyebrows, nostrils, the part of the abdomen below the
navel—and rid them of the unnatural ugliness of dark hair. One
member of the Italian audience seemed to take this personally,
shaking his head and making huffing sounds after the second and

third time the ad was shown. The fourth time, he could no longer contain his irritation. He laughed, mockingly, at the almost hairless body of the male actor and said to the woman across the room from him, "Do you like that look, Rosa? That feminine look in a guy?"

Rosa answered to the effect that various looks were appealing to her, made a joke with sexual overtones, then glanced over her shoulder at us to see if we had understood. Throughout the rest of the afternoon she would be teased, in a kind way, and would more than hold her own. She was a fan of Ernie Els, still very much in the tournament, and whenever Els stood over a putt, one or two of the men would say, "Shh! Shh!" loudly, and grin at her.

The clubhouse at M&C was the only place on the lake where you could watch the tournament, and it was nice to be sitting there with Amanda and the girls, watching in real time, surrounded by a library of golf books that rivaled the one at St. Andrews. But the day had an odd tone to it. By that point, we had been at Lake Como for several weeks and I had been trying in vain, for much of that time, to arrange a meeting with Vittorio Roncoroni, the president of the club. We'd had some e-mail contact before my arrival in Italy, even one brief phone conversation, because I'd wanted to make sure the course was open to the public. "Yes, of course, play as much as you want," Signor Roncoroni had said. "We're looking forward to meeting you." So, naturally enough, I had tried, via Doris the *segretaria,* to find a way to say hello in person. This proved to be something like trying to say hello to the president of the Olympic Committee on the night of opening ceremonies. "Doris," I would say, when I was checking in for a round at M&C, "would it be possible for me to meet with President Roncoroni, just to introduce myself, perhaps ask him a few questions about the course?"

And onto Doris's face would come a look of the most profound doubt. So much so that I would, at first, wonder if a language problem was involved. Maybe in my faulty Italian I had inadvertently asked to see a record of Signor Roncoroni's Internet favorites, or his bank statements, or had misused a word and called into question his taste in clothes. So I said the same thing again, in English, but the look of doubt remained. "Ooh," she said, "I doan know. He is not here very frequently."

"He doesn't live here?"

"Oh, no. He lives near Milan."

"But he must come up to play in the summer months."

"Oh, yes, but he is always very busy when he comes. So many business, and so on. Phone calls. But I will try."

"Thank you."

This conversation, or some version of it, was repeated a few times, and then, at last, a meeting was arranged, at ten thirty on the morning of the last day of the Open. In fact, it was not through Doris but through the second secretary, Francisco, that final word came to me of Signor Roncoroni's availability. By then, however, I had been in Italy long enough and had played at Menaggio and Cadenabbia often enough to understand that, rather than show up at the club at ten thirty, I should call first. I don't mean this as a criticism, exactly. I believe it may simply be a matter of cultural eccentricity. Many times in Italy we'd arrange to meet with people at a specific hour—for dinner, a tour, a glass of wine—and they would be there waiting for us when we arrived. Sometimes, however, plans that felt concrete to us would, to our Italian friends, be general approximations of what might happen, within a few minutes, or a few hours, or a few days of the appointed time.

Once we understood this fact of Italian culture, I came to like it. I came to like it, in part, because it could be discerned in other areas of life, not just social engagements, and because it gave one a sense of freedom that is often lacking in the more efficient Anglo-Saxon nations. If cars were supposed to park within certain lines, then, we came to understand, these lines were to be considered general suggestions as to the possibilities of places the vehicle might temporarily be abandoned. Parking, like so many other aspects of life, was an opportunity to assert one's independence over the greater powers, whether those powers were housed in Rome, Vatican City, or the local *polizia* headquarters. There was no meanness in this, no bitterness: it was a happy game, a carnival. A sport and a pastime.

You'd be in a restaurant for a dish of pasta and a glass of wine, and you'd notice, once the bill was presented, that the waiter had forgotten to note down the glass of wine, forgotten to charge you. "Excuse me," you'd say, acting the part of the scrupulously honest visitor, "but I believe I owe you for the glass of wine." The waiter would pause a moment, then shrug, raise his eyebrows in an expression of mild amusement. "It's nothing," he might say, *niente.* "It's a glass of wine."

At the Hotel Royale, just across the road from Andrus and Elsa's house and a little ways downhill from La Baita, Mario, the preternaturally friendly owner of the gourmet restaurant there, practically had to be begged to bring the bill at the end of the meal. We had come for lunch and were not guests of the hotel, but he told us our children were welcome to use the pool, of course. They were using it, and we were sitting up on the hillside with a magnificent view out over the lake, and Andrus and Elsa had come by for a drink, and we were talking about our children, about American politics, about European food regulations, and Mario kept walking by and I kept suggesting we were prepared to pay for the meal we had finished ten minutes, twenty minutes, then half an hour earlier—ravioli in a cheese-and-walnut sauce, perfectly prepared fresh trout, white wine from Trento, homemade apple torte—and he kept smiling and saying, "*Sì, sì, certo.* Yes, yes, of course," until finally he ran out of patience with me and stopped and said, "You must listen to me. We have a saying in Italy: There will always be time to die, and there will always be time to pay."

This attitude applied absolutely to the rules of the road, where cars might pass on blind corners or they might not, where speed limits were considered to have a margin of error of approximately 30 percent, and where bicyclists, pedestrians with children in strollers, speeding motorcycles, Lamborghinis, and trucks carrying a thousand bottles of spring water shared the mountain road to Porlezza without any white lines for guidance, or any obvious rules beyond a generally accepted give-and-take that seemed, much of the time, to work. When it didn't work, the results could be catastrophic: Italy has one of the highest motor-vehicle fatality rates in Europe.

You could observe this anarchic tendency while standing in line, too, and there it was not charming. If you let your attention wander, the person behind you would suddenly be the person in front of you. Rules, after all, were only rules. One time that summer, waiting in a long line for tickets at Milan's *stazione centrale,* I saw a grown man move up twelve positions simply by waiting until the people in front of him suffered a momentary distraction. He did this without apology, with a poker face, devious as the devil, until he reached a certain American whose wife and children were waiting upstairs in the hope of catching the 2:40 back to Como after a hot, tiresome day in the big city. At which point he could go no further in his sneaky game because the American was twice his size, and not in a particularly generous mood, and kept shifting from one side to the next to block the man's stealthy advances, then turned around to fix him with a stare that would have paralyzed a stalking cheetah.

At the golf courses, I found myself hurrying to make a tee time, only to discover my Italian playing partners still up at the range at the appointed hour, perhaps talking on a cell phone, perhaps not. Twice in the early days at Menaggio and Cadenabbia, when I did not yet know the course well, and lacked a full understanding of the different pace of play, I accidentally hit into the group in front of me. This is something I am usually careful about, but the people were playing so slowly, and hidden from my view—in the first instance by a stand of trees well below me, and in the second by an elevated green well above—that I assumed they'd made their shots long before and moved on. On both occasions I apologized profusely, and on both occasions the apologies were waved off with the same calm, casual, impossible-to-disturb equanimity that Emilio, the second-tier caddy master, displayed when I arrived for an eight-thirty tee time at M&C. The *segreteria* had not yet opened at that ungodly hour on a summer weekday (in the States, the assistant pro would have been dusting sleeves of balls half an hour before sunrise with golfers lining up at the front door, stamping their spikes and sipping hot coffee), and not only was the credit-card machine not yet working, but no one was in the office to even mark down that I was heading out to play and add that to my debt. "There's no one in the *segreteria*," I said to Emilio, when I went to his shop for my pull cart. "What do I do?"

"What do you do? Go! Go! *Va! Va!* Just go out and play. That's what you do! What are you worried about? You can pay when you get in."

It seemed to me that time expanded in Italy. This may have had something to do with the extended lunch hour, the six weeks' annual vacation, the proximity of thousand-year-old buildings, or the aversion—everywhere except on the road—to any kind of hurry. Whatever the reason, time expanded. There was more of it. Eating, playing golf, perhaps even making love, who knew?—these things were done at a pace that was fundamentally different from the pace I was used to, and promises having to do with the opening and closing of shops, the starting of a golf round, the meeting with an American guest, and so on carried something less than the weight of a marital vow.

All of which led me to call the golf course before my scheduled meeting with President Roncoroni, just to be sure. At nine thirty, half an hour before we were to leave the house, I telephoned Doris and told her I was calling to confirm my ten-thirty meeting with her boss. "Oh, yes," she said, in a tone meant to imply that she had been meaning to call me at that same minute, "he has just gone out onto the course to play a round with a friend. Could he meet with you on this afternoon?"

"What time?"

"You say the time."

"How about three fifteen?"

"Very good. He will meet with you then."

We changed our plans, took a swim, had a great salad and pasta at the restaurant owned by Harold's pal Alberto, and drove up to the club to watch golf and hair-removal commercials. At exactly 3:14, I left the room where the British Open was being shown, walked across the stone patio to the *segreteria,* and told Doris that I was there for my meeting with *il presidente.* The shadow was upon her. "He will be here," she said, "in fifteen minutes." Then she added the fateful words "More or less," and I realized that all hope was lost. For whatever reason, Signor Roncoroni preferred not to meet with Jack Merullo, the visiting American golf writer who had shot 90 in the Coppa di Consiglio. Which was fine. It was merely a courtesy visit in any case. I abandoned hope, told her I'd be in the TV room, and headed back there, where Sergio was beginning to stumble, and Padraig Harrington, Andreas Romero, and Ernie Els were all coming on strong, and where the group of golf fans had swollen to fifteen souls, representing not only Italy and America, but South Africa, the Netherlands, and Great Britain as well.

But then, at four o'clock, to my surprise, I was summoned. I met with Vittorio Roncoroni in a sort of storage room behind the *segreteria.* Fresh from his game and his shower, dressed in lime green shorts and a tailored white shirt, Roncoroni was hospitable but unsmiling, long on eye contact and short on warmth, a 4-handicap golfer whose family had been associated with the course since before the war, and who had entertained kings, queens, princes, an American member named George Clooney, and various Milanese big shots.

"Should we speak in Italian or English," I asked, in Italian.

"In English, of course," he said, gesturing for me to sit.

We talked about J. H. Taylor, five-time winner of the British Open, who'd had a hand in the laying out of M&C. About water problems (they'd sunk a well three hundred meters and come up with nothing). About other courses I might play nearby. About the fact, obvious to both of us, that M&C's 122 slope was about six or seven points too low. I decided not to voice Rudy from Philly's (!) question about mismanagement, told him how much I liked the course, how kind everyone had been, and with some pride he said, "Driving up here, you'd never expect to see a golf course in this place, would you?"

I told him I realized that I might be putting Doris, who had been particularly helpful, in a difficult position by asking her so often, but that I would really like to play with some club members now and then and hadn't been able to arrange it.

"We will arrange it for you," he said. I thanked him, said I would take up no more of his time. He presented me with a coffee-table book printed for the course's centennial celebration, and together we stepped into the *segreteria*. "He wants to play with a member," Roncoroni said to Doris, in the voice of a kindly king. "Set that up." Then, pointing to a young man sitting in the corner, he said, "Here, right here is my nephew. Andrea. He's a good golfer. Perhaps he could play with you."

I turned to Andrea and suggested we make a tee time for the following day.

"No, no, tomorrow is not good for me," he said without explanation. "Tomorrow is impossible."

"Well, maybe later in the week, then."

"Yes, maybe," he said without enthusiasm.

On the counter between Doris and me was a sheet listing all the members and their handicaps. Alphabetically arranged, it showed only the first sixty names. Among them were two people in the single digits. Most of the handicaps read 50.0, which seemed to be the maximum allowed. I wondered if it could be possible that the members were worried about playing with a 10 handicap. This struck me as next to impossible. Ten is not exactly an intimidating number where I come from, and I had repeatedly made it clear that I didn't care about the ability of the people I golf with. I was out there to have fun. If someone hacked their way around at a reasonable pace, it didn't matter to me. And, of course, as the Coppa di Consiglio debacle had shown, a number of golfers at the club, or at least in the area, played much better than I.

But, somehow, due to forces beyond anyone's control, my longed-for game with one or more of M&C's 345 members was never arranged. I played with a wide variety of folks there, including Harold's generous friend Alberto (who gave us a discount when we ate at his Villa Linda, who judged Olympic ski competitions, who said, "No! No! No!" when he hit a bad shot, who once spent fourteen minutes looking for stray golf balls on the thirteenth hole while I waited a hundred yards ahead), but all my requests made through the *segreteria* withered in the summer sun like seeds cast upon stony ground.

IN ANY CASE, WHEN I RETURNED to the TV room from my talk with *il presidente,* the big tournament was taking on that electric intensity you feel on the back nine of the majors. More people were in the room by then, including a trio of South Africans who may have had one or two drinks too many at the bar and who were giving loud advice to the players on the screen. Garcia was stalled at minus 8, Harrington had come down to minus 7, Romero, after a series of miraculous putts, to minus 6, and Els to minus 5. President Roncoroni joined the small crowd and sat down a few feet from me without so much as nodding in my direction.

On Carnoustie's treacherous eighteenth, scene of Jean Van de Velde's legendary follies in 1999, Harrington hit his drive too far. It reached the water, ran most of the way over a bridge, bouncing and bouncing as if carrying every bit of Irish luck with it, then kicked sideways into the drink. Twenty-five strong by then, the crowd at M&C was on its feet, yelling, moaning, enduring a kind of vicarious suffering for the pain the cruelest game can inflict. Harrington hit another into the water, giving the tournament away, it seemed at the time, and Roncoroni shouted, in a pained voice, *"Come il francese!"* Just like the Frenchman!

Only the South Africans seemed unaffected by the misery of Padraig's position. "He should have hit a three wood," one of them said calmly. "He forced it," intoned another.

By that point, though, with the girls watching, and Amanda watching, and Jack Merullo having just enjoyed a wonderful cappuccino and apple torte to take the edge off his nervousness, we had been joined in the rear of the room by Andrus and Elsa, had exchanged our views on the course, and on golf. When Harrington finally holed out on the eighteenth, the camera offered an unforgettable shot of his wife and young son at the edge of the green. His wife seemed to understand that all hope was lost, but the little blond boy, finally released, ran out to greet his father as if Paddy were ahead by four strokes and king of the world. Seeing him, the famous smile burst out across Harrington's face. He tilted his head sideways as if to say, "Well, I did my best." And the boy leapt into his arms.

Beside me, Elsa said, "It is much better to have a boy like that than to win." I asked if she and her husband would like to play a round of golf with me sometime, at Menaggio and Cadenabbia, and that was how we became friends.

By the time the tournament ended in the four-hole playoff— glory for Harrington, tragedy for Garcia, all the joy and heartbreak of the game of golf played out there on a flat piece of land in Scotland—the room was mostly empty. The South Africans, Americans, and Dutch remained, and three Italians. The rest of the club members were on their way home to Milan, hoping to beat the traffic.

The afternoon of that day ended on another odd note. On the way down the road toward the main gates, we passed an elderly woman moving along at a slow pace, and it occurred to us that she might not just be walking to her car in the lower lot. We passed her, stopped, backed up, asked if she would like a ride. *"Sì, grazie,"* she said without hesitation, and with a warm smile that made me wonder if she was related to the man who'd guided us to our dinner in Genoa. Apparently unconcerned about climbing into a car full of strangers, she squeezed into the back beside Juliana, and we made a little conversation as we rolled down the hill. She was on her way home from her job at the club, where she had worked for sixty years. We drove her more than a mile down the zigzag road to her house, and it seemed strange and sad to me that she would otherwise have had to cover that distance on foot after a day of washing dishes and cleaning bathrooms. She'd been there sixty years; surely someone at M&C knew where she lived and knew she didn't have a car. What kind of a club was this? When we let her off near the Hotel Adler, she had trouble opening the car door and laughed. She thanked us three times, offered a blessing, and got out.

16

TO ST. MORITZ

The best salad I had, during our time in Italy, was in Switzerland.

One of my many theories about food is that salads are an essential and often overlooked part of the meal and point us back toward our origins. If we have, in fact, become the creatures we now are through evolution, climbing through the slow parade of life from single-cell organism to human, then it makes sense, chronologically, developmentally that we are in the habit of having some raw greenery before we get to the grains and meat. And it makes even more sense to follow the greenery and grains and meat with coffee and processed sugar, products of more recent times. Eating a salad reconnects us to the days, eons in the past, when we must have been grazing on the plains of central Africa or Asia Minor, our digestive systems scrubbed clean by the harsh bristles of half-chewed steppe grasses. The present-day passion for sushi and raw bars highlights the same progression: in the midst of the frenzy of twenty-first-century existence, some deeply buried piece of us wants to remember, in a visceral way, the millennia spent in the sea. So, after a day in the artificial light of an office on the eighteenth floor of a skyscraper in a city packed with five million souls, what do we crave? Raw oysters, raw fish, seaweed, eel.

In Italy, there is a simple dish called *insalata mista* (which sounds, to my ear at least, more interesting than "mixed salad"). This dish almost always consists of a bowl of fresh greens and radicchio, sometimes watercress or chicory, topped with tomato wedges, shredded carrots, a pepper or two, and a few kernels of corn. The dressing options are limited to oil and vinegar, to which I like to add a large helping of salt and the juice squeezed from *un pezzo di limone.* What separates these salads from many similar-looking ones I've eaten at home is the fact that the vegetables and greens are fresh. The salad itself is made by hand, not pulled from a plastic bag, not thrown together ahead of time by the restaurant's bottom-rung cook/apprentice and then left to sit out in the air until you happen by. More often than not, the vegetables come from a garden within walking distance, not some megafarm harvested by giant machines and nomadic work crews.

In Italy, I like to eat these salads with a thick piece of crusty bread slathered with cold butter, with a few sips of white wine, a pinot grigio, a Vernaccia. Add to that a dish of pasta with tomato sauce, and you have, in my opinion, one of the Three Perfect Meals.

But we were going to Switzerland, and I have to admit that enjoying a salad there was not foremost on our list of motivations. Before we even decided to make the drive, I'd felt that there was a certain romantic notion attached to the name of St. Moritz. Monte Carlo. Paris. Marseille. Venice. St.-Tropez. St. Andrews. St. Moritz—I imagined it as one of the grand tourist capitals of the

Western world, with Jaguars and Bentleys cruising crowded streets, with restaurants hidden away behind dark glass, internationally famous actors dining there, designer villas tucked back in the mountains, and snow on the peaks year-round. And I made the mistake of describing it to the girls in something like that fashion.

On the way up to Menaggio and Cadenabbia, I always got a small thrill when I saw the blue rectangular sign, pointed on one end, that read ST. MORITZ 98. After passing it a number of times, it occurred to me that ninety-eight kilometers was not a great distance, that we should make a road trip there. On a rainy Monday—the only rainy day we encountered that summer—we decided to do that.

After another satisfying breakfast on the covered patio, looking down at the mist-edged lake, the girls gathered some reading material, favorite stuffed animals, notebooks, and sweaters, and we were soon driving up the western shore. Just north of Menaggio the mountains slants down so close to the water's edge that the *statale* passes through a series of tunnels, one of them two miles long. You wind through the shadows and patches of light into Pianello, then Musso, then Dongo, where Mussolini was actually captured on the day before he was brought to Mezzegra to be shot, then the ancient burg of Gravedona, where the girls and I had found the old church but failed to find pizza.

Though the guidebooks had played down the northern end of the lake as a not-so-pretty province spoiled by swarms of German campers, it had, on that day, beneath the swirling dark clouds, its own beauty. Yes, the lakeside towns there weren't as large or as "characterful" (to use guidebookese) as Menaggio or Bellagio; and, yes, the mountains retreated from the shore, stepping back behind a few hundred hectares of marshy flatlands; and, yes, there were some Winnebagos with women grilling sauerbraten beside them, and some of the signs were in German. None of this seemed "uncharacterful" to me. As you left the lake behind and continued north on a flat, two-lane highway with pencil-thin, three-hundred-foot waterfalls splashing from cliff faces, a few small factories, the Do It market, and one exotic-dance club by the side of the road, you could sense the Alps' higher peaks looming just ahead. Long, narrow valleys cut into the landscape. It was not hard to imagine Austrian and Italian troops in the World War I trenches, Hemingway's ambulance bouncing along these roads, or lines of German soldiers retreating northward in World War II.

Beneath a natural stone outcropping arching over the road and then through Chiavenna we went (there, a wiry man and his young assistant were gluing up circus posters on the telephone poles), past the customs checkpoint, such as it was—an Italian swing of the chin, a Swiss wave—then up and up and up and up. At that altitude, only stunted fir trees and a few white birches survived. The Swiss drivers seemed tamer than their Italian counterparts, the houses were roofed with thick stone slabs instead of red tiles, the whole of the landscape with its green mountainsides and granite chalets was half a degree more orderly than what we'd left behind.

The air grew cooler as we climbed, from the seventies near Menaggio to the fifties as we moved into the Engadin valley and passed Lake St. Moritz. For a hundred Februarys an event called the White Turf Horse Races had been held there on the ice. But on that July day, the lake still in its liquid form, we saw only a few people hiking along the shore in the rain with their walking sticks and ponchos—sturdy Swiss, we guessed—and one brave soul surf-sailing on the whitecapped water. Then we made a left turn and climbed into the precious village of St. Moritz Dorf itself. The small town center with its lopsided streets and old ski hotels was peppered with steel-and-glass shops: Bally, Rolex, Hermès, and the like. In Gothic script on the exterior wall of one hotel was written TO TEACH THE BLESSINGS IS THE MAIN THING IN LIFE. I had told the girls ahead of time that we would be seeing some great wealth on that day—it is the oldest winter resort in the world—but, really, St. Moritz reminded me more of Lake Placid, the sleepy Adirondack ski town, than Beverly Hills or Palm Beach.

The rain stopped. After making two circles through the construction-clogged downtown, we found a parking spot. It was two fifteen by then, toward the tail end of the European lunch hour. I worried we would carry our empty bellies into a Swiss café and encounter the greeting we'd had once, trying to get lunch after two p.m., in Verona: *"A quest'ora?!"* the proprietor said, aghast that anyone should wait so long to eat. *"At this hour?!"*

I tried the technique that had worked for us in Bellagio weeks before: going into a clothing store and entertaining the bored salesperson there with a request for restaurant recommendations that stood outside the usual tourist fare. In the shop in St. Moritz the price of the sport jackets approached my monthly income. The person selling them was a trim, kindly, strikingly pretty middle-aged woman who took immediate pity—I could see it—on our hungry girls. "There is a place right here on the corner," she said in perfect Italian, swinging a braceleted arm, "but I would recommend the Hotel Steffani, which is a short walk down the street. You will eat better there."

Those wonderful words. *Là si mangia più bene.*

We walked down a couple of blocks, made a dangerous crossing on the wet, busy Am Sonnenplatz, and were greeted, inside the door of the Steffani, by a blue-jacketed waiter who spoke Italian with his colleagues, and French, German, English, and Romansh with clients. The pale wood booths gave the Steffani's restaurant, Lapin Bleu, a decidedly Germanic feel, and so, once we were seated and had looked over the menu, I decided on a northern-European lunch: salad, soup, beer, bread.

A simple meal, but what a salad it turned out to be! Arugula, watercress, red cabbage, red leaf lettuce, kernel corn, diced beets, shredded carrots, huge fava beans. "Where," I asked Amanda, "do they get such fresh produce here, at the top of Europe?" A superb yogurt house dressing, and dark German bread. The beer, a draft Himelmann, fit in with the food as perfectly as a hiker's hut into a cleft in a high alpine valley. The girls went with pasta and fried chicken. Amanda ordered a mild veal sausage with pan-fried potatoes, and in a few moments we were oohing and aahing in embarrassing fashion. I followed my salad with a bowl of thick, salty/sweet barley soup that reminded me very much of a sort of porridge called *farro,* served mainly in the Italian city of Lucca and the surrounding area. The efficient waiters, the good beer, the beautiful young woman in a milkmaid outfit at the hotel desk— even a 48-euro ($68) *conto* and the freshening rain couldn't dull the shine of that simple lunch.

For dessert, we fluffed out our umbrellas and walked across the street to a *Konditorei* called the Hanseranhaus, where Amanda and I shared a tort with boysenberries, Juliana and Alexandra poured sugar into their extremely chocolaty hot chocolates, and we looked out at the cold lake and chatted with an American-born man and his Swiss family. When we told them we'd made the drive from Lake Como that morning, he said, "We live in Geneva, where it's been raining all summer. We've been wondering where the sun line is. We're desperate. We've had nothing but gray, gray, gray all summer so far. We're thinking of just getting in the car and heading south."

AS IF THAT CONVERSATION HAD GIVEN an idea to the gods who rule the skies, the weather turned awful as we headed home, unusually awful in a town known for having three hundred days of sunshine every year. Gusts of wind pushed against the brave little blue Renault, and the rain beat down so hard we had to put the wipers on their highest setting and slow to half our normal speed.

I watched the temperature gauge drop from thirteen to seven to four as we climbed. "Four degrees," I said to Amanda. "What's that in Fahrenheit? High thirties, isn't it? It's almost cold enough to snow."

And then—this was mid-July—it did snow: big, wet flakes flopping hard against the windshield. This only increased the pleasure of the endless series of hairpin turns that took us up the pass and then down again. In Italy, the precipitation changed back to rain, and even the rain turned softer. Tired from the difficult mountain crossing, I pulled over at the entrance to a state park, and we walked up a muddy path to the base of a waterfall that slammed down into huge cold fountains of spray. There was thunder and lightning, creeks sprouting alongside the pavement, a real *torrente* beside us, threatening to overflow its banks.

The storm stayed with us as far south as Domaso, where, hungry again so soon, we stopped for another installment in our pizza competition. Maddonina, the place was called, and it was filled with happy German families drinking beer. A solid *margherita,* a very good sausage and garlic, but still not quite up to the level of the Baba Yagar in Bellagio, or La Rampa in Dolceacqua.

The sun broke through as we made the last leg home, through the tunnels, through Menaggio. A rainbow arced over our side of the lake. I thought of Harold saying, "Italy isn't made for rainy days."

WE MADE A FEW OTHER SMALL excursions during the summer, all of them in good weather. In Milan, searching for a bookstore that sold the latest volume of Harry Potter, we tried to visit the famous cathedral, built in 1387, but Amanda was wearing shorts. Although men in shorts could clearly be seen coming out the door, the guard refused to let her in ("God doesn't care if you wear shorts!" Alexandra wrote in a letter addressed to him, which she never sent. "You will go to hell!"). We rode the subway a few stops and found our way to Piazzale Loreto, where, in April 1945, the bodies of Mussolini and his mistress had been hung upside down in front of a gas station. Furious mobs had spat on the corpses and beaten them with sticks, but the *piazzale* was quiet on that hot afternoon. The gas station was gone, Mussolini's name nowhere in evidence. On the spot where he and Clara Petacci had dangled, a monument had been erected to resistance fighters who'd been hung there in 1944: on the front a Christlike figure with arms spread wide, and on the back the names of the murdered fifteen.

Amanda and I searched for a restaurant called Brek, where we had enjoyed several meals on a visit in 1995. But Brek seemed to have gone out of business long before—even the policemen we asked hadn't heard of it—so we settled for a place called the English Football Pub. The girls had hot dogs and hamburgers, and instead of asking for *tè con pesca,* iced tea with peach, I asked for *tè con pesce,* iced tea with fish. The waitress was kind enough not to laugh.

There was, on another day, a family hike up to a cliffside chapel in Breglia, recommended by the kind woman in Menaggio's tourist information office; and another to a church where Mary was said to have appeared; and another, with Harold, along a narrow path above a river, past the ruins of a 250-year-old iron factory in the pasture behind la Barcola.

There was a ride down to Cernobbio, where at the Enoteca Vini and Affini I purchased a magnificent bottle of Vino Nobile di Montepulciano.

And, near the end of our vacation, there was a visit to the wilderness refuge high up in the mountains behind our house. This ill-advised trip took us, for hours and hours, along dirt roads wide enough for one small car. As was the case on the ride to La Baita, I sounded the horn three times as we approached each of the hundred or so hairpin turns. "Feel free to do that as much as you want," Amanda said, because, unlike the road to La Baita, the road to the *rifugio* featured five-hundred-foot slanted drop-offs separated from the passenger side of the car by two yards of loose gravel. At one point, when we were traveling a somewhat wider section of road, a car came barreling down the hill so close to us that our mirrors banged hard against each other. "That's why there are so many broken mirrors and pieces of plastic along the road when we walk into town," Amanda said.

It was a nightmare ride. Even weeks of mountain roads hadn't prepared us for it. Even the spectacular view from a cow-pie-spotted pasture at forty-five hundred feet didn't compensate for it. We arrived home exhausted, and contented ourselves, after that, with walks into town for pastry and the *Herald Tribune*.

17

PACE OF PLAY

We were moving toward the final weeks of our time in Mez-zegra, and it was beginning to seem that I would never complete a round of eighteen holes in less than eighty strokes in Italy. Why this was important to me I can't say, though I think most golfers will understand—whether they play to break 110 or 70. I have shot in the 70s probably thirty times at home, and though it's always a good feeling, it's not as if I leave the course in a fit of pique after shooting 81. In fact, at my home course, the Crumpin-Fox Club, the best I'd managed to that point, from the blue tees at least, was 83 (though I did shoot 82 upon returning home and 80, twice, the following summer) and that never bothered me.

It bothered me in Italy, however. I suppose it had something to do with Menaggio and Cadenabbia being only 6,000 yards from the back tees, a par 70. Looking over the Web site at home before we left, I just assumed I'd be shooting in the high 70s and low 80s there: 6,000 yards, par 70, slope of 122.

The course record at M&C is 62, but that didn't matter much to me. I'm not good enough to be in the business of playing against course records. I'm in the business of playing against my own unpredictability, my own inconsistency, my tendency to mess up when things are going well, to fluff my way out of bunkers, to leave birdie putts short, to push drives deep into the rightside woods, or line a grounder into the barranca after having made five straight pars. If golf shows you nothing else, it shows you the cracks in your interior architecture, the bad welds and rusty rivets, the places where you doubt or limit yourself, fail to trust in your abilities, worry about another's opinion, or struggle under pressure. And what, exactly, is that pressure composed of? Why is a three-foot putt to win a match so much more difficult than a three-foot putt on the practice green? It has to be that creating goals for ourselves, in the presence of others, is a natural human enterprise, and that investing those goals with meaning helps us to sharpen some interior blade. Maybe we are built to move toward perfection, at whatever pace and in whatever arena and according to whatever definition. Who knows? I know only that one of the beautiful aspects of golf is that the movement toward perfection, or at least improvement, can be measured with absolute precision: 81 is 81, it is not 79.

But the perfection I was after on the trip to Lake Como was the perfection of relaxation, not of my golf game. And so, though I wanted to break 80, though I'd set that goal for myself, I had enjoyed every round of golf that summer, even the hackfest at Lanzo, just as, despite the soggy crust, I'd enjoyed the pizza at Il Cris and, despite the rain, enjoyed the trip to St. Moritz. If, upon arriving in Italy, my relaxation handicap had been 20, by then I'd whittled it down to 15 or 14—not mastery, by any means, but a level of competence, at least. A 15 handicap, I've always believed, can keep up with anybody.

For the last round I played with my German friend Karl, we decided to make a relatively early *appuntamento,* eight a.m., thinking we might be first off the tee and move along at a reasonable pace, for once. What would turn out to be a most unusual day started off in the usual fashion, with my traditional morning meal at the Bar Roma, then the soothing drive along the lake, up through Menaggio and Croce and beneath the gates of Far and Sure. I left the required euro coins on The Smiling Matteo's desk, carried the *carrello* down to the parking lot, and began the enjoyable ritual of moving small objects from the pockets of my pants to the pockets of my golf bag, and vice versa.

Like most golfers I know, I have my quirks in this respect. I always put three balls in the left front pocket of my shorts, then half a dozen long tees, two Sacagawea coins (for markers), and a divot tool in the right pocket. I always mark up the balls around their equators with angled double dots. I used to do this in blue ink but have recently made the difficult transition to black. One or two of the guys I've played with have considered this marking excessive, but I like it because I never have to turn the ball over to identify it, and it's nice to watch the blurred black ribbon as a putt rolls.

Karl drove up in his sports car convertible, which I had never before seen, and which turned out to be a Ferrari Spider. "Nice wheels," I said, and he smiled in his humble way and told me that, when he'd sold his business, he had been thinking of just buying something reasonably nice, "a Porsche, maybe." But then, "I thought it would only be one time in my life, and that I would have a very special car."

"What's the fastest you've gotten it up to?"

"Well, I have not still done 300 kilometers an hour in this car. I have done 280, but not yet 300. Even in Chermany it iss getting to be that there are places where you can not go so fast anymore. I did make 280 on my motorcycle, but at that speed, you know, the road gets a bit . . . narrow."

"Two-eighty is 174 miles an hour."

"Yes. What kind of car do you drive at home?"

"Oh, a family car," I said. "Just a Toyota Camry, you know. Nothing special."

At the first tee my fast-driving friend and I encountered some confusion. A few days earlier, I'd told Doris we wanted to play early in the morning and asked about making a tee time. "I think," she said, "it will not be necessary at that hour."

But, necessary or not, it would have been nice, because when Karl and I arrived at the *partenza*, two women were on the forward tee, and an unusual couple on the back. I had noticed this couple in the parking lot. It would have been hard not to notice them, because the man was between sixty and sixty-five and his female companion about thirty. She was as trim and pretty as a magazine model and carried herself with a posture befitting a princess. She was pulling a golf cart with one hand and, with the other, leading a small white dog, a cockapoo I think it was, on a leash. When the man saw us approaching, he asked, in thickly accented English, what tee time we had.

"Eight o'clock," I said.

"We are eight o'clock, also."

"Are you with the women on the tee?"

"No. I thought that you were with them."

I shook my head. "Go ahead. You follow the women. You were here first. Or we can play together if you like."

"No, I don't think so. We are not good golf players."

"Well, it's up to you. We're happy to play with you, or you can go ahead."

He considered this a moment, then said, "We can play to-gether?"

The gentleman half of this couple, Valter, was a Swiss citizen who'd moved to Austria due to unspecified financial considerations.

"He's a German living in Switzerland," I said, pointing to Karl.

"And I'm Russian," the woman said, "Olga."

"And I'm American but I speak Russian," I said. "Orlando."

And so we had our multinational foursome.

Valter was stockily built, with receding gray hair and a rough-cut, well-put-together face that was a mixture of Mike Ditka and Don Shula. Olga was dark blond, with classic Slavic features. Everything in the right place, as a friend of mine says.

I started off with my club of choice on that tee, the two hybrid, and made a nice enough swing. "About the perfect position, I think," Karl remarked, as we watched the ball roll to a stop on the only flat part of that fairway. One of the things I liked about playing golf with Karl was that his commentary—on my shots and his own—was unfailingly straightforward and factual. He remarked on good shots and on bad ones, never flattering in the former case and never demeaning in the latter. "We can be happy now, yes?" or "That, I think, was not so good" or "Golf can be a frustrating game, do you think?"

He went up on his toes, settled back, and hit a solid drive that ended up a few feet behind mine.

Valter stood on the tee, set his feet, waggled, looked up, reared back onto his right foot, brought the club up around his ear with a bent left arm, and slashed a low line drive that disappeared into the trees to the right as if it were afraid it might be hit again. "Iss out?" he asked.

"No, but it's going to be hard to find down there. Why don't you hit another one?"

So he slashed another, not quite as deeply into the trees, and we walked, three men, one woman, one dog, four countries, five or six languages, down to the forward tees. Olga had a choppy, upright swing—it was almost as if she lifted the club straight toward a point above her head—and hadn't ever played much. She hit a ground ball toward the place where her husband would soon be looking for his.

We went off, then, on the first of what would turn out to be many, many searches for Valter's golf ball. Eventually we found one of them, and he and Olga began thrashing their way, like peasants scything wheat, in the general direction of the green. It is easy, in a situation like that, to have certain thoughts, chief among them being that the woman married the man for his money. That may or may not have been true—it was none of my business, and I knew that; but there was a courtly kindness and gentleness between them. As our round went on, I noticed that they seemed, really, to wish each other well on the course, while at the same time being unafraid to state the painful truth.

"No!" Valter would cry out bitterly as he blasted the ball this way and that or threw up clods of turf behind a shot that went only a few yards. And Olga would tell him something like "You cut down some of the tree with that one" or "That one was no good." Their dog, Patsy, was an amicable and for the most part silent companion, well trained and affectionate, and absolutely thrilled if one of us happened to stop for a moment between shots and scratch his belly. He barked only twice during the whole round, both times because the golf bag blocked his view of Olga. This I found understandable.

Right from the start of that day, things went very slowly. Karl and I finally reached the point in the long trip down that first fairway where we were able to hit our approach shots. He struck another low, hard liner into the difficult rough just to the left of the green, and I managed the best iron shot I'd hit in Italy, a high four iron that dropped down hard onto the green, rolled a bit, and stopped on the back of the upper tier, leaving me with a smile on my face and a thirty-foot downhill putt. I would baby the first of my three putts and make bogey. En route to the dance floor, our new friend Valter would cut down a few tree branches, uproot a few fistfuls of M&C's high rough, and end up with some number he did not make public. Karl would begin what would turn out to be a personal-worst day for him by putting uncharacteristically poorly. And on that hole, Olga, though she'd hit a couple of good shots on her trek down the fairway, would demonstrate for the first and not the last time the uncanny ability to not be able to put the ball into the hole once she had it on the green. Later in the day she would occasionally miss right and left, but on probably ten out of the first thirteen, she'd putt the ball halfway to the cup, then halfway again, then half the remaining distance, then pick up. But, on the first green and afterward, she did all this with such grace, and such a pleasant, unflappable demeanor, that no complaints were heard.

On the second, from twenty-five feet, I missed birdie by an inch, and Karl said, "It's good you didn't make a birdie like that right away on the second hole. I would have been intimidated."

But he wouldn't have been intimidated by the shot I hit off the third tee, that simple, downhill par three, all of 180 yards to a wide-open green. After starting off with two greens in regulation, I stood up there confidently and hit a vicious shank into the trees on the right. I will not say any more about this shot.

Valter found my ball in the heavy grass beneath a pine tree, and I hit a sand wedge to the green and was overjoyed with bogey. He landed in the back left trap in two and took three shots to get out of it, mostly because his sand technique consisted of bringing the club back a few feet and more or less shoveling the ball forward, scooping a few cupfuls of sand with it. Like Olga approaching the hole, his first stroke got him about halfway to the edge of the trap, his second shot half the remaining distance, and his third popped up onto the rough. Since the more sadistic of the golf gods seemed to be in charge that day, he would end up in four bunkers in the first five holes, but though he'd throw out an occasional *"Schiessa!"* he really handled things fairly well.

I am not someone who takes pleasure in seeing my playing partners struggle. In fact, like most golfers, I play better when those around me are playing well. So it would prove to be a long and difficult day for everyone involved. It was like a dramatic production in which the lines are forgotten or misspoken: with each new error a silent frustration builds among the company of thespians, so that you come to the point where you *expect* things to go wrong. Then, of course, they do.

I holed a fifteen-foot putt to par the easy fourth, then hit a nice drive on the short, par-five fifth that just trickled into the rough.

"You would from there go for the green in two if you had a better lie," Karl observed, and he was right. Then, as sometimes happens, I got so focused on the good layup, on the idea of making birdie, and Valter and Olga were playing so slowly, that I ended up walking up to my ball and standing there and only then looking back fifty yards and realizing that Valter hadn't hit. I moved out of the way. Valter grounded one to third base, otherwise known as the savage patch of ankle-high grass at the bottom of the hill on which the green sat. While he walked up to us, I asked Karl how to say "I'm sorry" in German. This proved to be a difficult word, *Entschuldigung,* or something like that. I worked on it with him as we waited.

"*Int chuli en,*" I tried.

"*Entschuldigung.*"

"*Intz hooligan.*"

"*Entschuldigung.*"

After my fourth try, my honest friend Karl could no longer keep his mouth from twisting into a smile. "That is . . . understandable," he said.

"*Intz-hooldijen,*" I told Valter. He waved it off, shook his square head as if to say, *No problem.* I missed the birdie putt.

On that morning the downhill, par-four sixth was notable for damage done to the fairway by the nighttime marauding of a batch of wild boar. (I love the word in Italian, *cinghiale,* and have often enjoyed the slightly spicy meat in tomato sauce over pasta, so I suppose they were only taking their fair revenge.) It looked as if someone had walked around a fifteen-yard-square area with a pool cue, jamming the wider end into the ground. Their hooves, perhaps. Or perhaps the holes were made by their snouts as they searched for truffles. In any case, I flopped around near the putting surface and finally ended up making a nice fifteen-footer from the fringe for bogey. By that point, Karl was digging himself deeper into his maddening round, and Valter was already sweating so profusely that he'd soaked through most of his shirt and the upper part of his pants. This was the first time he and Olga had ever played at M&C, and it turned out they should have taken a cart.

On the seventh, the straight, uphill, 201-yard par three, Valter clunked his way up the left side fifteen yards or so at a time, and Karl wasn't doing much better. "Tough pace today," I said to him, while Valter and Olga were searching for a ball in the bushes. "Did you and Harold play yesterday?"

"No. Harold said he was going to choin me, and then—"

"And then he couldn't make it."

"Yes. Well, I walked thirty-six holes here yesterday. I sink I'm a bit tired."

"You *walked* thirty-six? Here?"

He nodded. "And I stayed at the Hotel Adler last night. The man who owns it and I, vell, we had a bottle of vine at dinner."

"That wouldn't help."

"Yes, and three grappas afterwards." Then, with a perfectly straight face: "I think this was a mistake, yes?"

On the eighth, Valter yanked his drive dead left off the tee, almost sideways. It ended up way over near the first green, separated from its proper fairway by a forested mound probably twenty feet high. The trees were thick of trunk and closely spaced, and when, with my help, he finally found the ball, Valter tried a shot Arnold Palmer couldn't have pulled off one time out of five in his heyday, shooting it straight up out of deep rough and between two trees that stood about three feet apart. He succeeded, miraculously enough, but the ball sailed all the way across the fairway into the rough on the other side. I couldn't bring myself, I just could not bring myself, to walk over there and help him look for it. He did find it, though, knocked it out of the woods, and hit a beautiful approach shot onto the green. Olga, meanwhile, had settled into a rhythm and made it up the hill in four shots. I punched out and carded a bogey. Karl continued to struggle.

On the demonic ninth I missed birdie by two inches and settled happily for a frontside 38. And then I started to think about my score.

I know you are not supposed to think about your score. My excuse is that I had an abundance of thinking time on that day. Karl and I might have made up some excuse and hurried on forward. But we shared a gentlemanly trait, I suppose, and I suppose there was a way in which we felt for poor Valter, there with his gorgeous wife, soaked with sweat, playing like an old man, in front of two younger men, one of whom drove a Ferrari. Karl and I are not the flirting type. In fact, all through the front nine, as much as I missed the language it had taken me twelve years to learn, I held myself back from speaking Russian with Olga except for the occasional two-word expression here and there. The two women in front of us had long ago disappeared; we hadn't caught so much as a glimpse of them after the second hole. It would have been a simple matter to say, "We really have to move on. I have young kids at home to get back to." Karl, in fact, had a date with Sandra at the golf school at Lake Garda, which was one of the reasons we'd made an early tee time in the first place. But it was an international foursome, after all, and a certain degree of diplomacy and compromise seemed to be called for, and I'd shot 38 for the first nine, so maybe the slow pace was helping, and it occurred to me that if we continued at this pace I might shoot 78, or 76, and go home happy. And I shouldn't have been thinking about that at all.

The deadly slow forward movement was ruining Karl's game. On the par-three tenth, he pushed his tee shot far to the right. His provisional hit a tree and bounced back almost to where he was standing, so he decided to go look for the first ball. He found it on the other side of the wooded hill that separated the tenth green from the eleventh tee, tried the difficult uphill pitch three times in a row, only to move the ball a few yards each time, then picked up. There was a sprinkler on the green, and using that as an excuse to myself, I made a careless bogey. Olga finally sank a long putt. Valter was really huffing and puffing, and I confess to having thoughts about whether I would end the day reviving him with some improvised version of CPR. It was hot, we were thirsty and could have used a quick bite, but the *casetta* was closed. Why it was closed remained a mystery—there was no sign, no schedule saying CLOSED ON FRIDAY MORNINGS. Nothing. "They have excellent food there, I think, yes?" Karl lamented. "I do not understand why they are always not open."

I made bogey on the eleventh, out of a fairway divot, then hit into another divot on the twelfth. I waited an inexcusably long time while Valter searched for his ball on the other side of the fairway, found it, advanced it a few yards, looked for it again, slapped it another few yards, then, after what seemed like the better part of a month, hit a brilliant approach shot from 140 yards to about eight feet. It was the kind of shot that would have made anyone happy, and I was happy for him, except that I was sure it would mean he'd keep trying impossible shots for the rest of the afternoon, keep looking for lost balls as if he had a chance to shoot his lifetime low, keep trying to repeat the eight iron on the twelfth.

This is what golf does to you. Instead of realizing that the eight iron on the twelfth is an aberration, a shot you will make once out of fifty tries, you convince yourself that it is the shot you should really have been making all along, you are that good, you will be that good from now on.

Of course, I don't know if Valter actually had any of that in his mind. I know only that the heat and the hills were really taking a toll on him. Olga wasn't doing too well, either. As we approached that green, she and I finally began to talk a little bit, in Russian, about Russia, and her general feelings could be summed up in the phrase *Ani vsye banditi.* They're all bandits. "We've always lived with bandits," she said, as if she were still in St. Petersburg, walking along one of the canals there, with the gilded onion domes casting their shadow over Nevsky Prospect and trolley wires snapping and sparking and kerchiefed *babushki* disappearing into the mouth of the metro. "First it was the KGB. And then all the *KGBezhniki* went into business and got rich. Then the Mafia. Now Putin, who is KGB, and appoints all his old KGB friends to ministry posts. They're all thieves, all of them. *Vsye.*"

"People were very kind to us when we worked there," I told her.

"Yes, the people are kind. But the leaders have been always *banditi.*"

Parred the twelfth. Bogeyed the thirteenth with a missed five-foot putt. The sprinklers were going strong on the fourteenth tee, and no representative from the bathing-suit-and-work-boot-wearing maintenance staff was there to turn them off, and between that and the rash of foolish bogeys, and the slow and getting slower pace of play, I was starting to feel a certain kind of frustration building, and it was not in any way good. "We would have finished in three hours and a half, maximum," Karl said, as we were walking up the fairway. Normally a good, straight driver of the ball, he had hit yet another grounder off the tee, sending it over near one of the four-hundred-year-old stone houses that could be found here and there in the foliage. These *casette* were picturesque structures, formerly shepherds' cottages. The roses winding up the exterior walls, the neat red tile roofs, the simple shape and elaborate stonework, the way they half hid in the trees alongside several fairways—it was almost enough to take your mind off other things. "Three and a half hours, maximum," Karl repeated quietly, and I nodded and then made another awful bogey.

As he grew tireder, our Swiss friend's previously poor golfing ability slipped into the category of absolutely pitiful. Worst of all, he seemed unaware of the effect his slow pace was having on his playing partners, and several times even teed up another ball after hitting a findable bad one, for practice. This happened on the fifteenth, after I had just put my eight iron into the trees and listened to it knock around there and then crack off the paved cart track near the out-of-bounds stakes. "That is a bad sound," Karl observed. He hit one into the trees as well, and when we were finally up on the green, I drained a long putt for triple bogey.

Both of us thought Valter had picked up. He'd hit a terrible tee shot, a thirty-yard bounder into the left rough. But instead of walking up and hitting that one, he'd dropped a second ball on the tee and tried again. Forty yards this time. And he had been working his way up the steep hill with such deliberateness, playing one or the other of those balls, and had fallen so far behind the rest of us, that we assumed he would just pick up at some point, as Olga had done, and finish the hole, as the golf saying has it, "in his pocket." But he was a determined fellow . . . and I think he had the eight iron on the twelfth in his mind. From a point near the crest of the hill, twenty yards short of the putting surface, he drilled a pitching wedge over the back and made his way laboriously around the green to his ball. The rest of us had holed out by that point and were standing on the putting surface awaiting Valter's surrender. But from his spot behind the green, after setting his feet and sizing up the play, he drilled another one, and—I couldn't help myself—I stuck out my foot in a clumsy imitation of the famous goaltender of the Soviet-army hockey team, Vladislav Tretiak, and stopped the ball from going all the way back down the hill. Though I had saved him a long hike and at least three more strokes, and saved the rest of us another five-minute wait, Valter did not seem pleased. He mumbled something to Olga in German, made his two putts, and we headed off to the next tee in an awkward silence.

I bogeyed sixteen after a bad tee shot. Karl and I were slogging along in silence. A threesome that had teed off probably an hour behind us had caught up and we waved them through, but they waved back and told us to go on. No hurry.

"At least ve aren't holding them up," I said to Karl, shocked that they wouldn't want to pass.

"Right, but it is not them I worry about," he said. "It is the people behind them, and the people behind them. And the people behind them."

There was nothing left for it but to finish out the round. On the seventeenth tee, Olga said, *"Ochen' oostala,"* I am very tired. Valter didn't have to say it. He was sweat-soaked and beaten, a boxer who knows he can't win, but is determined to finish the match on his feet, bloody, exhausted, triumphant. I hit a nice seven iron. Karl made a good shot, too, at last. Olga had given up for the day and was concentrating on Patsy, while Valter searched and searched and searched for his ball, which, after several whacks, had taken refuge in the left-side woods and was hiding there in terror. "I think it must have bounced from there onto the road and rolled all the way down toward the gate," Karl suggested, as a sort of hint that Valter should give up the search, drop one, and move on. But Valter continued to look long after any ordinary man would have surrendered. I made par. Too late now. All was lost.

In a kind of last gasp of the golfing day, I reached the fringe of the eighteenth in two shots, chipped on, but then missed a two-footer for par. "That's fitting," my honest friend Karl said, and it was.

We shook hands all around. Our exhausted playing partners shuffled down toward the parking lot. Karl and I found a table on the shaded stone patio and sat there, trying, with the help of something from the bar, to regain our mental equilibrium. I had shot 45 on the back for an 83. Karl had stopped keeping score somewhere around the fourteenth hole.

FOR MOST OF US WHO LOVE golf, the pleasure of playing is sandwiched between the before-round anticipation and after-round postmortem. Following a game at my home club, I like to sit out on the back porch with a turkey Reuben on grilled rye bread, and an iced coffee, look out at the last difficult hundred yards of Roger Rulewich's marvelous eighteenth hole, and listen to people at the other tables talk about the rounds they've just finished. Most of the analysis tends to be of the "if only" variety, with a dozen excuses offered here and there between sips, but there is the occasional recounting of the best shots of a best-ever round, the blow-by-blow provided in an excited voice by the player himself, with highlights added by one of his friends. It's not hard to tell who has played well and who hasn't. You can see it in the way a golfer walks out to the car, puts the bag in the trunk, takes off the shoes. There is a spring in the step and a small smile of satisfaction, or there's a hangdog look, a slump in the shoulders, a disgusted tossing of soft spikes into trunk.

Golf leaves a certain kind of deep bruise, or a certain kind of happy glow. I suppose it is a bit like lovemaking in that whatever mysterious psychic terrain you have just navigated, whatever physical pleasure you have just experienced, echoes in your mind like the notes of a piece of music after it is finished. Like lovemaking, golf can leave you exhausted or invigorated, wanting to quit or smoke or smile or come back soon for a repeat performance.

In this instance, our round with Valter and Olga left Karl and me with the simple and straightforward need of a drink. We secured a table on the shady patio—a great place, really, a place of peace; you could imagine Scotsmen in caps and plus fours sitting there a hundred years earlier. He bought the first round, and we talked about what we might have done differently and decided we'd really had no good options.

"The first time I ever played golf," Karl said, across his beer and with his precise but accented English, "was in Thailand. I was on business there and the person who was hosting us was Japanese. He invited us to his course to play golf. He was a very good golfer, 3 handicap, I think. He went up onto the tee and hit a big drive. Very big, tremendous. I had told him that I had never played, but I think the man did not really belief me. Another person ve did not know came up and asked if he could choin us. He was Korean, I think. Zo I went up on the tee. I missed the ball five times, completely missed it. I brought up big pieces of dirt and grass from the tee. The Korean guy saw this and he pretended to look up the fairway and he said, 'Oh, I think I see a friend up ahead,' and he hurried up away from us. After that moment I wowed it would never happen again, and I began to take lessons."

"Good story," I said.

"Yes. We could have done that."

"We could have. It would have been awkward."

"Yes."

We sat there for another little while, drinking and talking and letting the frustration leak out of us. I told Karl to be sure to give my regards to Sandra, to come visit America and be our guest for a while, and we shook hands and said good-bye next to his Ferrari.

IT WAS A PLEASURE ON THAT day, as it had been after every other round of golf at M&C, to make the slow ride down the mountain and then go along the lake. Past the hotels with their wrought-iron-railing balconies. Past the stone houses standing opposite the shore. Past the church in Tremezzo, the Bar Roma, and an unnamed private villa sitting back on its vast grounds, the gates locked and the windows shuttered and the flowers and lawn perfectly cared for. I took the right at Bar Tre Archi, went along the narrow uphill road, left the Renault in the garage, climbed up into the sunlight, and found Amanda and the girls, as I expected, at the pool. By then the frustration of the Endless Round had entirely faded.

"Come in, Dad! You have to come in!"

"Dad, how'd you play?"

A kiss from my wife, a quick change of outfits, then I was standing on the edge of the diving board, and Alexandra and Juliana were coming up behind me because they derived a peculiar thrill from pushing me into the water. The big splash, the paddling around, and the swimming of a few laps, a race or two, a game of tag, the obligatory "Watch this, Dad! How was that dive?" and then I climbed out and lay on a chaise lounge in the hot sun and replayed the round in my mind. I wasn't thinking about pace of play, I was thinking about the score. Was there a pattern to my mistakes? Something I could change to shave off a few strokes? How many tee shots found the fairway? When I missed putts, did I miss them long, left, right, leave them short?

We dove in and baked, dove in and baked in the afternoon sun, and when we'd had enough of it, we changed clothes and drove back into Menaggio to have a go at the miniature golf course there. We play miniature golf wherever we travel, the girls and I, and sometimes Amanda. At home, we bring our own putters—

always a surprise to the attendant—and play so often that we have punch cards at the local minicourse (ten games earns you a free one) and can whip through the eighteen holes at a lightning pace.

But, in all our days of golfing—Massachusetts, Florida, North Dakota—we had never seen a course like the one at Lake Como. The holes were sometimes thirty yards long, played on smooth concrete that appeared to have been covered with a thin coat of rubberized paint. Eighteen or 20 on the Stimpmeter, I'd guess. To complicate things, few of the holes were straightforward and flat. You'd have to hit over small water hazards or dry gullies, bounce the ball around doglegs or off high tees, or hit your first shot into a narrow opening that would lead to a tunnel that would kick the ball out somewhere near the hole if your aim was good. And the greens (painted red, usually) were lined with metal tubing that killed any lucky bounce you might be hoping for.

It was a spectacular layout. Sometimes you had to hit up narrow ramps on the first leg of the hole, and if the ball wasn't perfectly struck, it would roll all the way back down to your feet and you'd have to try again. One sorrowful day it took me eleven tries to get the ball to go along the fast fifth fairway and up the narrow ramp at just the right speed to fall into the square opening on top. On the twelfth shot it went up the ramp, into the square, down the chute, then fifteen yards to the right, straight into the hole.

We played that evening, in the late-day heat, with men fishing nearby at the end of short metal walkways the town had built for them, casting with their long poles and catching nothing. Ferryboats churned through the shadows, headed for Varenna Gravedona, or Lecco, and it was late enough that you could start to feel the town gearing up for its Friday-night revelry. A rock band was playing, loudly and well, outside one of the hotels nearby. The music set off a car alarm, which blasted away for ten minutes until someone came and turned it off. Near the fence of the mini-golf course a car with POLIZIA on its side drove up and parallel-parked,

with atypical difficulty. Four muscular young men got out, changing into their dress shirts as they appeared, chests and backs bare
and voices loud. They were off duty, headed for a night on the
town. Their drinking and fun might possibly have started even
before they left the barracks.

Measured yard by yard, the game took us probably as long as
the real round at M&C had taken that afternoon. By about the
fourteenth hole, Juliana was so hungry we almost decided to walk
off. Instead, I went into the little restaurant and asked the girl behind the counter if they sold potato chips. No, but a glass bowl of
chips was there, on the bar.

Could I take some?

"Yes, of course," she said. *Sì, certo.* "Take the bowl if you
want."

No "But be sure to bring it back." No suspicious look. No
request for payment or maneuvering for a tip. Your daughter's
hungry, take the bowl!

I took the bowl. Juliana ate, her mood improved. Soon the
game was finished, and we were all hungry to the point where our
collective good humor was in danger of evaporating.

Andrus and Elsa had recommended a place called the Albergo
Bolsena, which was housed in a square, two-story, stucco, lakeside
building right on our way home. It had a pretty balcony with tables
on it, and colorful painted decorations in floral patterns on the outside walls, and we made the mistake of arriving there, at the Friday
dinner hour, without reservations. After some hesitation, the host
found a table for us, far back in the room, away from the water
view. That would have been fine if he hadn't tried to tell us what a
bel posto it was, and if the menu hadn't been full of things the girls
would never in a thousand years eat (fish mostly, caught in the lake
and prepared in various ways), and if it hadn't taken the waitress so
long to come and bring us water, and if Juliana and her dad weren't
the type of people whose blood-sugar level determines their mood.

After ten minutes of unpleasant indecision, we left a tip, stood up, and walked out. We went across the street to a place called Il Timone, for another round in the pizza contest. Il Timone came close to winning. For an appetizer I ordered smoked duck breast, which was served in thin, round slices, the meat as red as the skin of a cherry, greasy and strong, and accompanied by a sharp-tasting local honey and sprigs of parsley. It went well with the buttered bread and heavy red wine, served chilled. The pizza arrived. We sliced it and ate it, drank two pitchers of water, had ice cream and *torta* for dessert.

"Sorry, Dad," Juliana said.

"For what? You saved us money and there was nothing great in that place anyway."

"Really?"

"Sure, really. We're all happier here, aren't we?"

A three-quarter moon was rising over the lake, the strip of restaurants there bustling with guests from the hotels. Darkness had fallen but the air had not cooled much, and when we went home, and when the girls were in bed and quiet in their downstairs rooms, I went out the back door and had a solitary swim, then a cold shower there beside the pool, and all the frustrations of the day were gone.

18

AT THE POOL

It was a little society all its own, the pool at the back of our place on Via Pola. Four houses shared swimming rights, and there were two apartments in each house, and though most of them were used only on weekends, and some never used at all while we were there, still, we had a coterie of regulars. As time went on, we got to know these neighbors—no golfers among them—and to depend on them for, among other kindnesses, food recommendations.

Piero and Carla were an older couple who had moved to the lake ("Paradise, it's paradise here," he was fond of saying) from Milan after he retired from the municipal water company. He was a small, stocky man, somewhere in his sixties, and he had owned our half of the house and done all the plumbing there before selling out to an Englishman a year before. "He still thinks he owns it," Harold would complain, and, in fact, Piero would come by unannounced and cut pieces from the rosemary plants that grew beside our patio. But he'd also be the one to turn on the sprinklers when the lawn went brown from the heat. He and his wife, Carla—a shy woman who bore some resemblance to Sophia Loren and was as trim as someone half her age, and who usually had a cigarette in hand—would rake the pinecones from the backyard after a windy day, and they appreciated it, I think, when Amanda and I got up and helped them. Once, with the peculiar downward clawing gesture favored by Europeans, Piero motioned for me to come with him and took me on a tour of his house and poured me a glass of a potent limoncello in midafternoon. I repaid him with chocolate. I would practice Italian with them as we lay in the sun, asking about the retirement age (fifty-eight as long as you'd put in thirty-five years of work), the crime situation (no trouble here, though Como had its bad moments), the safety of children (they'd heard of three or four abductions in the past five years, in all of Italy. It was still very safe, though not quite the way it used to be), the cost of medical treatment (zero), college (about five thousand euros a year for the best schools), and, of course, asking them for restaurant recommendations.

They liked a modest eatery called the Trattoria San Stefano, in Lenno, and so we drove down there one night for dinner. We could have walked to Lenno and often did. If you turned right on Via Pola and strolled down the road a few hundred yards, with the lake and the mountains below and to the left, the road came to an end and you found yourself at the top of a steep, ancient path that squeezed between the walls of houses. The path had been made from thousands of small stones set in concrete, and you could still see that one side of it was crude steps, and the other side a sort of ramp along which a donkey's load could be rolled or slid. On this downhill walk, you went past the elaborately decorated stucco home that had been the headquarters of the local Nazi officers a generation earlier, then you descended again through a damp, shady section, where a bridge crossed a stream coursing down from the mountains. Just beyond the bridge you turned left and soon found yourself in the labyrinthine walkways of the hamlet of Pola itself. Right and uphill to the town library; left toward the lake. It was a few steps to the *statale*, and after making the dangerous crossing, you came into the lakeside town of Lenno.

But it would have been a steep climb on the way home, a lot to ask of a six-year-old and a nine-year-old at the end of a long day, so on that evening we took the car. In Lenno, we found a place to park near a monument to those who had died during the war years.

In our experience, these monuments, which were everywhere—alongside the road, in the center of town squares, next to churches—never made a distinction between those who had been lost fighting with the Fascists and those who had died fighting against them. The victims had been in the prime of life, most of them, and men, most of them, and their deaths had been part of an enormous tragedy, of course, whichever side of the fence they had been fighting on. Or, at least, that is what the monuments seemed to be saying in their stubborn insistence on not making that one crucial historical distinction. In fact, like our own Civil War, the Second World War had torn Italy in two, cost almost half a million Italian lives, and it was a miracle that the country had ever managed to sew itself back together again. There were men and women living as neighbors now who had laid their sympathies on different sides of the battle lines, whose fathers, mothers, grandfathers, or grandmothers had been resistance fighters or Fascists, German sympathizers or victims of the SS, whose aunts and uncles had been shipped off to camps or been the guards on the trains. But that layer of Italian life remained impenetrable to us. Once in a while, that tortured history would lift its head from the dark past and show its face in the sunny everyday world around Lake Como. You would hear a certain note when someone told you that the resistance fighters weren't universally loved, that people were afraid then, always afraid, and that the resistance operatives sometimes did things, good things perhaps, that nevertheless resulted in vicious German reprisals, a mass execution, the hanging up of bodies in the town square. Or you would see a postcard of Mussolini in a bar or pizza place, a gesture of defiance. Or you'd come upon a monument by the side of the road, with old sepia photographs encased in glass and the dates—1943, 1944, 1945—saying almost everything that needed to be said. Beside the church in Tremezzo stood a monument to the nephew of a local priest who'd been sent off to the extermination camps, and, not ten steps away, a plaque on the church wall with Mussolini's name on it, right below the pope's. Present-day Italy, sunny, happy, well-fed, gorgeous present-day Italy, rests upon that mottled history, the way the glorious architecture of the Roman era rests upon the broken backs of forgotten slaves, the way American's power and prestige rests upon the slaughter of Indians and the enslavement of blacks, the way modern Germany and Russia and Cambodia and Turkey and Japan all have their ghosts.

I was thinking about that as we got out of the Renault in the town square in Lenno and went into San Stefano to have our meal.

I was in an adventurous mood that night; the girls were not. Alexandra and Juliana split a perfectly decent if not particularly Italian meal of beef and french fries; Amanda chose the asparagus and ravioli, which she liked very much. I began with *missoltini*, two smoked shad from the lake, which, to the consternation of the girls, appeared on the plate heads and all. This local delicacy had dark red flesh and an extremely strong smoky, fishy taste. It was unfortunate that the rectangular block of polenta served with the *missoltini* also had this fishy taste and seemed as if it had been lying around for a while. But the main course was penne in a heavy, delicious Gorgonzola sauce, and with cold white Sorsasso wine it was a satisfying meal of strong flavors, and the next day we thanked Piero and Carla for the recommendation.

SOMETIMES IN THE LATE AFTERNOON, another neighbor, named Vittorio, would appear and climb into the pool, where he would stand and wave his arms back and forth beneath the surface. Vittorio, a retired cook, was another of our food consultants. He had a salesman's way about him, ebullient, speaking in a slushy, rapid-fire Italian, and you could see an odd, square lump beneath the skin of his chest where a pacemaker had been implanted. "Your girls are *gioielli*," he said to me on more than one occasion. "Jewels. Just jewels, I tell you. They remind me of my daughter when she was that age." Sometimes his daughter, a pretty young woman who lived not far away, would come and visit, sitting with him on the park bench in the shade at the diving-board end of the pool. Once in a while his wife would make an appearance, but she would never swim and almost never smile. It was as if Vittorio had been given too large a measure of personality and she too small. After we'd had several conversations ("Once," he said, making a face, "some English tourists asked me to put marmalade on pasta! *Ma, mi schifo*"), Vittorio told me that we absolutely had to go to the restaurant where his friend was a chef, a place called the Hotel Lario. He would set it up. All we had to do was tell him what night we wanted to go and he would arrange everything and we would be treated like royalty. He had been a chef himself, he knew good food from bad, and we simply had to go to the Hotel Lario and have dinner there. After a while, every conversation we had turned to the Lario and the meal he would arrange for us there; it was the chorus of a song. And so, finally—though Carla made a face when she heard me mention Vittorio and his recommendations and said diplomatically, *"Io dico niente,"* I say nothing—I told our voluble friend that we might be able to get to the Lario on Tuesday night. "Tuesday," he said. "Wonderful. Good. *Benissimo*. Tuesday night. I will tell him. You'll see the meal you'll have there. You won't forget it." In our next conversation he told me he had made the necessary arrangements. It would be a special night. We'd arrive and there would be a fish risotto for four, all ready for us, made specially by his good friend the chef.

"Oh," I said. "That's a problem."

"Why, what problem? You'll see what a meal it is."

"But the girls don't like fish, or risotto. Amanda is not much of a fish eater either. I love risotto, but they'll want something else."

"But you can't make a risotto for one person."

I could see a spasm of hurt cut across his face. He'd gone to some trouble to set up the risotto, called his friend the chef and told him that the American family would be arriving on Tuesday night, and could he give them a good table, make them a special meal?

He shrugged, turned his eyes away, then back. "You can't ask the chef to make risotto for only one person," he repeated, as if I might have been mistaken about the girls' taste, or as if I might not have heard him the first time.

"No, I know you can't. I'm sorry."

He paused for a second and, recovering his ebullience, waved a hand. "It's not a problem. It's nothing. Don't worry about it. It's not a problem. There are plenty of other good places you can go to eat. Plenty of places. Plenty." And so, on that Tuesday night, we ended up at another of the lakeside hotels, a humble eatery called the Belle Isole, where I had a not-so-good bottle of Bardolino, and the girls discovered they did not like pasta Bolognese.

A COUPLE FROM MILAN, CARLOTTA AND Louza, came up only on one or two weekends, the woman blond, plump, and pretty, and fond of swimming; the man aloof and averse to it. They were not locals, so we never asked them for restaurant recommendations, but we saw them in church one Sunday morning, and the woman was kind enough to lend us a coffee-table book about the history of San Abbondio up on the hill, and this book was to play a humorous role in our lives a week later.

At home in Massachusetts, we have in our family what might be considered an odd tradition, a strange way of celebrating good news from the publishing world. It started almost a decade ago, when I had gone a long stretch without selling a book. Day by day, week by cold week, the financial pressures were leaning in against the walls of the house like fifty tons of snow. My agent at the time was sending around a novel into which I had put years of work. I thought it was a good novel, but it was bringing back only rejection after rejection. So I put a bottle of vodka in the freezer and made Amanda the promise that, when the book was finally bought by a publishing house (*if* it was finally bought, I should have said, though that is not the thing to say to a pregnant wife when you are both worried about money), I was going to take off my clothes immediately upon hearing the news, go out into the yard, even if it was the dead of winter, and run around the outside of the house butt naked, come in and have shots of straight vodka as a way of warming up again, then call every person in our lives who cared and give them the happy news.

And that's the way it played out. On January 20, 1998, the novel was bought by Henry Holt & Co. Alexandra was thirty-three days old. There were three feet of snow in the yard. I came home from an afternoon of cross-country skiing, and Amanda met me at the door holding Alexandra and said, "Tell Daddy the good news."

Upon hearing this good news—to which the word *good* was hardly sufficient—I stripped down to my Sorel snow boots, stepped back out into the 5-degree air, and jogged around the house, barking my shins badly on a pile of lumber buried in the snow. And then I came inside, put my clothes back on, and, relieved beyond measure, began working my way into the cold vodka, treating the open wound on my leg in a haphazard fashion and calling old friends.

As the girls grew and we told them this story, they made the transition from thinking their father was completely crazy to thinking he was only partly crazy, to hoping for good news so that they could see him running around outdoors without any clothes on and join in the fun themselves. The next time I sold a book it was winter again, and nighttime thankfully (though we live in the country and the only neighbors who might see us naked in the yard would probably understand), so we all stripped down in the kitchen and sprinted around outside, Amanda with the video camera on, the girls shrieking in delight.

It happened, during our summer at Lake Como, that some good news arrived from the New York book world. The girls, of course, insisted we celebrate, despite the fact that I told them I could be arrested for running around outside this particular house with no clothes on. "This isn't like home," I said. "We're not in the middle of the woods here. People will see us. I could get in trouble."

They considered this a moment, as if to say, *But, Dad, why would you get in trouble for showing your body?* then came up with a compromise, "Okay, then we all have to go in the pool naked. You, too, Mom."

After a bit of back-and-forth, and some sensible reluctance on our part, we designated a certain Sunday night for our skinny-dip. We waited until we thought the neighbors had all gone to dinner or to bed, and we went up to the pool wearing only towels. We shed the towels and jumped in. And naturally, Carlotta and Louza from Milan chose that moment to come back to the pool to get their lawn chairs and bring them inside. They saw our smiling faces above the water and stood there in the half dark making conversation with me about the service at the church that morning, about my impressions of the book they'd lent us, about the best way to return it, while the girls dissolved in laughter, and Amanda and I surreptitiously worked our way into the deep end.

SOMETIMES HAROLD AND SARA AND THEIR children came up for a swim. Harold would throw his son and our daughters this way and that in the pool, do backflips off the diving board, and repeat a phrase I often heard from him: "There is nothing as good as hearing the happy noises children make. Nothing in life is better than that."

Sometimes, lying on the chaise lounges or standing on their patio, we'd see two thin men, in their thirties or forties, both of them blind, and their sighted teenage nephew Giovanni, and his mother. One afternoon Giovanni went fishing in the lake. An hour later he knocked on the door with a prize bass, asking Amanda if we had a scale so he could weigh it.

ORDINARY AND ECCENTRIC, THESE RELATIONSHIPS ALWAYS began by one of the parties saying *Ciao* as they walked along the path. And then *Ciao* again or *Buon appetito* if they walked past while we were eating on the patio. And then a few tentative phrases about where we were from, and how long we were staying, and wasn't it a *bella giornata*? I began to feel that we were sending out roots into the soil of the Tremezzino, becoming familiar with our various neighbors and with the different moods of the lake: the way it could be torn into whitecaps on some mornings, or grow busy with water-skiers and pleasure boats on a Saturday afternoon; the way the moon would appear from behind Monte Legnone (2,609 meters) on the opposite side, the way the afternoon and evening light struck the faces of the ocher buildings in Bellagio; the enormous black bees that came to the mustard and rosemary plants near the patio; the sound of sirens echoing up the hillside from the *statale;* the slight speech impediment of the redheaded librarian in Pola, where we went to check our e-mail messages when we did not want to drive to Harold's office; the way the wind moaned at night in the awnings, as if an animal in pain were there; the enraged voice of a neighbor across the road shouting at her children; the sound of the landscaping crew trimming the hedge at seven a.m.; the shadows on the green pyramidal summit of Monte Galbiga behind the house, the ground hornets, the cold shower, the way Carla held her cigarette and Piero lay facedown on the chaise; the way the putts broke at Menaggio and Cadenabbia and the proud posture of Alessandro when he served a drink at the bar. Italy was working its way into us, and we all noticed, after several weeks, that we were beginning to be able to separate one word from the next when two Italians were speaking, whereas, even to me, the best speaker of the bunch, it had previously seemed like a single ribbon of baffling syllables.

WE HAD THE MOST CONTACT WITH the family that lived in the house right next to us, Davide, his six-months-pregnant wife, Paola, and their two young boys, Pietro and Luca. Davide was a famous folk musician in that part of Italy, a handsome, athletic-looking, sometimes brooding man with a raspy voice. Paola was a classic Italian blond-haired beauty, who was somehow able to care for the two rambunctious boys all day while in her third trimester. The boys were cherubic creatures, walking around with their little chests thrust out, borrowing and lending toys, learning to swim and crowing about it to a small audience of neighbors, throwing tantrums, coming up to you, the picture of innocence, and asking where the girls were, or why you were stretching, or why you didn't understand everything they said, or why you liked to dive into the pool that way. Once, when I was worried that the ground hornets who liked to fly about near the pool would bite the children, I killed a few. Luca strutted over and with his three-year-old's Italian told me, "If you leave them alone, they'll leave you alone." After that I stopped killing them and none of us was never bitten.

We had met the Bernasconis early in our stay. I'd gone over to Davide, complimented him on his boys and asked their ages, and we'd moved from there to talking about the weather, and the history of the lake.

A few days after that first meeting, he came by when we were having breakfast on the patio and brought two of his CDs and a small book he'd written, which had recently gone into its seventh printing. "Would you want to walk over to the Villa Balbianello with us in a little while? It is a beautiful house, right on the water, and they give tours. Afterwards we could have lunch."

Later that morning we started out on our excursion—down the path into Lenno, along the lake for a few hundred meters, then up another steep road that led over the green promontory and up to the gates of the mansion. "The people in this area are very *particolare*," Davide advised, as we went. "If, at times, they seem to be unfriendly to you, it is not so. They are not unfriendly. They are shy. Most of them have never been anyplace else. Sometimes, in the presence of visitors, they assume you are much richer than they are, that you have seen the world and they haven't, so they act cold, reserved, they don't say anything to you. But it isn't who they really are. It is a protection."

Villa Balbianello had been built in the late 1700s on Punta di Lavedo. Home to Capuchin monks for a time, it had passed down through various owners until it came into the possession of Guido

Monzino, a Milanese businessman and explorer. The house, complete with a music room and library, stood on a stone promontory, surrounded by gardens of plane trees, wisteria, and boxwood bushes, and it offered yet another spectacular view of the lake and mountains. Inside, there were cherry- and rosewood writing desks, secret passageways, tiny balconies cantilevered out over the water, marble mantels, four thousand volumes on alpinism and polar exploration, and rooms filled with memorabilia from Monzino's various expeditions: Chinese vases; African, Aztec, and Mayan relics; flags that had been planted on Everest, Kilimanjaro, and the north pole; Buddhas from Java and tapestries from Nepal and pre-Columbian statuettes from Belize and the Amazon.

After a while, despite being in the presence of these treasures, the girls grew restless and the boys came perilously close to jumping up on the roped-off beds. The fast-speaking tour guide watched them carefully, and Davide ended up carrying them outside, and we soon followed. The person manning the booth near the tall iron gates had been a friend of his and hadn't charged us admission. When the tour was finished, another friend met us at the Balbianello's private dock with his boat and ferried us back into Lenno, also at no charge. These things seemed to be arranged almost by telepathy, with the raising of an eyebrow or the wave of a hand, as if invisible contracts were being drawn up in a silent Comasco of hospitality, old debts repaid, this good deed done today, for the Americans, in exchange for a good deed to be named later, tickets to a concert perhaps, who knew?

I remembered this amicable barter system from my childhood in an Italian neighborhood outside Boston. In that place and time life was conducted in a constant give-and-take of favors that fell somewhere into the gray territory between perfectly legal and obviously illicit. My father understood this language the way he understood how to pronounce his last name: he'd make a phone call and get a friend's daughter a summer job as a lifeguard at the beach, or find something on the city payroll for the cousin of a boyhood pal, someone down on his luck and not capable of anything too taxing. After a day of work, my father would shower and dress up again in suit and tie and go to visit a neighbor's mother in the hospital, or attend a wake, or he'd find a sport coat on sale for a fellow usher at church, a man who didn't have time for shopping, and who could pay him later, when his ship came in. He'd talk the police into forgiving a few parking tickets for an errant nephew or put in a word for someone applying to college; he'd get the brother-in-law of his cousin's husband to do some electrical repairs for his sister's mother-in-law, who was too old and frail to find someone on her own and didn't speak English well enough in any case. In the grand tradition carried over from the old country by his mother and father, he lived in a complicated and many-layered web of friends and acquaintances—and a few lifelong blood enemies—and he knew how to maneuver his way around the bending silk threads, giving and helping and counseling, and, in the process, building up a kind of trust fund of favors on which he'd draw when it came time to find his own boys a summer job, or his brother or sister a discount at the local car dealership, or his mother a place in the nursing home.

Here, thousands of miles to the east, the silken web was constructed in just the same fashion, and Davide maneuvered us through it with the same ease and unself-consciousness. His friend with the boat dropped us on the shore in Lenno. There was a large white tent there, a more or less permanent structure with an excellent view up the lake. It housed a fancy restaurant called Lido di Lenno, and of course Davide was friends with the people who ran it, and of course we would have lunch, and of course it would not be possible for us to pay. "This is my day," he said in English. "Another time you will pay, but not today."

Pasta for the girls, and for me, tabbouleh shaped in a pyramid, then tagliatelle with tiny shrimp in a curried tomato sauce and a glass of red wine. And then the long, hot walk back up a stone path that had been used from the days of the Romans.

AS OUR TIME AT THE LAKE grew shorter, we tried to find a way to return the favors Davide and Paola had done for us: the day at Balbianello, the lunch at Lido di Lenno, the CDs of his music he'd given us, the T-shirts from his line of clothes, the advice on how to fix our cranky satellite TV, her talks about Italian life and help with language questions, the stories about the lake. Not until our last week in Mezzegra did Davide's touring schedule have him home for a few days. We were at the pool when we saw the chance to have a last meal together, and Davide and Paola stood there thinking of places we might go. Il Cris was raised as one possibility, but I knew what the girls' reaction to that would be. "No," I said with some diplomacy, "we want some place fancier."

"Fancier? How fancy?"

"As fancy as you want. We want a special meal. Our treat."

"The place in Schignano," Paola suggested.

Davide nodded thoughtfully. "Do you mind driving for fifteen minutes?"

Following an Italian driver in a two-car caravan is something like going out for a jog with a Kenyan marathon runner: even a dramatically slowed-down version of his natural pace is your top speed. For the first few kilometers along the *statale*, Davide seemed to understand this. He was moving along at only five or ten miles an hour over the limit. Through Lenno, through Ossuccio. But then he forgot or decided we might be able to keep up, or he worried we wouldn't get to the restaurant in time for our reservations, and we zipped down into Argegno at a fast clip.

In Argegno, not far past the bar where Mussolini's picture stood on a shelf, we made a sharp right turn and began another of the zigzag ascents we had become accustomed to by that point. We were climbing into the Schignano valley, where the locals held a kind of Mardi Gras celebration in early March, a *carnevale* famous throughout northern Italy for the elaborate wooden masks that the Schignanese designed and wore. The masks were divided into two basic categories, *il bello* and *il brutto,* the beautiful and the ugly, the latter as disfigured and asymmetrical as the surrounding land was gorgeous.

As daylight slipped into dusk, we came to a sort of preliminary summit, a flat place with a cluster of houses on it. Davide turned into a gravel parking lot. I followed, and when we stepped out of the cars, we were in a wonderland of old fruit trees on gently sloping lawn, and below us spread yet another version of the impossibly beautiful landscape. The hillsides folded down against each other with the roofs blood-red in the last light, and, beyond them, still sparkling in the sun, the blue water and green mountains on the eastern shore. It was almost narcotic, that view. Turning your eyes to it was like walking into a familiar room in a favorite museum and standing, at various angles, in front of a Cézanne or Bouguereau. It was no surprise to hear that the building in which we were about to have dinner had once been owned by the archdiocese of Como and used by nineteenth-century prelates in need of a contemplative vacation.

Locanda Santa Ana was a grand old two-story building the color of a ripe apricot, three main doors with half-moon windows over them. As if posing for a tourist brochure, a grandmother sat out front at a table, folding napkins. She was a kind of bouncer. You went past her and she inquired, in a pleasant way, if you had reservations, as if she were only trying to save you the walk in case you didn't. Inside, you were happy to have reservations because there were a dozen tables covered with lemon-colored cloths and gleaming glasses, and the walls were decorated with wine and grappa bottles, and many of the tables were already full.

We were seated at a long table against the back wall, chairs on one side, and on the other a cushioned bench that was immediately taken over by the boys and girls. The "meal of meals" as I would describe it in my notes, was elegantly simple: it began with a superb risotto (the girls passed; Amanda enjoyed it) made with zucchini and a local cheese called *tarlezza*. This was a stunning piece of culinary artistry—creamy, rich, light on the tongue—followed by an entrée of sliced, herbed beef served over lettuce with carrots and zucchini, and a bottle of Carai, a dry red wine that Davide was deservedly excited about. He had played a concert at the vineyard years before and claimed to have been looking for the wine ever since.

He was the effusive, not the moody, Davide on that night. As we ate, he talked about playing in New Orleans with an old bluesman named Sugar Blues, about performing for groups all across the spectrum, from neo-Fascists to Communists, because he wanted his music to transcend politics. He talked about non-violence, about his love for Led Zeppelin, Jethro Tull, Tom Waits, John Hiatt; about his struggle to find quiet and peace of mind and raise young children at the same time. We sat there for two and a half hours, eating and drinking and listening to him, the younger kids fading toward sleep on the bench. They awoke for the finishing touch, a chocolate-and-peach *torta*. The adults had a last glass of strawberry grappa, and we all bade each other good-night.

Like some sort of cosmic second dessert, as we were heading down the road on our way home, a full moon rose from behind the eastern mountains.

19

THE UNREACHABLE
SEVENTIES

The last round of golf I played at Menaggio and Cadenabbia was with Andrus and Elsa. On the day before that golf game, they had taken us up into the hills—not far from Locanda Santa Ana—to have lunch with the friends they'd mentioned at La Baita, an internationally admired painter named Petrus and his writer wife, Piera. Billed as "a light lunch," this turned out to be another entry in the encyclopedia of lakeside hospitality: a tuna soufflé, pasta with various sauces, homemade coleslaw, green salad, fruit, cheese, bread, an abundance of wine, and a *torta* from the same renowned *pasticceria* that had provided Juliana's birthday cake. The light lunch had been followed by a tour of Petrus's painting studio, then of the seventeenth-century murals on the interior walls of four tiny *cappelle* that stood there, open to the air, beside the steep dirt roads of their neighborhood.

I had high hopes for a happy farewell round at M&C. So high that I arrived an hour early. Doris, who had gotten the credit-card machine working on my previous visit and given me a generous discount on the summer of golf . . . and a smile . . . was not on duty. The friendly Francisco was manning the desk in the *segreteria* on that day. I shook his hand, thanked him for his hospitality, and paid the day's greens fee with my credit card. In the caddy master's shed, there was a bit of bad news: my hybrid headcover, which I'd sent flying up onto the roof of the stone house next to the first tee while making a practice swing a few days earlier, had not been turned in. *"Non riporta niente,"* The Smiling Matteo informed me. Nothing has been reported. Which was strange and dispiriting news—stealing is such an ugly human activity. I'd seen the head-cover up there, caught against the tiles, and I was almost sure that it had to have fallen off the roof and right onto the first tee in the strong winds of the day before. Someone had to have seen it. But, no, *non riporta niente*.

As if I knew that the Bettinardi would save me on that day, I warmed up by hitting dozens of putts on the badly chewed-up practice green. My Dutch friends arrived and we walked down to the *partenza*. For once—another parting gift—no one was in front of us. We all hit ideal drives: a long fade for Andrus that caught the slope just where the fairway bent to the right and rolled and rolled toward the hundred-yard marker; a long, straight drive for Elsa off the forward tees; and for me, the usual high draw, up over the pines, sailing and sailing, then bouncing agreeably from the edge of the fairway toward the middle. As we walked down onto the fairway, I took a last look around. Whatever my quibbles with certain attitudes at M&C, it was surely the most picturesque place I'd ever played golf, a magical kingdom, a little mountain paradise.

But paradise was tilted in places. My nice drive had left me with an approach shot from a sidehill lie, and swinging with the ball well below my feet, I pushed a gap wedge into the greenside rough, just short. I chipped to eight feet and sank the first in what would be a series of unlikely putts, and my friends made par, too, and we went to the second in an upbeat mood.

This mood, in my case at least, did not last long. There was something about the air on the second and third tees, something about the landscaping, the way the grass grew, the color of the tee markers, the pattern made by previous players' divots, something . . . because I almost never shanked a ball when I wasn't on the driving range, and I'd had two or three absolutely hideous snap-slices on those tees. On that fine morning, yet again, I hit my six iron sideways. Unbelievable. Andrus and Elsa maintained a diplomatic silence, but I was muttering to myself as I walked after it: "That's the way to break eighty. Right. Beautiful. Excellent." That type of thing.

Still muttering, I hit a sand wedge over the bunker and onto the green, probably twenty-five feet left of the hole, pin-high. It would be nice, I was thinking, as I made my way onto the putting surface, marked the ball with my lucky Sacagawea, cleaned it, and watched Andrus make a lag putt from the back fringe that stopped four feet short of the hole, it would be nice to make par here after that abominable tee shot. What a recovery that would be. And a par-par start with three easy holes coming up would be an excellent foundation on which to build a good round. I was thinking that as I watched Andrus's ball travel down to the lower section of the green. It seemed to me that his putt should have been quicker coming down that slope. The green slanted toward the tee, after all, and he seemed to have struck it fairly hard. It was still early and the sun wasn't at anything near full power yet. Wasn't that a thick layer of moisture on the green?

All this was clattering around in my mind as I replaced the ball, aligned it, slipped the coin into my right front pocket, and stood over the putt. I made a good, authoritative stroke, putting like a grown-up, but the ball skidded past on the high side. Five feet past. Trying to take the small right-to-left break out of the comebacker, and still having in my mind the notion that the green was slow, I hit the next putt like a grown-up again, four feet too firm. Missed the next one also. Four putts, in all. A triple-bogey six. Three over par after two.

I tried, after that disaster, to keep the forces of despair at bay.

On the downhill third, I hit a decent seven iron to the right apron and then, traumatized by the ugly display on the previous hole, left the birdie putt eight feet short. Eight feet. And I'd been only twenty-five feet away to begin with. More mumbling. A relaxed "Who cares anymore?" stroke, and the ball curled into the cup. All right. Three over after three wasn't so bad.

I parred the fourth and could feel a seed of hope sprouting. Three over after four now, three out of four pars, with a definite birdie opportunity coming up.

On the definite birdie opportunity I made a double. I shall not provide the details.

On the par-four sixth, I hit three wood into the left rough but then a gap wedge to eight feet and sank the putt. Four over.

On the seventh I lipped out a three-foot putt and carded a bogey. Five over.

On the uphill eighth, another par. Five over, still.

On the brutal ninth, I hit the best three wood I am capable of hitting. Benefiting from a topspin bounce, the ball climbed up onto the plateau, leaving me only about 175 yards from the uphill green. I thought and thought, figured and considered and pondered, then settled on a five iron and laid the sod over it, as the Irish say. Lot of turf, not much air. Eighty yards still to go. My pushed sand wedge got a lucky hop onto the green, which was in terrible shape. So terrible, in fact, that Elsa's comment on the first of my two putts was "That bounced and bounced!"

All right, bogey on nine wasn't so awful, even after the good drive. And 40 on the front side—par 34—wasn't really awful either, considering the four-putt, the unmentionably sloppy double bogey on five, and the ugly five iron on nine.

Andrus and Elsa were having an atypically bad day, angling shots into the right woods or yanking them into the left, missing makeable putts, hitting their irons fat. Elsa, with the sweetest of all swings, was spending time searching in the places where the snakes and spiders lived. I tried, within the borders of politeness, not to think about them. I made the usual small talk, complimented them on their good shots, rooted for their putts to go in the hole, but I could see that they were both off their game, and though I cared for them and felt bad for them and wished that our last round together could have gone on the way it started, with all three of us hitting different versions of the perfect shot, I had to harden my heart a bit in order to keep my focus.

There was a sign posted on a tree near the tenth tee that said the stone house was closed, again. I complained about it, briefly, wondering why they couldn't keep it staffed in peak season. Elsa said, "Yes, but once we called and they came out and opened it for us," which seemed so perfectly Italian to me, that mix of inefficiency and kindness, of breaking the rules in both directions—not opening when you're supposed to be open, but making an exception, especially in the case of food, and sending someone all the way down from the clubhouse to serve a hungry visiting player. I was sad that there would be no last piece of *torta di nocciole*. But maybe it was just as well: I tend to play poorly after I eat, and I'd brought along a sports drink from the Bar Roma, and in any case the day was a few degrees cooler than most of the summer had been, and there were no slow players in front of us, and I had plenty of energy for the back nine.

On the narrow, uphill, par-three tenth, as if that club had decided to apologize for its performance on the previous hole, I hit a solid five iron. So solid that it sailed all the way to the back of the green and bounded over into the rough. Determined to leave nothing short that day, I sent the chip ten feet past. Then sank the ten-footer coming back. "Right in the center," Elsa remarked. I gave the Bettinardi a quick kiss. Still six over.

We now faced a series of downhill holes—eleven, twelve, and thirteen—with daunting tee shots. As we stood on the eleventh, we felt a slight headwind, and the hole measures a solid 409 yards, so, though I was tempted to hit a three wood and keep it in the fairway, I decided to go with my old Titleist 970D, for which I had paid exactly $49.50 several years earlier. I sometimes think about switching to one of the larger, newer drivers. But then I'll have a stretch of five or six long, straight tee shots, where I can feel the ball hit the middle of the clubface, and I'm left with short irons to the green, and I'll think, If you can do that once, or six times, then you can do it every time. It's the swing, not the club. Yes, a larger head might mean another eight yards, but do you really need another eight yards if you hit this club well? And aren't there better ways to spend $500?

I tried, on the eleventh, just to slow everything down, to give the arc of the swing all the time it needed. And I hit a drive that stopped just short of the bunker that crosses the fairway near the three-hundred-yard mark. "Wonderful," my generous friend Andrus said. "Look at that, look at it. Spectacular."

My wedge to the green was less than spectacular. "You didn't finish your swing that time," Andrus said, and he was right. Thanks to another sloppy chip, I needed another long putt, twelve feet, to save par. The bad news was all the long par putts. The good news was that all of them—including this one—were finding the bottom of the cup.

On twelve, while Elsa was getting ready to hit her approach, she was assaulted by a ground hornet—it was a good summer for them, even in the States—and it whirled and zipped around her as she danced and wriggled. Eventually, Andrus came over and shooed it away, but Elsa was obviously shaken and made another poor shot. I hit gap wedge to five feet, then yanked the birdie putt so badly it did not even graze the hole.

"Then you want to have it on a string," Elsa said. "And have it come back."

It reminded me of a friend who missed an easy putt, then when the rest of his foursome had putted out, put his ball down in the same spot, missed it again, and declared, "It's not makeable."

Six over.

Even with the flubbed birdie opportunity, I thought I still had a decent chance to break 80. But on the thirteenth, a birdie hole, par five and only 508 yards, I hit a humiliating ground ball off the tee, a ball that by all the laws of fairness should have bounded down and down into the woods on the left side, unfindable, unsalvageable. I would have given up on it, but Andrus said he'd seen it smack against a tree trunk and carom out onto the side of a dry hill. After a short search, we found it, in knee-deep grass. I banged it out twenty yards or so into shorter grass, then hit a hybrid that stayed just right of where I wanted it to land and seemed, from our vantage point up on the hill, to end up in a patch of rough. "We'll find it there," Andrus said, but I wasn't so sure, and hit a four-iron provisional. We looked and looked and never found the third shot, so I was lying five. And it was a tough approach from there, about 155 yards over a big swale. Too short, and you'd watch your ball roll back down the steep hill on which the green sat. Too long and you were OB. I left a seven iron a few feet from the putting surface and walked toward it thinking, "Up and down for eight. Nice going."

Then I lined up the shot and chipped it in.

The par-five fourteenth starts the long climb back toward the clubhouse. It was reachable in two, with a good drive, but I was always afraid to hit driver there because if you pushed it right at all, you'd be back in the deep, sloping rough where I'd just lost a ball on the previous hole. So it was three wood, five iron to sixty yards short of the green. A slightly fat sand wedge. A weak chip. Seven feet left. That putt, too, went in.

On the uphill, par-three fifteenth, the hole that had so heartlessly ruined my hopes the last time around, the hole where I made a kick-save of Valter's eleventh or twelfth shot, I hit a nice eight iron, pin-high, but a bit left. Andrus hit an awful tee shot, duffed his way up the hill, and was as upset at himself as I'd ever seen him. In a kind of inadvertent spousal sympathy, Elsa pulled her tee shot far left, put her difficult uphill pitch into the greenside bunker, then drilled her bunker shot over the green and through the woods, out-of-bounds.

The maintenance crew had been watering on that day, and there was a puddle between my ball and the hole. I saw the puddle, but for some reason, instead of flying my ball over it, I chipped right through it. The ball lost all its speed and ended up fifteen feet short. I hit the first putt thirteen feet and was walking up to it and saying, to Andrus, "Now this is a really lousy four," and I didn't take enough time and lipped out the two-footer, and I was done. Finished. Three tricky holes to go and if I parred my way in, I shot an even 80. All right. So it was.

I sank a ten-footer on the sixteenth for par.

On the short, serpentine seventeenth, Andrus took out his driver.

"I don't have the courage to hit that club here," I told him.

He paused for a second, seemed to be considering one of life's deep questions, then looked at me and said, "It's not courage, it's stupidity."

"Sometimes there's a thin line."

He sent his tee ball flying into the woods.

I hit eight iron into the middle of the narrow opening between the top branches of the trees, then sand wedge onto the green, leaving me ten-foot downhill putt for birdie. Missed it.

Because of the way the holes were set up, we always left our bags on the path near the seventeenth green and carried a club up to the eighteenth tee. On that day, wanting to make my decision when I got there, I took a handful of clubs—driver, three wood, hybrid, seven iron, eight iron. At first, I kept the eight iron in my hand and set the other clubs on the ground. I figured the play here was to make another safe tee shot on another short, narrow par four, just put the ball in the fairway, a hundred yards out or so, then hit a wedge close from there and at least give myself a putt for birdie and 79. But I wanted to think about it for a minute, so I let Andrus go ahead. He sent his tee shot into the parking lot. Hit another one in that same general direction and it found the bunker. Elsa, who never cursed, said, "I have played like such shit," and let Andrus hit the last ball in her pocket. Toward the patio. I had been watching all this and thinking. Driver, maybe. It was 240 to the hole, and though it was a slightly elevated green with a bunker in front and the patio off to the right, I thought it might be wise, just this one time, to go for it. After his poor third shot, Andrus said in disgust, "And the tees are up today," and so, instead of the driver I picked up the three wood, which I almost always hit left. Even if the draw turned into a hook, the worst that could happen was that I'd end up in the woods, and the woods were preferable to the patio. And it was the last round for me at that course, in any case, and it wouldn't have felt right to have played there all summer and hardly ever have taken a risk on the reachable eighteenth.

Standing over the ball, I thought about Anthony Pierni, a close childhood friend who'd given me my first golf lesson and who'd had a crippling stroke just before we left home. For you, pal, I thought, and I hit the three wood onto the fringe of the green.

Andrus went off into the right woods for a quick look. He and Elsa had already x-ed out the hole and ended up just dropping a ball each and playing it out for the fun of it. I was focused on my own miniature challenge. My tee shot had come to rest twenty feet below the pin just at the edge of the rough, but it was sitting well.

I chose a nine iron instead of my usual pitching wedge and hit a chip that had the right speed and headed straight at the hole, then veered off to the right as it slowed and ended up two feet away. I knew the putt would have a small break. Right edge probably. Just long enough and just enough curl to keep me nervous. I had to wait for Andrus and Elsa to hole out, then I walked up to the ball and stood over it and felt my hands start to shake as if I were putting for the lead in the British Open. Let me hit it, I thought, before I start to shake so bad I yank it a foot left. I hit it, and in it went. Seventy-nine. My little triumph, my small revenge over the short, tricky mountain course. I asked Andrus to sign the card.

In the well-appointed locker room at Menaggio and Cadenabbia there are three urinals, all with small signs above them. The sign over the right-hand urinal says ZAPPATORI, the rough equivalent of "hacker." I had never used it. The sign over the middle urinal reads HANDICAPS 10–25. And the sign over the left-hand urinal: LESS THAN 10. No one was there to check, or to care, but, until that day, I had always used the middle one.

AT HOME, THE GIRLS HAD SET up a restaurant complete with a written menu. Aspiring golfers themselves, accustomed to hearing a report after all my rounds of golf, they squealed and hugged me when they heard about the 79, then served Amanda and me a great, celebratory meal of smoked Gouda on crackers with white wine, then a salami, cucumber, and cheese sandwich garnished with cherry tomatoes, followed by a plate of dark chocolate.

Alexandra had drawn up the menu in a fancy script and presented it to us with a flourish of nine-year-old pride. "If you were writing about our restaurant, Dad, would it make the cut?" she and her sister asked.

Absolutely.

20

A TASTE OF THE LAKE

Middle-aged men have certain needs. Among them, it seems to me, is the need to prove to themselves that they are not yet old. This proof can take various forms: a red convertible; a new, younger wife; business triumphs; shooting a certain score in golf; climbing a mountain; finishing a race; riding a hot-air balloon across the ocean. I say this as a sort of introduction to the Como Lake Jump, because I can find no other good explanation for my having done it, except that it was pure fun, and pure fun is a rare event at any age, on either side of the gender line.

We had found the lakeside park in Tremezzo after a visit to the Church of San Lorenzo, which stood just on the other side of the *statale*. The interior of that church, like so many of the churches near the lake, like so many in Italy, was chockablock, as Harold would have said, with marble. White marble, black marble, orange, pink, and brown marble—floors, walls, altar rails, columns. Maybe we will learn one day that marble has a healing quality, that its electrons spin a mysterious rhythm that works its way into our minds and settles whatever troubles might be brewing there. I don't know. But we liked the church in Tremezzo with its abundance of marble, its cool interior and murals and dark wooden confessionals, its complete quiet a few yards from the busy lakeside road.

Afterward, we crossed the *statale,* wandered into a patch of greenery called Parco Mayer, and found, right on the water, a little eating place called La Coupole. It was nothing more than a one-room café with a grape arbor offering shade, but it had three outdoor tables hard against the railing and served a good sandwich of ham, cheese, tomato, and arugula on a soft roll. With a glass of Friuli sauvignon, the sight of a hawk soaring over the water and boys jumping into the lake, it made for an exceptionally pleasant lunch.

From La Coupole, a walk of only a few meters along a shady path brought us into the heart of the park itself. There was a tattered lawn with a fountain at its center, and worn stone steps that led down into the water. We saw a woman sunbathing in her bra, and a family with a little girl, dressed all in pink, who looked to be the same age Alexandra had been when we'd first brought her to Italy. Teenagers preened and glanced around, lying on blankets with iPods attached to their ears. A work crew was doing some repairs, and one of the workmen wore a T-shirt that read THE MAN with an arrow pointing up to his chin, and THE LEGEND with another arrow pointing down toward his belt buckle, and there was a fortyish fellow with a weight lifter's build, wearing only a pair of tight blue gym shorts, the hems of which he folded up with great care, as if giving himself another half inch of flesh to admire, or maximizing the skin surface exposed to the sun. This showing off of a good physique was his way of proving to himself that he was still young. Or a manifestation of absurd hope: maybe, if he flexed his impressive quadriceps often enough, one of the bikini-clad young women would find him especially attractive, leave her blanket and her peers to come up and ask him what kind of car he drove.

Then there were the teenage boys, for whom the frailties of middle age lay unimaginably far in the future. Some of them were lying on blankets so close to the teenage girls that the priests at San Lorenzo and the girls' fathers would have strenuously objected had they been there. But most of the boys were lounging about on the steps, or swimming a hard crawl stroke straight out into the lake, where sticks and leaves floated in small eddies of debris, and the wakes from commuter ferries rolled the water into fat ribbons. Or they were standing up on the stone wall, five meters above the surface of the water, and jumping or diving in.

I was feeling, I suppose, a bit domesticated on that hot afternoon, so I walked over toward the boys on the wall as if their daredevilry and happy cries might conjure memories of my own youth. I had never been much of a daredevil—no jumping out of airplanes, no 120-mile-an-hour rides on dark highways. But I had been in good shape like that once, and I had shouted and splashed like that with friends, in the days when life seemed to be opening out in front of me without boundaries. I leaned on the wall and looked over, and for some reason my heart started to beat faster. A minute earlier, I'd had no inclination to jump off the wall. A broken upper back, a disc taken out at L4-5, a history of muscle spasms that kept me off the golf course for weeks at a time in prime season, even the man a few years younger than I who was showing off his thighs and making a fool of himself—these seemed like good enough reasons to avoid pretending to be someone I was not. I would allow the fright and fire of youth to fall behind me and try to do it with as much dignity as I could manage.

But then, as I was standing at the wall, I felt my heart start to change its rhythm. The boys were so full of joy as they leapt out into the air. They appeared to hang suspended there for seconds before splashing hard into the lake, disappearing beneath its choppy surface, then showing their faces again, breathing and happy, alive. Amanda and the girls looked over at me. And so, for the fun of it maybe, or maybe for some other reason, I climbed up onto the wall. It felt so much higher there, so much farther from the sparkle and plash of the waves. Boys with flat stomachs and hair that was not turning gray were climbing up the stairs, dripping. In a moment they would be forming a line behind me, waiting for the old American, *il vecchio americano,* to do something or get out of the way. Then I realized that it wasn't the type of thing you should think about, that the chances were at least fifty-fifty you could do it without sustaining any golf-career-threatening injuries, that it wasn't an opportunity that came along every day in a life like mine. And then I was airborne.

Really, the only courage involved—a small amount compared to so many other decisions—was the courage it took to make that one step. After that, things were out of your hands. Time seemed to pass slowly, your stomach pressing up toward your mouth, and then there was the cool surprise of the water, a world of bubbles and green shadows, and the slow rise to the surface. A simple thing, but there was a strange, narcotic joy to it. I swam over to the steps and climbed out, dripping, apparently unhurt, secretly ecstatic. Alexandra must have seen something in the smile I sent her, because she announced that she wanted to jump, too. Nine years old, ordinarily a careful child, she wanted that ecstasy, and who were we to stop her? So we climbed up onto the wall and I warned her to make sure she pushed out toward the deeper water, away from the rocks at the base. Hold your breath, go in straight, you'll be fine. She hesitated a few seconds and I thought she'd change her mind, but then she pushed out and away and hit the water hard, and nothing was finer than seeing her face appear above the surface, safe, happy, shining with pride. On a later visit we both went again, as did Amanda. Juliana, all thirty-four pounds of her, made noises about wanting to try, but we wouldn't let her.

Afterward, Amanda and the girls drove home in the Renault, and I made the hot, steep trip on foot. A hiking route marked with stone squares led up behind the Bar Roma via an ancient, stone-paved walkway, up through the hamlet of Bonzanigo, with its banana plants and oblong houses dating back to the sixteenth century. At the church of Sant' Abbondio, part of which dated to the twelfth, I stopped in for a rest and a meditative half hour. There were more black marble altars and, on the domed ceiling above the nave, a mural that showed Sant' Abbondio being lifted up to heaven. Around the painting's circular base was the ordinary world of men and women, then, partway to the summit, the milky dimension of saints and angels, and finally, at the higher central point, where all fear, doubt, and vanity had been conquered, only light.

21

LEAVING

"*Paga tranquillo,*" the sweet woman in the Bar Centrale told me as I carried our coffees, juices, and pastries from the counter to one of the sunny tables. Pay in peace. It seemed just the right note on which to leave Mezzegra and the shores of the lake. We had said our good-byes to our neighbors at the pool, the Renault was packed to the roof, and the girls were already missing the diving board and the house and their undersized boyfriends. We were to take our time in settling up with her, the woman gave us to understand. We were to enjoy our breakfast and sit there as long as we liked. We were to pay in peace.

The plan was to head across the northwest part of Italy—that section where a bulge of trouser seems to fluff out of the top of the boot—and to play one last round of golf at a nine-hole course in the shadow of the Matterhorn. I had a 1:45 tee time in a tournament that was open to all comers. We sipped and talked, tucking the memories away, then made a final ride down the *statale,* turned one last time to look at the blue and green spectacle, pointed the nose of the Renault due west, and spent several hours on the autostrada.

On the map, the unnumbered road that climbed from St. Vincent on the autostrada to Breuil-Cervinia at the foot of the Matterhorn looked as crooked as it turned out to be. Signs said that chains were required on all tires after October 15, and the surreal sight of snow-topped mountains moved into and out of our view as the road curled. There was a campground called the Dalai Lama, gondolas crossed above the road on tight cables, and a small hotel where we stopped for a quick pasta lunch and where at 1:10 the waitress said she thought it was only twenty minutes more to the end of the road and the golf course. This turned out to be an Italian twenty minutes. We pulled up to the crowded course at 1:43. I trotted over to the registration desk while Amanda unloaded my clubs and shoes. "You have to go across the street to register," the gentleman there informed me.

"But I called. I made a tee time. One forty-five."

"You must register first, across the street."

By the time I found the pro shop, I was, a gentleman there said, *squalificato.* Too late, too late. Your foursome has already started.

They were right, of course, but it was ironic, considering the lack of punctuality I'd encountered all that summer, and it seemed a sour note on which to end the season of Italian golf . . . until I went back outside and noticed that every hole on the well-groomed, treeless, rather plain-looking course was packed tight with three foursomes of players. Suddenly, it did not seem like such a bad alternative to spend the afternoon strolling the streets of the ski town and hiking up the bare, stony slopes. Coated with snow on its higher, shaded faces, the fourteen-thousand-foot Matterhorn (Cervino, it is called, on the Italian side) looked like a gray sandcastle tilting under the assault of the tide. Below it spread an alluvial plain of green and brown, with fast streams coursing toward the valley where the highway ran, and with furry creatures—marmots, we guessed—scurrying from burrow to burrow and eyeing us as if we were a family of hunters and had come all that way to make them into hats.

That night, at a corner restaurant in the heart of the touristy town, we had a meal that would have stood only a few points lower than La Baita and Locanda Santa Ana in a rating system of the trip's culinary highlights. The place was called Da Paolo, and the waiter, once he heard my American-accented Italian, called for his boss. The boss insisted on speaking English and referring to me as "meester."

"Meester, we have for you and your fahmily *salsicce* and polenta you will like very much, meester, and for the childrens some pasta with the tomato, yes?"

"*Va bene.*"

Salads all around with Boston lettuce, the first we'd seen on the trip. Then sausage and a superb polenta, light and soft, "like couscous," Alexandra suggested. A great white wine from Piedmont. Chicken marsala for Amanda and a pizza for the girls, and at the end the manager's hearty handshake and linguistically fractured good wishes.

A solid night's sleep in a small ski hotel roofed with three-inch-thick slabs of granite, and the next day we made the curving ride back down to the highway.

I was feeling, I don't know, something like bereavement, and it had nothing to do with having missed out on the tournament at Breuil-Cervinia. It is always nice to be heading home, and yet, in a way-time spent in Italy colors everything that happens afterward with an urge to return. Amanda and I seem to have been made to travel; it is when we feel most ourselves. We've had enough bad trips to know how fortunate we'd been during that summer, how many things—Harold, the house, our health, the string of sunny days—had gone right.

Still, the more enjoyable the trip, the harder it is to leave for home. At some point on the autostrada, sailing along with the other cars and trucks in the 80–85 mph range and wrestling with a small demon of sadness, I called over the back of the seat, "You guys want to see what going one hundred feels like?"

"Sure, Dad."

Amanda, who has ridden hundreds of thousands of miles in the passenger seat with her generally careful, eminently responsible, law-abiding husband behind the wheel, did not raise an objection. I pushed the pedal down. The Renault did not shake. No one screamed. For a few seconds we went along the smooth pavement at 170 kmh, the passing hills and clusters of houses taking on a surreal quality, as if we were making our own fast little world and they approved and had agreed to serve as the background; as if we were locals now, entitled to at least one moment of road recklessness.

I eased back on the gas. We settled into the general flow of traffic, letting the big sedans roar past in the fast lane, and the memories of that summer began to fall away behind us.

EPILOGUE

Because the whole idea of the summer at Lake Como was to learn to live in a more relaxed fashion, Amanda and I had decided, during our planning, that it would make sense to come back across the Atlantic on a boat rather than by air. We had enough time for that before the school year started. Thanks to the shipping lines' discounts on the eastbound airfare, it was not much more expensive (actually less expensive, if you counted the six days of onboard food and lodging) than flying would have been, and I hate to fly. Amanda had made a transatlantic crossing when she was just Alexandra's age, and my paternal grandparents and maternal grandmother had come to America by ship, so there was what might be called a family tradition of a little time at sea.

This idea complicated things, however. Taking into account

cost, schedule, and comfort (I'm not sure the girls would have done well on a freighter), the most attractive plan was to sail home on the *Queen Mary II*. But the *QMII* left from Southampton, England, and we had to return our rental car in Paris, so all sorts of arrangements had to be made—the flight from Paris to London, a place to stay there, a way to get from London to Southampton with all our luggage, then home from the docks in Brooklyn at the end of the trip. For a while, with all the airplane and boat schedules in front of me, the long list of lodging options in England, and the dollar's weakness against the pound, it seemed as if this might be a risky attempt to wring too much pleasure out of the summer months; instead of making things more relaxed, it would mean ending the trip on a note that was chopped-up, overly busy, and hard to arrange.

But then I had an e-mail from a friend of a friend who is an editor at one of the better-known national golf magazines. This friend of a friend, John Barton, wrote to say that, if I happened to be in London in August, he'd be pleased to have me to his club for a game of golf. The name of his club was Wentworth.

We booked passage.

The drive across southeastern France was without incident, and pleasant enough—the long, low mountain ranges and fertile fields, the small-town pastry shops, the mellifluous, impenetrable language. We did not have much luck with eating places, I am sorry to say. One night we ended up at a restaurant at a small hotel that shall remain unnamed. There, the menu had been translated into English, which might have made things easier except that the translations went like this (not the slightest exaggeration here):

APPETIZERS
Laminated of mussels to the Maseillaise "heat"
Tomatos mozzarella with the Parisian one

Crystallized sarladaise fray and its gizzards and monsoon
Its mesclun and meat pie "Richelieu" ravigote'

ENTREES
Saddle of lamb roasted with the crystallized shallot
Farm chicken Poelee' creams chive aciduated in Jerez
Pight language to soft garlic savours
Paving stone of Rumsteak roasted "Henri 4"
Net of pike perch to the sorrel with the fresh fettucinis

DESSERTS
Brie of the area on salad
Burned cream
Baked Alaska "horse" with the three perfumes
Cut negresco to the hot chocolate and its meringue
Cross of the Owner
Marrowy cream coloured chocolate English

As tempted as I was by the paving stone of rumsteak roasted "Henri 4," or perhaps the pight language followed by the cross of the owner or some burned cream, I ended up playing it safe that evening and ordering what I thought was a basic grilled sausage. Amanda and the girls went with the *poulet* because, even without the translated menu, we were all pretty sure what that meant.

It is rare for me to order something in a restaurant and not eat it. As much as I like good food, as particular as I can sometimes be about its preparation and freshness, I have spent a number of years living in parts of the world where good food—at least by my definition—was not available, where one ate to fill one's belly, not to tickle one's palate. I have consumed, on those occasions, fermented mare's milk, calves tendons, roast dog served in a plastic bucket, sea snails, pig fat, cold lard for breakfast, and variously prepared internal organs, intestines, and animal skin. So I tend to balance off the guilt I feel about my fussy culinary requirements with a pride in my ability to eat almost anything that is put in front of me. That *almost* came into play at the Hotel X, in central France, where, as Amanda and the girls picked apart their various *poulets,* I took one bite of the grilled sausage, chewed, managed to swallow, then left the rest of it lying there, looking like nothing so much as a curved pink tube stuffed with uncooked scraps from the floor of a meatpacking plant.

In London, the food was better, but the pound oppressed us. It cost $150 to take a cab in from Heathrow. For a similarly outrageous price, we secured a place to stay in Westminster: four sleeping spots in one large, homey, third-floor, slope-ceilinged room, with an interior stairway so steep, narrow, and serpentine that you were likely to simultaneously rupture a couple of disks and knock out a piece of the railing as you carried your suitcases up. The management did kindly agree to keep my heavy golf bag behind the counter downstairs. And it was a spectacular neighborhood for walking, with a pub on the corner that served excellent ale, and row after row of shops with colorful awnings, restaurants with menus that made you feel, even as you were about to board the *Queen Mary,* like a beggar, and little cars racing by on the wrong side of the tree-lined streets.

We enjoyed a wonderful Indian meal in a newly opened place, hidden away in a basement, and the next morning—after a breakfast of beans and watery eggs—I was standing out at the curb with my clubs beside me, listening to the garbage trucks making their loud rounds, and noticing the morning commuters eyeing me with obvious envy.

Two minutes after the designated time, John Barton drove up. Tall, genial, speaking in the kind of British accent you wish you had been born with, he shook my hand and lifted my bag into his trunk. We had never met each other but soon realized we were linked by a love of golf, identical handicaps, and a shared passion for traveling in Italy. Both of us had married women from the state of Connecticut. I had two daughters; he and his wife were expecting their first.

On the long ride west through London's suburbs we talked about Italy, writing, fatherhood, our respective home clubs, and I think we both felt that eagerness to be out on the course. John was taking a rare day away from the office, and I had not played in a week and would not play for another week, or more.

At last we turned into Wentworth's rhododendron-lined entranceway and drove slowly toward what seemed to be a low-set white castle. This turned out to be the former home of a Spanish countess, with a last name—Morella—similar to my own. In what might have been interpreted as another promising sign, the Ryder Cup had been played at Wentworth in the year of my birth, 1953, and Sam Snead—whom I'd met at the Greenbrier shortly before his death—had been part of the winning team. Hogan had played here. So had Peter Alliss, my favorite television golf announcer. Wentworth had been the site of the World Match Play Championships since their inception in 1964 and was the home of the gentlemanly Ernie Els. Clearing skies, mild temperatures, lightning-fast putting green—everything pointed to a fine day of golf.

"Let's just have a match," John suggested, as we stood waiting beside the first tee of the older East Course. "None of these presses and Nassaus and that sort of thing. Just an old-fashioned match."

Once the twosome in front of us had cleared the fairway, we moved onto the tee and I hit probably the best drive I am capable of hitting, 250 or 260 yards with a little draw on the end of it. My host hit the worst drive he would hit that day, a snap hook into the foliage. So as we headed off on those old links, the mysterious magic of match-play psychology was already at work on both of us: I was thinking my opening drive was a sign of good things to come, and John might have been worried his opening drive had been a sign of approaching disaster. I ended up winning the hole, after a sloppy approach shot, with a one-putt par, but it took only about another fifteen minutes for my nice balloon of confidence to deflate. John had a textbook swing and went the rest of the front nine hitting fairways and greens. I lost the second, third, sixth, and ninth holes with a series of small miscues—a weak lag putt, a half-mishit drive—and lost, too, my nice relaxed rhythm as one less-than-good shot after the next went into the books. It hurt to be playing that sloppily, because the course had an old-land feeling I love, its holes fit into the natural landscape like neatly chiseled tenons into their mortises. There was lush foliage, gorse, heather, a beautiful variety of shot options, and eighty-three years of golf history.

I loved Wentworth and thought the chances were good that I'd never play there again, and it seemed a shame to express my gratitude for John's hospitality by giving away one hole after the next.

When we stopped for a snack at the turn, I was three down and giving myself a silent lecture about at least making a decent game of it. Maybe that worked, or maybe it was just the predictable ebb and flow between two evenly matched players, but with a bogey I won the par-three tenth—a strange hole with a sort of low levee running diagonally through it—and the twelfth with another bogey, then the fifteenth and sixteenth with pars. On the seventeenth tee we stood even.

The seventeenth at Wentworth's East Course is a long, difficult par three, 210 yards from the tees we were playing that day, though it was downhill with a bit of a helping wind. John was kind enough to give advice about aiming the tee shot right of the green and letting it bounce on, and my long iron rolled up and onto the putting surface, while his found the right-side bunker. When he drilled his sand shot over the green and to the edge of the heather behind, I thought the hole was mine. Going into the last, I'd at least be dormie. More match-play mindfulness than that was called for, however, as I three-putted for a four, and he made a miraculous half with a forty-foot snake from off the fringe.

I hit a long, straight drive on the eighteenth, he pulled a short one left, and it was a kind of replay of the first hole, except that he hit a 230-yard three wood to six feet and two-putted, while I pushed a six-iron right, chipped on, and missed my putt. "I feel like I've robbed you at gunpoint," he said sheepishly as we shook hands.

"No, you just beat me. Two great holes."

DESPITE THE SEVENTH-LEVEL JOGGING DECK, a good-size gym, and several swimming pools, I believe it is impossible to spend six days on the *Queen Mary* and not gain weight. As evidence, I offer the following sample of two nights' dinner menu:

Pastrami smoked salmon and jumbo shrimps on Russian salad
Roasted sea bass
Strawberry Napoléon

Or:

Chilled vichyssoise
Chateaubriand béarnaise
Baked Alaska

There was a golf simulator (or "stimulator," as the girls called it) on an upper deck. I had the pleasure of "playing" the Old Course at St. Andrews there, smashing shots into a rubber mat on which views of terrifying pot bunkers were projected. After an opening eight, I settled into my typical rhythm of pars, bogeys, and a couple of "others," birdied number thirteen, then, if the computer doesn't lie, hit a nice long draw over the hotel on seventeen, the famous "road hole." I finished somewhere in the 90s, though, from the looks of the pot bunkers, even the make-believe pot bunkers on the mat. My score at the real St. Andrews would have been about twice that.

In mid-Atlantic we came across an overturned sailboat, a surrealistic sight after three days of empty ocean. Our genial captain put the brakes on. It took the ship a good half mile to stop. He turned her around and went back, dispatched a rescue crew, who looked like insects in their tiny orange boat in the middle of the sea, and made sure there were no survivors or bodies. Once we had started up again, the good captain came on to say, "Let us hope the craft simply drifted out from harbor somewhere in Nova Scotia." Then, as if considering the unlikelihood of that, since Nova Scotia was five hundred miles to the northwest, he added, "Or perhaps the crew came to grief at sea."

With our lobster tails and chateaubriand, our breakfast buffets and afternoon teas, we came to no grief during the crossing, unless grief can be defined as the gaining of a couple of kilos of excess weight. There were drama classes for the girls, family swims in a pool where the water sloshed back and forth like a miniature ocean, cool, windy loops around the deck, reading time in the glass-walled library, and formal dinners where all of us had to dress in our best outfits. On the sixth night we approached the east coast of the United States in darkness, fattened and happy and anxious, in my case at least, for the open spaces and perfectly stable ground and the stimulation of actual golf on an actual course. At three a.m. on that last night we joined several hundred other passengers on the top deck and watched in awe as the great ship passed beneath the arch of the Verazzano

Narrows Bridge—with a clearance of only eleven feet between the steel girders and the smokestack. After the slow docking and a few hours of sleep there was a last breakfast, a welcome from the Statue of Liberty herself, and the docks of Brooklyn Harbor.

THAT WOULD BE THE END OF the happy tale, except that not long after we arrived back home, I had two of the best golf rounds of my life. Which led me to the sensible conclusion that the summer in Italy had not only thrilled and relaxed all four of us, but made me a better golfer. That was more than enough to start me thinking about going back someday, in the not too distant future, to the place my father's parents had sailed from in order to give their descendants a happier life.